THE KING OF ALL,

SIR DUKE

THE KING OF ALL,

SIR DUKE

ELLINGTON
AND
THE ARTISTIC REVOLUTION

⌒〰〰〰⌒

PETER LAVEZZOLI

CONTINUUM
NEW YORK | LONDON

2001

The Continuum International Publishing Group Inc
370 Lexington Avenue, New York, NY 10017

The Continuum International Publishing Group Ltd
The Tower Building, 11 York Road, London SE1 7NX

Copyright © 2001 by Peter Lavezzoli

All rights reserved. No part of this book may be reproduced, stored
in a retrieval system, or transmitted, in any form or by any means,
electronic, mechanical, photocopying, recording, or otherwise,
without the written permission of the publishers.

Printed in the United States of America

Library of Congress Cataloging-in-Publication Data

Lavezzoli, Peter
    The king of all, Sir Duke : Ellington and the artistic revolution / Peter Lavezzoli.
        p. cm.
    ISBN 0-8264-1328-5 (alk. paper)
        1. Ellington, Duke, 1899–1974—Criticism and interpretation.   2. Jazz—History and
criticism.   I. Title.

ML410.E44 L37 2001
781.65'092—dc21   00-069390

Dedicated to Duke

In memory of

Mark Tucker	Kenai Perry
(1953–2000)	(1957–2000)

Contents

Acknowledgments

ABOVE ALL ELSE, I WISH to thank my family for their unconditional love and support. I also wish to thank those who directly contributed to this book in one form or another: Jack Towers, Maurice Lawrence, China Valles, Morris Hodara, Frank Waddy, Butch Ballard, Luther Henderson, Gunther Schuller, and Jerry Valburn. Others who made suggestions and offered encouragement include Jamie Levin, Dianna Collier, Evander Lomke, Philip Kapleau, Kristie Vullo, Lindsay Planer, Dino and Katherine Polizzi, David Hajdu, Ann Kuebler at The Smithsonian, Sam Brylawski at The Library of Congress, Nancy Nolen for the idea, Charles Shaar Murray for inspiration, and Rico for the tape machine!

Foreword

"Music knows it is and always will be one of the things that life
  just won't quit.
Here are some of music's pioneers that time will not allow us to
  forget:
There's Basie, Miller, Satchmo, and the King of All, Sir Duke!
And with a voice like Ella's ringing out, there's no way the
  band can lose!
You can feel it all over!"

☙❧

STEVIE WONDER SINGS THESE WORDS in his hit song "Sir Duke,"
released in 1976 on his number one LP *Songs in the Key of Life.* "Sir
Duke" was an international success, a celebration of the universal language and power of music. It was also a tribute to one of the greatest
musicians in history, Duke Ellington, coming from an equally powerful
and individual voice in modern music, Stevie Wonder. Written and
recorded shortly after Ellington's death, "Sir Duke" is one artist's heartfelt expression of gratitude to another. Stevie's tribute to Duke is significant for several reasons. This pop song communicates in many ways,
musically and lyrically, how Duke Ellington has influenced modern
music beyond the boundaries of jazz. Now that the world has recently
celebrated Ellington's one hundredth birthday and moved into a new
millennium, Stevie's "Sir Duke" remains a perfect affirmation of how
Duke Ellington continues to impact the way people communicate
through music—in ways that many of Stevie Wonder's own fans may
not completely understand.

Born in the late sixties, I did not have the privilege of growing up
with Ellington's music as it evolved over the decades, nor did I get the
chance to see the Ellington orchestra perform live. But I knew of
Ellington by the time I was five, shortly before his death in 1974. My
father gave me a liberal musical education as a child, and played me
his Ellington records among other classics. Along with the Beatles, I
took a strong liking to Duke from the very beginning. His music was

filled with the colors, rhythms, and sounds that could easily inspire and stimulate a young child's imagination. The music was alive.

As I grew older and began seriously collecting music myself, I deepened my knowledge and appreciation of this man. The more I listened and learned, the more I was in awe of his groundbreaking achievements and diversity. Everything Duke did, he did so well—as a composer, bandleader, pianist, performer, conductor, arranger, producer, and businessman. By my late teens, I had more Ellington records than my father. But growing up in the seventies and eighties, my friends in school were too busy listening to Top 40 radio, heavy metal, disco, and punk rock. Many of them had no idea who Duke Ellington was, and even if they had heard of him through their parents, they certainly had no interest in hearing anything related to big band jazz. How ironic that many of their favorite artists on the radio were making music that would not have been possible if not for Duke Ellington. My friends all knew "Sir Duke" by Stevie Wonder, but they had no idea who or what Stevie was singing about.

I collected rock records and listened to the radio as much as my friends did, but Ellington's music gave me something richer and deeper than what was being pumped out on the airwaves. As I grew and became a musician myself, and began to experience life, Duke's music grew with me. It was the sound of life itself. I would hear elements of Duke in so many different places outside the realm of jazz. It astounded me how pervasive Duke's influence has been on today's music. I was discovering links between Ellington and younger artists that even my fellow musician friends did not know existed. But aside from his impact on other artists, I always came back to Duke himself. I wanted to learn more about how he went about making music, how he assembled his musicians, and how he inspired them to make their contributions.

I began talking with people who had listened to Duke all their lives. Despite the age difference between these people and myself, we became friends based on our mutual love for this timeless music. As I began to meet and interact with older Ellington fans, I realized that many were unaware of the connections between Duke and modern popular music. Most had little interest in the rock and soul music of the younger generation. When they were not listening to Duke, they listened to other jazz artists, or classical music. It reminded me of my friends in school who had no interest in Duke or other music from the older generation. Only in the twentieth century has there been such a generation gap in music, particularly since World War II.

This made me wonder if Duke Ellington would be recognized in the future as the master that he was. He had broken so many important barriers in music, in ways that have since been taken for granted. Would his music be listened to and performed hundreds of years from now, after those who lived through the Ellington era have long since passed? Would people only recognize Ellington as a prominent twentieth-century jazz bandleader, and perhaps composer? That would be like saying that William Shakespeare was simply a prominent English playwright. But Shakespeare is so much more than that: he is possibly the most influential writer in the history of literature, whose work transcends boundaries and continues to speak to people in a universal language of human experience. This is Duke Ellington. Far from being simply a great jazz composer and bandleader, I feel that Duke may be the most well-rounded musician of all time. A strong statement, to be sure, and of course it is beside the point to try to label any one musician as the greatest. But in my research and experience, I cannot find another musician who excelled in as many different areas, with such consistency and longevity. Without at all being hyperbolic, it can be said that he embodied everything that defines the word "genius." His achievements are completely "beyond category," a phrase that Duke himself was fond of using when describing his music.

Duke's music has touched me on every level: spiritually, intellectually, emotionally. There is a full range of human expression to be found in his work, in a language as universal as Shakespeare. Duke's innovations as a composer and communicator are also evidence of how we progressed in the last century. If there is one thing we learned in the twentieth century, it is that our planet is actually very small. People of different cultures and beliefs from every corner of the globe communicate with fewer barriers. As our world continues to evolve into a global community, we are learning to understand and respect our differences while recognizing our underlying unity. Duke Ellington was a student of human diversity. He traveled around the world and received inspiration everywhere he went—America, Europe, Asia, South America, Australia, and Africa—then incorporated elements from all of these cultures into his own music in a way that was completely "Ellingtonian." It was the music of the world, but it was also unmistakeably "Dukish." No composer before Ellington had embraced so many different ethnic musical traditions so effortlessly. Granted, no composer would have been able to achieve this before the development of global travel and communication. But has any composer after Ellington been able to encompass such a wide range of musical expression with such ease and originality?

I knew that it was important to share my love for Duke Ellington, and help others discover the same connections between Duke and modern music that I discovered. It was also important to give a clear and balanced picture of this man, with the help of people who were directly involved with Ellington and with the preservation of his legacy. My goal was partly to shed some new light on Ellington for experienced listeners who have been familiar with his music for a long time. But I especially wanted to communicate to people my age and younger, about who Ellington is and what he represents. There is no reason why Duke cannot be appreciated alongside today's popular music, not just within jazz. And it all begins with Stevie Wonder's "Sir Duke."

ᏻᎶᏬ

Before we take a closer look at Stevie's tribute—as well as several other instances where Ellington has influenced modern music—the simple question must be answered: Who is Duke Ellington? This book is not a biography, and cannot tell the whole story of Ellington's life. Several biographies have already attempted this difficult task. But a brief summary of his life is necessary before getting to the heart of the matter— straight talk from Ellington experts on his professional life, working methods, and legacy; an examination of how Ellington broke new ground and became the role model for a new breed of composer/ bandleaders in jazz, rock, and soul music; and an appraisal of Ellington's role in creating a global musical language, as well as how modern society can learn from his skills as a communicator.

We begin with Ellington's life. Then we consider how Ellington has influenced a generation of composer/bandleaders, including jazz artists Miles Davis, Sun Ra, and Charles Mingus; as well as a powerful lineage in pop music beginning with James Brown and continuing through Sly Stone, Frank Zappa, Stevie Wonder, Steely Dan, George Clinton, and Prince—all of whom have permanently changed the course of modern music. Rock and soul music fans who are unfamiliar with Ellington will be surprised to learn the degree of Duke's influence on these pioneers. Although, like Ellington, they each created their own musical language, they all learned many important and specific lessons from Ellington on leadership, innovation, and excellence. Drummer/vocalist Frank Waddy, who has the unique perspective of having worked with James Brown, Sly Stone, and George Clinton, helps us trace the evolution from Ellington down through these three artists.

We also discover a surprising and important link between Ellington and Indian composer/sitarist Ravi Shankar in terms of their global impact on twentieth-century music. Their parallel achievements are such that Ravi Shankar could be seen as Ellington's only true peer in the creation of music that successfully broke through cultural barriers and opened new doors for "world music," as well as a renewed emphasis on spirituality in modern music.

I have been privileged to interview people who discuss Ellington from completely different angles. Gunther Schuller is a world famous composer, conductor, and scholar who conducts live performances of Ellington's music throughout the world. Jerry Valburn is the world's foremost collector of Ellington recordings, whose collection now resides at the Library of Congress. Morris Hodara is a senior member of the world's largest Ellington Society, based in New York City, which unites Ellington listeners from around the globe. Butch Ballard is a former Ellingtonian drummer who continues to perform Ellington music today. Luther Henderson is a composer and arranger who translated many of Ellington's extended works for performance by symphony orchestras. These people each tell their own stories about their experiences with Duke Ellington, and their efforts to preserve his legacy for the future.

We are finally faced with some important and challenging questions. How can Ellington's capacity for spiritual expression through his music, his revolutionary methods of leadership and communication, and his refusal to acknowledge boundaries, all serve as positive examples of how people can live and interact with one another in the world? Apart from his music itself, is there something more fundamental that people can learn from Duke Ellington as a person?

But a brief summary of Duke Ellington's life and career is necessary before we can explore these issues.

Edward Kennedy "Duke" Ellington

EDWARD KENNEDY ELLINGTON ARRIVED on the eve of the twentieth century in his nation's capital city. He was born in Washington, D.C., on April 29, 1899. Coming from a modestly well-to-do family in a middle-class black neighborhood, he enjoyed a comfortable and pampered childhood where he was always encouraged to be himself. His relationships with his parents and younger sister, Ruth Ellington, were filled with closeness and warmth. His father was a successful butler who sometimes worked at the White House, and later designed blueprints for the Navy. He taught young Edward about the importance of eloquent speech and proper dress. Edward became a sharp dresser and soon earned the nickname "Duke" from one of his schoolmates.

His bond with his mother was the strongest, and her death in 1935 was the agonizing blow that would inspire him to compose "Reminiscing in Tempo," one of his earliest extended works. Ellington would continually refer to his departed mother throughout his life. She was the defining influence on Ellington's spiritual beliefs, escorting him to church and Sunday school as often as possible, instilling in young Edward a strong belief in a loving and benevolent God. It was her unshakeable religious devotion that laid the foundation for her son's own spiritual expression, and toward the end of Ellington's life his Sacred Concerts would become the crystallization of his faith. Until the Concerts were composed and performed in the sixties, only those closest to Ellington knew of his love of God and intimate knowledge of the Bible.

Ellington was always exposed to music at home and in the church. His mother and father were both musicians, and he soon learned the basic fundamentals of piano. Yet he never received any significant formal musical training. He learned how to play mostly by hanging around local poolrooms and observing other pianists who would befriend him and show him the basics. This was back in the days when professional musicians would freely give younger players advice and encouragement. Ellington was a great listener with a natural aptitude, and had no trouble finding mentors. Such people included Oliver "Doc" Perry and Henry Grant. Ellington's piano style was rooted in two-handed stride, but would develop its own unique characteristics over the years: a highly percussive approach that left a good deal of space between the notes and chords, and a distinctive bell-like tone. Thelonious Monk, Sun Ra, and Cecil Taylor are some of the prominent pianists who would learn from Ellington's technique. As Ellington developed his piano skills, he also began writing his own music.

The fact that Ellington did not receive formal training is significant. It means that he developed his methods without an awareness of restrictions. He simply played and wrote what he heard and felt, with nothing but his inner creative impulses as his guide. Ellington became widely known as an innovator and rule-breaker, mostly because he never learned the established rules of composition to begin with. His lack of training became a source of pride for him, because he felt that his creativity would have suffered in a structured educational environment.

Ellington's first compositions were "Soda Fountain Rag" and "What You Gonna Do When the Bed Breaks Down?" Within a short time he acquired a taste for the show business lifestyle, when he realized that being a professional musician could enhance his relations with women as well as boost his income. Eventually Ellington became a regular performer around Washington who displayed a gift as a showman and businessman. He also tried his hand at painting. Although he never fully pursued a career as a visual artist, his natural affinity for color manifested itself in many of his titles: "Mood Indigo," "Azure," "Black and Tan Fantasy," "Sepia Panorama," "Blue Light," "Black Brown & Beige," and others. This emphasis on color carried over into his composition as well, as Ellington became a master of *orchestral* color, giving the music a visual quality and sense of place. The pensive melody of "Mood Indigo" vividly conveyed the melancholy images of dusk implied in the title.

Before he was twenty, Ellington was a family man. On July 2, 1918, he married Edna Thompson, who had lived across the street from Ellington and attended the same school. The next year his only child, Mercer Ellington, was born on March 11. Duke's business acumen inevitably improved in direct relation to his growing financial responsibilities, and he began to make money booking local bands around Washington in addition to his own musical engagements. At one point he had taken out the biggest yellow page advertisement under listings for musicians and bands.

His marriage with Edna would prove unsuccessful, and although they never divorced, they separated after only a few years. His only other long term living companion would be Evie Ellis. Inevitably, this is where many Ellington biographers begin to encounter difficulty. Ellington's private life is a subject quite beyond the scope of most biographies. Too much simply remains unknown about Ellington's personal life. Suffice it to say that although Duke always had an eye for beautiful women, none could match his devotion to his music. Of course, Ellington was fond of stating: "Music is my mistress, and she plays second fiddle to no one."

Ellington nurtured a strong personal charisma, and would soon attract the people who would form the nucleus of his first band, beginning with drummer Sonny Greer, banjo player Elmer Snowden, and saxophonist Otto Hardwick, who was Duke's neighbor. Together they formed the core of Duke's Serenaders, later to change their name to the Washingtonians. Greer had a reputation for flamboyance, and boasted of connections in New York from previous gigs. This would eventually help the band find work in the City with bandleader Wilbur

Sweatman, and although paying gigs were scarce at first, they decided to take their chances in the burgeoning entertainment capital of the world. This was the environment where Ellington received his most valuable education. In the house parties and barrooms piano masters such as Willie "the Lion" Smith and James P. Johnson were to be found—both of whom had enormous musical and personal impact on Ellington, who had learned to play Johnson's "Carolina Shout" note for note by studying the piece from a slowed down piano roll.

The Washingtonians finally landed a job at a Harlem club called Barron's, where they quickly learned how to make extra money by playing for tips. Ellington also learned how to generate income as a composer, and was soon selling the rights to songs like "Blind Man's Bluff" to Broadway publishers on Tin Pan Alley. His first complete score was a collaboration with lyricist Jo Trent on a musical production called *Chocolate Kiddies*, which ran for two years in Germany. This was also the time (November 1924) when Ellington made his first professional recordings: "Deacon Jazz," and "Oh How I Love My Darling" on the short-lived Blu Disc label.

The band soon upgraded to the classier Kentucky Club in midtown Manhattan. Two New Orleans musicians came aboard at this time: bassist Wellman Braud, and clarinetist Barney Bigard, who would go on to collaborate with Ellington in 1930 on "Mood Indigo," perhaps the most widely known Duke Ellington piece of all time. Trombonists Joe "Tricky Sam" Nanton and Charles Irvis, trumpeter Bubber Miley, and legendary soprano saxophonist Sidney Bechet (also from New Orleans) all joined the band and helped create Duke's "jungle" style by employing wah-wah and "growling" techniques on their horns with the use of rubber plunger mutes and braying sounds. It was their unmistakeable sound that helped inspire Ellington's compositional methods. For the first time in music history, ensemble and composer joined forces to create a unified work of art. For the rest of his career, Duke and his musicians would enjoy an intimate relationship that would define the way Ellington would structure his music. Each player had his own voice, and Duke composed with those individual voices in mind.

Another important person at this stage is Irving Mills, a businessman who became manager of the Ellington band for over a decade, and who was instrumental in transforming Duke's band into an international success. Although the relationship between Ellington and Mills was sometimes strained, Ellington would very likely not have progressed as quickly without the help of this shrewd negotiator. Two important saxophonists from the Boston area also arrived at this time. Harry Carney played baritone saxophone, clarinet, and bass clarinet.

Not far behind was Johnny Hodges, the master of alto saxophone, as well as soprano saxophone for a brief period. Both musicians were indispensable additions to the orchestra, bringing new colors to Ellington's palette. Carney also became very close personal friends with Ellington, and remained in the band for the rest of Duke's life. Hodges became the most celebrated soloist in Ellingtonian history.

Jazz gained wider public acceptance in the twenties as more white artists such as Paul Whiteman developed a softer and more sophisticated approach. Ellington's music expanded upon this evolution. "East St. Louis Toodle-oo," first recorded on November 29, 1926, was a landmark composition that would become the band's theme song until the arrival of Billy Strayhorn and his classic, "Take the A-Train." Soon Duke was able to reach a larger audience, and every year from 1926 all the way to his death in 1974, the Ellington orchestra always broke the Top 5 rankings of jazz bands. The next year the orchestra won the lucrative position of house band at the prestigious Cotton Club in Harlem. Beginning with their debut performance on December 4, 1927, the Ellington band was now reaching people across the nation on a nightly basis with the classic hour-long radio broadcasts from the Cotton Club. Ellington could not have asked for better exposure. It was during this period that crucial new additions to the band were made with the arrival of Hodges, trumpeter Cootie Williams—who would replace Bubber Miley—and trombonist Juan Tizol.

New innovations came with pieces like "Black and Tan Fantasy," "The Mooche," and "Creole Love Call," which featured a "wordless" vocal by Adelaide Hall. "Black Beauty" was one of Duke's first musical "portraits," written for deceased singer Florence Mills. "Mood Indigo" introduced new concepts of color and harmony, an abstract and introspective piece that featured a trio of muted trumpet and trombone with clarinet—the clarinet playing in the lower register as the trombone played in the upper. The unprecedented inversion of the standard range of these instruments created a sound previously unheard in music.

The following year, in 1931, Ellington wrote his first "extended" work, "Creole Rhapsody," which stretched over two sides of a 78 rpm disc. Another productive year was 1932 with more Ellington classics like "Sophisticated Lady" and "It Don't Mean a Thing (If It Ain't Got That Swing)," both of which would become standards for musicians around the world. Comparable only to George Gershwin and Cole Porter, Ellington wrote thousands of songs in his lifetime, the exact number of which remains unknown. He would also reinterpret many of his standards over the years. "Mood Indigo," for example, would be rerecorded with new arrangements in 1957, 1966, and so on. Ellington left the Cotton Club in 1931 and, unlike Gershwin or Porter, henceforth established his orchestra as a consistently active touring band.

As Ellington broke new ground musically, Irving Mills broke new barriers in his promotional efforts for Ellington and the band. Soon there were film appearances such as *Check and Double Check*. Ellington's roles in films from the very beginning were never stereotypical or racially demeaning. He was always portrayed as the intelligent, "gentleman genius." Then came the highly successful tour of Europe in 1933, an important turning point. Ellington was astonished by the degree of familiarity and affection European audiences felt for his music. He made his first connections with royalty, and soon the Duke of Ellington was sharing his piano stool at parties with the Duke of Kent.

It was also at this time that Ellington was being compared with European classical composers ranging from Delius to Bach—although as Gunther Schuller points out, Ellington was not familiar with classical music at this time. He simply continued following his own path. The individual voices of his players increasingly excited his musical imagination as never before. He continued to establish the previously unknown practice of composing pieces that would incorporate a given player's unique sound into his own musical vocabulary. "Clarinet Lament" was a type of concerto for Barney Bigard. "Trumpet in Spades" for Rex Stewart, "Echoes of Harlem" for Cootie Williams, and so on.

There were also more structured works for the entire orchestra. "Reminiscing in Tempo," written in mourning after the death of Ellington's mother in 1935, was a one-movement variation piece that stretched over four 78 rpm sides. It was attacked by critics who felt that Ellington was straying too far from the "hot jazz" that was popular at the time. Many called it boring, self-indulgent, pretentious. This type of criticism would resurface when Ellington unveiled his magnum opus in 1943, "Black Brown & Beige." Such attacks on his extended pieces were a personal blow to Ellington, but he forged ahead in spite of criticism and a rigorous touring and recording schedule. In fact, constant travel provided Ellington with a great deal of inspiration and isolation for his writing, and kept his musicians employed. Ellington, always protective of his health, did not allow the relentless schedule to slow him down, and in 1937 he first encountered the doctor who would become his personal physician and one of his closest friends for the rest of his life, Arthur Logan.

By the beginning of the forties, three new musicians arrived that would help define one of the strongest units in Ellington's career: virtuoso bassist Jimmy Blanton, tenor saxophonist Ben Webster, and composer Billy Strayhorn. Growing up in Pittsburgh, Strayhorn played and studied classical music. Hearing the Ellington band in concert had an overwhelming impact on him. Within a few years he found enough courage to show Ellington some of his songs, including the incredible "Lush Life," written when Strayhorn was still in high school. Ellington was stunned at the quality of Strayhorn's work, and brought him into the organization without hesitation.

Although he was initially hired as a lyricist, Strayhorn's skills as a composer, arranger, and pianist enabled him to become Ellington's musical companion, creating one of the most unique partnerships between two composers in history. When listening to an Ellington–Strayhorn composition, it is virtually impossible to pinpoint who wrote what, such was their affinity for one another personally and musically. Strayhorn immediately contributed several classics into the band's catalogue between 1940 and 1942: "Take the A-Train," which would become the Ellington band's theme song, "Raincheck," "Day Dream," "Chelsea Bridge," "Passion Flower," to name only a few.

This steady stream of Strayhorn material came at a welcome time when Ellington's own material was being kept off the radio due to a dispute between ASCAP and radio stations. Mercer Ellington also began making important musical contributions during this period with "Things Ain't What They Used to Be," "Moon Mist," and "Blue Serge." As a young composer and trumpeter, Mercer was beginning to establish himself in his father's world, and the two experienced a complex relationship for the rest of Duke's life—another difficult area that suffers some misrepresentation in many Ellington biographies, including Mercer's own book on his father's life.

Tenor saxophonist Ben Webster and bassist Jimmy Blanton also made significant musical contributions at this unique juncture of Ellington's career (1940–42). Webster became Ellington's first major voice on tenor, influenced particularly by Coleman Hawkins. Suddenly Duke had to adjust his writing strategy to accomodate the new sound. The same changes were required for Blanton, whose approach to bass as a simultaneous solo and rhythm instrument created a whole new language for future bassists in jazz. The combination of these three newcomers (Strayhorn, Webster, and Blanton) with the ever-evolving strengths of Hodges, Cootie, Carney, Nanton, and company, gave Ellington one of the greatest ensembles of his career, inspiring him to new levels in composition. The classics poured from Ellington's pen: "Jack the Bear," "Ko Ko," "Sepia Panorama," "Warm Valley." There were "exotic" pieces with a Latin flavor such as "Conga Brava," and "The Flaming Sword," similar in flavor to Juan Tizol's "Caravan." There were musical "portraits" such as "Bojangles," and "Portrait of Bert Williams." And there were two pieces that anticipated the bebop movement by at least five years: "Cottontail" and "Main Stem."

All of these were masterpieces of the three-minute format. But Ellington was ready to compose more extended works and perform longer concerts, something his manager Irving Mills was against. Ellington soon severed his ties with Mills for this and other reasons including financial conflicts, Mills having received royalties on many Ellington songs. The William Morris Agency became Duke's new business representation. Ellington soon began work on a musical production called *Jump for Joy*. The show would express many social concerns of the African-American community in an entertainment context as opposed to outspoken political protest, which was always Ellington's preferred approach. The production was only performed in Los Angeles where it was created, not only because too many players had left to fight in World War II, but also because the show itself was simply too ahead of its time in 1942. Nevertheless, it was a milestone for Ellington because it gave him more confidence in producing more extended works.

He began work on his most ambitious composition of all, "Black Brown & Beige," with an eye toward unveiling the piece at one of the world's most prestigious venues for classical music: Carnegie Hall. But before this would happen, Ellington had to deal with the tragic loss of bassist Jimmy Blanton to tuberculosis, as well as the departures of important players such as Cootie Williams, Barney Bigard, Ivie Anderson, and eventually Ben Webster. New arrivals included trumpeter Ray Nance to replace Cootie, Jimmy Hamilton to replace Bigard, and arranger Tom Whaley from Boston. Duke was now working around the clock on his magnum opus for the Carnegie Hall performance on January 23, 1943.

"Black Brown & Beige" is a three-movement work that Ellington referred to as a "tone parallel to the history of the American Negro." Some of his ideas came from an unfinished opera with a similar theme he had been working on called *Boola*. The "Black" movement was the most fully realized and successful, contrasting the physical impact of the "Work Song" with the spiritual introspection of "Come Sunday," which featured a breathtaking alto solo for Johnny Hodges. "Brown" presents a musical picture of the black, notably Haitian, heroes of the Revolutionary War. "Beige," the least successful of the three movements, came to the present day with concerns regarding education, social advancement, and family. This final section received the most criticism, because Ellington had rushed to complete it before the deadline of the Carnegie performance, and it did not receive the attention and development given to the previous two movements. Many critics felt that the entire suite started off strongly, but tapered downward in quality as the movements progressed. Other critics rejected it altogether, saying that it was once again too pretentious and that Ellington was moving completely away from his proven abilities in jazz. Despite these criticisms, "Black Brown & Beige" was a major event not only for Duke Ellington, but for the entire world of music. The future implications of this would be enormous.

Carnegie Hall became an annual event for Ellington, and he would unveil his most ambitious pieces there. At the next Carnegie show in December of 1943, Ellington premiered "New World A-Comin'," which would later be rearranged for symphony orchestra by Luther Henderson. In years to follow at Carnegie there came Ellington–Strayhorn's "Perfume Suite," "The Deep South Suite," "The Liberian Suite," "The Tattooed Bride," and "Harlem," which would also be rearranged for symphony orchestra. These concerts helped establish Ellington as an American composer on a different level from other big band or jazz artists. And while jazz—and eventually rock—artists would begin performing in classical music venues much more frequently in the fifties, sixties, and seventies, it was Duke Ellington who first opened the door for these artists with the performance of "Black Brown & Beige."

Ben Webster left the band in 1943, only to return briefly in 1948. Although his place was taken by Al Sears, Ellington would now lack a distinctive voice on tenor saxophone until the arrival of Paul Gonsalves. Rex Stewart also left at this time, but Cat Anderson was a capable replacement. Anderson had his own sound, and was able to hit the highest register of any Ellingtonian trumpeter. The band enjoyed lengthy seasons at New York's Hurricane Club and Capitol Theatre, as well as the annual Carnegie performances, but the relentless touring also continued—as well as frequent recording sessions where collaborations between Ellington and his orchestra continued to develop. Later in the decade Ellington contributed to a musical called *Beggar's Holiday*, but it was a complete flop. Much more positive was Duke's return to Europe in 1949, although without the whole band due to union complications. He also played with the Philadelphia Symphony Orchestra. In the midst of this activity, Ellington could not have foreseen the problems on the horizon.

Bebop was developing as a musical form, and growing in popularity. Artists who had been profoundly influenced by Ellington such as Thelonious Monk, Dizzy Gillespie, and Charlie Parker, were pioneering a new style of jazz. Their bands were much smaller, usually featuring only five or six players. The post-war celebrations were over, and life was getting lean for the big bands. Promoters wanted to save money, ballrooms were closing, cinema theaters were only showing movies instead of presenting concerts. Many of the swing bands fell apart. Ellington was one of the only survivors of this period, but because of the recording ban there was not nearly as much new Ellington music on the market. Ellington had to make financial sacrifices to keep his musicians employed, and there were more significant personnel changes.

Tenor saxophonist Paul Gonsalves joined the band in 1950, and his warm and rich tone finally filled the void left by Ben Webster's departure. Gonsalves would remain with Ellington until his death. It was at this time that Ellington had a falling out with Sonny Greer, who had been suffering from a severe drinking problem. The two had an unhappy confrontation toward the end of a European tour. After his return to the States, Ellington completed work on what many consider his most successful extended work, "Harlem." The piece was commissioned by the NBC Symphony Orchestra, conducted by Arturo Toscanini. It was first performed at the Metropolitan Opera House as part of a benefit for the NAACP. But soon after this triumph, Sonny Greer, Lawrence Brown, and Johnny Hodges announced that they were leaving the Ellington band. Hodges planned to keep the other two players as part of his own group.

The music world wondered if Ellington would be able to recover from the loss. Ellington again proved himself a streetwise survivor with a decisive action known as the Great James Robbery. Ellington lured three important musicians away from bandleader Harry James: Willie Smith to replace Hodges on alto, Louis Bellson to replace Greer on drums, and Ellington's own former trombonist Juan Tizol to replace Brown. Tizol had been responsible for some of Ellington's best known tracks, including "Caravan" and "Perdido." Another trombonist named Britt Woodman also joined at this time, along with two outstanding trumpeters, Clark Terry and Willie Cook, and Butch Ballard on drums. These new voices, along with the incredible Gonsalves, gave Ellington new enthusiasm, although there were those who were not impressed with the new lineup.

With the changes taking effect in the early fifties, Duke began composing more steadily again. The most well-known piece from this time was "Satin Doll" with lyrics by Strayhorn and Johnny Mercer. He had also begun to take advantage of the new technology of long playing records, extending his studio arrangements for the new format. Two of his first twelve-inch LPs, *Masterpieces by Ellington* and *Ellington Uptown*, were successful and well received. The Ellington orchestra had never sounded so good on record before. He also recorded for Capitol as a solo pianist backed only by bass and drums on *The Duke Plays Ellington*. But Ellington had to swallow his pride to make ends meet in 1955, and spent the summer backing up an aqua show in Long Island called "Aquacades." Despite this apparent embarrassment, Ellington was able to complete the extraordinary "Night Creature," a new extended work performed at Carnegie with the Symphony of the Air. This innovative piece would be recorded in 1963 with various orchestras of Europe.

Everything turned around for Ellington when Johnny Hodges returned to the orchestra after his own group disbanded. Drummer Sam Woodyard also joined at this time. Ellington negotiated a new deal with Columbia Records and began a relationship with Irving Townsend, who would work on many Ellington projects in the future. The two met at Duke's legendary performance at the Newport Jazz Festival in Rhode Island on July 7, 1956, where the band performed the exotic "Diminuendo and Crescendo in Blue," with Paul Gonsalves nearly inciting a riot as he blew an unprecedented twenty-seven choruses. The crowd reaction was ecstatic. Never before had such a sustained improvisation from one player been heard in jazz. The remaining ensemble had also given one of their strongest performances, aware of the need to prove themselves. The victory at Newport landed Duke Ellington on the cover of *Time* magazine, and the live recording of the Newport Festival would become Ellington's best-selling LP.

Ellington was back, and he and Strayhorn immediately took advantage of this new momentum with new music, beginning with an extended work for the color television special "A Drum Is a Woman." The piece features picturesque narration by Ellington between songs, tracing the history of jazz in an allegorical fashion from the African jungle to New Orleans. Their next major work was "Such Sweet Thunder," a series of musical impressions based on the plays of William Shakespeare, who was a major source of inspiration. Duke trasformed Henry V into Hank Cinq, Katherine from "Taming of the Shrew" into Sister Kate, and Lady Macbeth into Lady Mac. Shakespeare had come to Harlem. Ellington and Strayhorn premiered the entire suite at the Shakespeare Festival at Stratford, Ontario, in 1957. It is regarded as one of the peaks of post-war Ellingtonia. The orchestra returned to Europe, and Duke was presented to Queen Elizabeth and Princess Margaret at the Leeds Festival. Duke returned to the States and recorded a new composition called "The Queen's Suite," and sent a special pressing to Buckingham Palace. In 1959 Ellington composed his first film score for Otto Preminger's *Anatomy of a Murder*. More film scores quickly followed, such as *Paris Blues*.

In 1960, Ellington and Strayhorn premiered "Suite Thursday," based on John Steinbeck's *Sweet Thursday*. The piece was first performed in Steinbeck country at the Monterey Jazz Festival in California. It was later recorded and released on an album which also featured an adaptation of Grieg's "Peer Gynt Suites 1 and 2." A similar effort with Tchaikovsky's "Nutcracker Suite" would soon follow. By this time, Lawrence Brown was also back in the band, soon to be followed by the celebrated return of Cootie Williams in 1962. In retrospect, the sixties would prove to be one of the most productive and creative periods of Ellington's career, with travel around the globe that would inspire some of his best work, arguably his most consistent lineup of musicians, new innovations in the studio, and Ellington's emergence as a composer of religious music—as well as pieces with a renewed concern for African-American expression.

The decade began with Ellington's involvement in many recording collaborations with other leading jazz figures: Ellington and Basie bands side by side, Ellington guesting on piano with Louis Armstrong, trio sides with musical descendants Charles Mingus and Max Roach, and joint sessions with Coleman Hawkins as well as John Coltrane. It seemed that everybody wanted to record with Duke.

Nineteen sixty-three was an especially prominent year, beginning with another triumphant European tour that would produce the brilliant live recording *The Great Paris Concert*. Ellington and Strayhorn also composed music for a production of Shakespeare's *Timon of Athens*. The hundredth anniversary of the Emancipation Proclomation was celebrated in Chicago, and Ellington was invited to unveil his newest extended work, the musical production *My People*. Composed and orchestrated entirely by Ellington, it was a logical extension of many elements of "Black Brown & Beige," with the "Come Sunday" section revised and expanded into "David Danced." The entire production divides its focus between spirituals and blues, until a climax is reached with a direct approach to social issues with "King Fit the Battle," and "What Color is Virtue?" "King Fit" is a direct reference to Martin Luther King's experiences in Birmingham, Alabama.

Then came the landmark Asian State Department Tour later in the year, taking the band through the Middle and Near East including Jerusalem, Beirut, Delhi, Bombay, Calcutta, Teheran, Isfahan, and Baghdad, among other cities. The reception was overwhelmingly positive, as was the band's experience of the tour, but the trip came to an abrupt and unpleasant halt on November 22 when President Kennedy was assassinated. Nevertheless, the sights and sounds of that tour provided the inspiration for what many feel is one of Ellington and Strayhorn's strongest collaborative efforts, "The Far East Suite."

The title can be misleading, because the band never reached the Far East on that tour, although they would visit Japan the following year—which inspired the closing piece of the recorded suite, "Ad Lib on Nippon." The suite was conceived as a series of musical impressions of the Middle and Near East, and was performed live but not recorded until 1966. When the record finally appeared, it was hailed as Ellington's most fulfilling studio LP to date. The unmatched genius of the Ellington–Strayhorn partnership produced a body of work that painted vivid aural pictures of the Asian landscape while still bearing the Ellington-Strayhorn stamp. Again Ellington's music conveyed a sense of place, but without succumbing to the limitations of any particular indigenous music. The success of this venture gave Ellington the encouragement to visit other areas of the globe. But the next major milestone of his career would be of an entirely different character, with the unveiling of his First Sacred Concert.

Ellington was invited to perform sacred music at Grace Cathedral in San Francisco on September 16, 1965. He responded without hesitation with a program that included many previous pieces such as "Come Sunday," "David Danced," and "New World a-Comin'." But Ellington also included new material such as "In the Beginning God." The first concert was performed many times in various churches of different denominations, and Ellington viewed this work with the hghest degree of seriousness. He would compose a second concert toward the end of 1967 using all new material with the exception of "99 Percent Won't Do." The Second Sacred Concert was premiered in New York's Cathedral of St. John the Divine on January 19, 1968. Duke believed that all of his sacred music—the Second Sacred Concert in particular—was the most important work of his career, expressing his most profound spiritual beliefs as never before. A third concert would be completed shortly before his death in 1974. Far from being "jazz mass," or traditional gospel or liturgical music, Ellington's sacred music was an individual expression of Negro folk music. As always, it was beyond category.

But between the creation of the First and Second Concerts, Ellington suffered a devastating blow with the loss of his close friend and musical alter ego, Billy Strayhorn. It was the most difficult experience of his life with the sole exception of the death of his mother. In 1965, Strayhorn was hospitalized for cancer treatment, and would never be able to travel with the band as freely as before. As his condition grew more critical, he continued to compose some of his most poignant music, and Ellington maintained steady contact with Strayhorn over the telephone. Some of Strayhorn's song titles at the time painted a picture of the painful circumstances of his life. "U.M.M.G." stood for Upper Manhattan Medical Group. "Blood Count" was the last piece he completed before his death. It was sent directly from Strayhorn's hospital bed to a Carnegie Hall performance, where Ellington held up the manuscript for Johnny Hodges to sight read. On May 31, 1967, Billy Strayhorn passed away in the early morning hours. Ellington immediately sat down and wrote a heartfelt eulogy, which can be found in the liner notes of the record the orchestra recorded as a Stayhorn memorial, *And His Mother Called Him Bill.* This record is regarded by many as one of the orchestra's finest, and features some of the most emotional playing from Johnny Hodges on pieces like "Blood Count," and "Day Dream." The original vinyl record closed with a spontaneous Ellington piano recital of "Lotus Blossom" that conveys the sense of grief and loss that permeated those sessions.

Becoming increasingly aware that his time in the world was growing short, Ellington began to drive himself with even greater intensity, with new compositions and appearances around the world. His first major effort in the aftermath of Strayhorn's death was the Second Sacred Concert. The extraordinary vocalist Alice Babs was brought in from Europe on soprano. The opening in New York, as well as subsequent performances, elicited audience response ranging from reverent to ecstatic. Highlights of the piece included "Supreme Being," "Heaven," and the finale, "Praise God and Dance." Ellington was pleased with the reaction to what he considered his most important work.

The next career milestone came in the form of Ellington's first Latin American tour in the late summer of 1968. Departing New York on September 1, the band took their first trip south of the equator as they played Brazil, Argentina, Uruguay, Chile, then back to the United States for a small string of one-nighters before returning to finish the tour in Mexico. As with the Asian tour of 1963, Ellington's sensitive mind absorbed the cultural aspects of the region, and produced an individual body of work based on his impressions. This time, Ellington composed the music so instantaneously that he was ready to debut the new suite in Mexico City before the end of the tour! The original title was "Mexican Anticipacion," but would eventually be recorded and released as "The Latin American Suite." One of Ellington's most exuberant works, it perfectly conveys the colors and rhythms of South America, again without reverting to the instrumentation or limitations of that region's indigenous music. Paul Gonsalves, who spoke fluent

Portuguese and served as official interpreter of the tour, was the chief soloist of the suite.

The following April, Ellington celebrated his seventieth birthday in his home town of Washington, D.C., at the White House, where he was awarded the Medal of Freedom by President Nixon. Ellington had been the guest of presidents Truman and Johnson in the past, but the birthday celebration of April 29, 1969, was of a much higher caliber. The ceremony began with a formal dinner, followed by the presentation of the Medal, and then an evening of music with an all-star lineup of musicians (Ellingtonian and non) playing selections from the Maestro's book. Some of the musicians included Count Basie, Benny Goodman, Cab Calloway, Gerry Mulligan, Louis Bellson, Dave Brubeck, Paul Desmond, and Billy Eckstine, among many others. The most poignant moment came during the presentation of the Medal, when Ellington declared, "There is no place I would rather be tonight except in my mother's arms."

Later in the year, the band returned to Europe and recorded the live record entitled "Duke Ellington's 70th Birthday Concert." It was given unanimously positive reviews. The 1969 European tour included Ellington's first performance in Eastern Europe with a concert in Prague. Sacred Concerts were also performed in Paris, Stockholm, and Barcelona. By this time, Jimmy Hamilton had left the band and was replaced by Harold Ashby, a fine saxophonist, but not the distinctive voice on clarinet that Ellington enjoyed with Hamilton—although Russell Procope continued to be heard on the instrument. It would not be long before Duke would lose the greatest Ellingtonian of them all—Johnny Hodges.

For the band's appearance at the New Orleans Jazz Festival of 1970, Ellington composed the first portions of what would become "The New Orleans Suite." Five sections painted aural pictures of the Crescent City, while four sections were conceived as musical portraits of some of the city's prominent native sons and daughters: Louis Armstrong, Sidney Bechet, Wellman Braud, and Mahalia Jackson. The festival performance was a success, and the band entered the studio to record the suite. But by this time, Lawrence Brown had once again left the orchestra. Then halfway through the recording of the album came the devastating news that Johnny Hodges had passed away in his dentist's office. The timing of this tragedy was especially poignant. Ellington was hoping to persuade Hodges to dust off his soprano saxophone for "Portrait of Sidney Bechet." Hodges hadn't played the instrument in at least thirty years, and Bechet was unquestionably one of Hodges' role models. Standing in Hodges' place, Paul Gonsalves gave a heartfelt tenor performance on the piece in memory of the greatest soloist the Ellington orchestra had ever known.

Despite this latest blow, Ellington had no choice but to continue moving forward. His itinerary was filled with more dates in Europe and Japan, as well as the orchestra's first visits to Australia, New Zealand, Thailand, and Laos. He was commissioned by the American Ballet Theatre to compose one of his most ambitious pieces yet, *The River.* His experiences in Japan and Australia helped inspire him to compose yet another unique series of musical impressions brought together in a suite called "Afro-Eurasian Eclipse." It was the last example of Ellington's individual approach to world music, and a worthy continuation of his works devoted to Africa, Asia, and Latin America. As a gesture of gratitude to the African nation of Togoland, which issued Ellington's image on a set of postage stamps, he composed the suite "Togo Brava— Brava Togo!" The suite was premiered at the 1971 Newport Festival. These aforementioned pieces would be among the last works of significance from Ellington's pen—with the exception of his autobiography, and one remaining extended work that would soon see the light of day.

With the loss of Hodges and Brown, as well as Cat Anderson, the orchestra seemed to be going through another difficult period of transition. Cootie Williams was soon to depart as well. Ellington, however, only expressed confidence in his personnel, and in 1971 the orchestra embarked on the biggest global tour of their career, with returns to Europe and Latin America, as well as their first voyage to Russia, which would last for five weeks and was a resounding success for Ellington. In 1972 the schedule was equally as relentless, with a mammoth tour of the Far East including more dates in Japan, Thailand, Singapore, Indonesia, and the Philippines. Ellington finally began completing his autobiography, *Music Is My Mistress*, which would mostly consist of anecdotes and stories about his many friends, associates, and favorite haunts. Not surprisingly, the book revealed very little about Ellington the private man.

In 1973, Ellington discovered that he had been developing lung cancer. In the face of this revelation, Ellington continued working with more courage and determination than ever before on what would be his final statement to the world—the Third Sacred Concert. The new piece would be performed at Westminster Abbey in London on October 24, 1973. Unfortunately, Paul Gonsalves had taken ill just prior to the performance, and Harold Ashby assumed Gonsalves's solos. The rehearsals were frantic, almost right up to performance time. But the Third Sacred Concert proved to be one of the most poignant and spiritually evocative pieces of Ellington's career, with more tremendous vocal performances from Alice Babs on pieces such as "Is God a Three-

Letter Word for Love?" and "The Majesty of God." Harry Carney and Ellington himself were also prominently featured throughout the concert.

While Ellington was still in the United Kingdom, his long-time physician and close friend Arthur Logan fell from his apartment window in New York under mysterious circumstances on November 25. This was the final blow. Only the losses of his mother and Billy Strayhorn were as devastating. Ellington confided that he would almost certainly not last another six months with Arthur Logan gone. He was off by one day.

In January 1974, Ellington collapsed during a performance in his hometown of Washington, D.C. He was taken to Columbia Presbyterian Medical Center in New York City, then returned to his West End Avenue home. But he was not the same Duke Ellington that his friends had known. In March, Evie Ellington was also diagnosed with lung cancer, and was hospitalized. Ellington returned to Presbyterian Hospital in April, never to see Evie again, or to return home. Once Evie left the hospital, Ellington maintained constant telephone contact with her. He was also working with Mercer to make changes and improvements on his Third Sacred Concert from his hospital bed.

With Ellington unable to attend, Brooks Kerr and Roscoe Gill were brought in to conduct a performance of excerpts from the Sacred Concerts at St. Peter's Church in New York in celebration of Ellington's 75th birthday on April 29, 1974. His health was steadily declining by this time, and it was the first time the Ellington orchestra performed without him. Unbeknown to him, Paul Gonsalves has passed away in London in mid-May. Nobody had the heart to tell Ellington, fearing that the news would only upset his fragile condition. Finally on May 24, 1974, one day shy of the six-month calculation he had given his own life expectancy after Arthur Logan's death, Edward Kennedy Ellington passed into the place where he most longed to be—his departed mother's arms.

Stevie Wonder

At THE TIME OF ELLINGTON'S DEATH, Stevie Wonder had just completed his 1974 LP *Fulfillingness' First Finale*. This was the fourth in a series of records where Wonder had taken greater creative conrol over his work, something which was still a new concept for his label, Motown Records. When he was signed in the early sixties as "Little Stevie" Wonder, Motown was building an empire in popular music by introducing black artists into mainstream pop music. Motown had staff songwriters, staff studio musicians, and staff producers, all of which guaranteed that everything released on the label bore the unmistakeable Motown stamp. Every aspect of the artist's career was predetermined. But as the sixties came to an end, some of the Motown artists were ready to take more control over their work. Marvin Gaye and Stevie Wonder were the first artists on the label who began making albums that were unified statements rather than a collection of singles. Motown resisted the change at first, but when the new directions taken by Gaye and Wonder proved to be even more successful than their previous hits, there was no turning back.

Stevie Wonder had developed into a multi-instrumentalist, composer, and lyricist of the highest caliber. His music was harmonically and melodically sophisticated, yet rhythmically accessible. His lyrics were personal and honest, and were often compared to Bob Dylan and John Lennon. Stevie had undergone a creative and commercial renaissance with a series of records beginning with *Music From My Mind,* continuing with *Talking Book, Innervisions,* and *Fulfillingness' First Finale.* He had broken many of the existing barriers in pop music. His music ranged from tender love ballads like "You are the Sunshine of My Life," to hard hitting funk like "Superstition." His message of love, spiritual awareness, and social consciousness resonated strongly with both white and black audiences on both sides of the Atlantic. By the mid-seventies, Stevie Wonder was on top, earning Grammy awards and platinum record sales. He had finally reached his highest potential as an artist—exercising full control over his music and reaching millions of people around the world. Soon he would produce one of his biggest hits by paying tribute to one of his musical heroes, Duke Ellington.

In 1975, Wonder signed a new contract with Motown, and began work on a sprawling two-record set that would take him almost two years to complete. *Songs in the Key of Life* was finally released in October 1976 and debuted at number one on the album charts. It was Stevie's most eclectic effort yet, with a range of styles largely unexplored in pop music. Unlike his previous one-man multi-instrumental albums, this record featured one of the largest collections of musicians on a pop album. There were arrangements for horns, strings, and singers. The studio musicians were the cream of the Los Angeles session crop. Stevie was going for a large ensemble sound, and appropriately used this to express his admiration for Duke. "Sir Duke" was one of the singles from the album, and soon dominated the airwaves. But on the actual album, "Sir Duke" is preceded by an instrumental prelude titled "Contusion."

Although radio listeners never heard it, this mysterious piece is crucial because it actually sets the tone for "Sir Duke," and the two songs flow together as one piece on the LP. "Contusion" is a short instrumental piece about three and a half minutes in duration, but it perfectly anticipates musically what Wonder has to say in "Sir Duke," with the most complex jazz-based harmonies of any Wonder composition up to that point. It features electric guitar and synthesizer over a propulsive rhythm section. The lead guitar plays a brief melody over four different major seventh chords in a 5/4 time signature, before settling on A-flat 7sus4, in 4/4 time. Suddenly there is a lightning fast run of descending major ninths. Then the lead guitar and synthesizer play a melody in unison, alternating between E9-flat5 and A-major7, with the rhythm section laying down a fast and funky tempo. The whole process repeats again, and eventually the descending run of major ninths repeats five times before crashing to a dramatic ending on F-sharp. Out of this whirlwind comes the opening horn fanfare of "Sir Duke."

What makes "Contusion" such an appropriate introduction to "Sir Duke" is the fact that Stevie takes these harmonies that had never been used in pop music before, and makes something so natural and effortless out of them. On paper, "Contusion" appears much too complicated to be on a pop album, and it certainly is an ambitious piece of music that is well beyond the traditional boundaries of pop. It could have easily been recorded by one of the jazz fusion bands of the seventies. But it flows so smoothly that the listener is lifted up by its buoyancy, virtually unaware of its complex structure. We are so taken by the sound, we are not concerned with attaching "rock" or "jazz" labels to it. We are too busy moving to the rhythm, and being moved by the alternating shades of light and dark implied in the harmonies—the kind of harmonies that were standard fare for Duke Ellington. This is what makes "Contusion" such a masterpiece, and an effective tribute combined with "Sir Duke." It is Stevie's use of advanced harmony and melody in a natural and accessible way, with a driving rhythm section, that is also the distinct hallmark of Ellington: experimentation and innovation with a groove. Stevie was indeed an honor student of the Maestro.

"Contusion" immediately gives way to "Sir Duke," which begins with an exuberant horn fanfare over a swinging drum beat. The rest of the band kicks in, and the message becomes immediately clear. Stevie is singing about the universal power of music to reach people from all walks of life, regardless of age or race. But Stevie cautions that if the music is going to move people, it has to have a beat: "Music is a world within itself, with a language we all understand/With an equal opportunity for all to sing, dance, and clap their hands/But just because a record has a groove don't make it in the groove/But you can tell right away, at letter A, when the people start to move/They can feel it all over!" Or as Duke would put it, "It don't mean a thing if it ain't got that swing."

Then comes Stevie's second verse cited at our beginning, where he pays homage to Count Basie, Louis Armstrong, Ella Fitzgerald, and "The King of All, Sir Duke." The music could not be better suited to the lyrics. Stevie essentially has an abbreviated swing band playing behind him, with an electric rhythm section. The horns swoop and slide with Ellingtonian exuberance and grace, with traces of Armstrong and the New Orleans parade bands. The melody is bright and sunny; the beat bounces and swings. Stevie again uses advanced harmonies, and as in "Contusion" there is a rapid series of descending and ascending ninth chords in the verses. But in "Sir Duke" these chords are played with such a funky rhythm that it becomes one of the main hooks of the song. Then the chorus where Stevie sings "You can feel it all over" is played over B, F-minor, E-major7, C-sharp minor7, and F-sharp11: another unusual sequence of chords that are once again so cleverly used with the soaring melody and lively beat, that we are too busy singing along and moving to the beat to notice the complex harmonies being used. After each chorus is a four bar melody played in unison by all instruments except for the steady drum beat. This particular melody has such a strong bebop flavor, but is so memorable and infectious that I can even remember my young friends scat singing along at school, and back then we certainly had no idea what scat singing even was! But it is such a catchy melody; it just seemed like a natural reaction.

Ellington could not have asked for a finer memorial. The Maestro, who spent fifty years making music that broke new ground and dissolved old boundaries, was now saluted by an artist of a younger generation who was breaking down a different set of barriers. Duke had done what Stevie was now doing: creating life-affirming music that would spread a positive message to anybody who listened; experimenting with complex harmonies without taking away the beat; and above all, being in complete control over the entire creative process. Stevie was also trying to break through the generation gap. He was telling his younger fans that the music of the older jazz generation was just as exciting as the music of the younger rock generation. Perhaps he was going the other way too. Perhaps he was telling the jazz listeners of the older generation that there was something just as vital and legitimate to be found in the rock and soul music of the younger generation, with Stevie himself a perfect example. He had achieved massive critical and commercial acclaim on his own terms with no need to borrow from anyone. He was creating his own sound, and speaking his own message. But he wrote "Sir Duke" out of a profound sense of respect and gratitude to the man who had set an example for Stevie by being true to his own inner vision.

Steely Dan

GOING BACK TO EARLY 1974, shortly before Ellington's death, is another fascinating tribute to Duke by an innovative force in modern pop music. Steely Dan was a group whose name came from Beat novelist William Burroughs's *Naked Lunch*. The group was the brainchild of two songwriting partners, Walter Becker and Donald Fagen. Becker and Fagen had met at Bard College in upstate New York in the late sixties. Both of them shared a preference for jazz over the popular music of the time, and Beat writers such as Burroughs, Kerouac, Ginsberg, and Ferlinghetti. They developed a unique songwriting style combining jazz harmonies and oblique lyrics with a modern rock sound. They wrote songs for the famous Brill Building in Manhattan before being hired as staff songwriters for ABC Records in Los Angeles, but it didn't take long for the label to realize that Becker and Fagen's songs were far too unusual to be recorded successfully by other acts. ABC offered Becker and Fagen a recording contract. The duo assembled a group of session musicians, and Steely Dan was born.

Their debut record *Can't Buy a Thrill* was released in 1972 to instant acclaim, and featured two hit singles, "Do it Again" and "Reeling in the Years." Steely Dan recorded and toured as a band for the next two years, but after the release of their third album, *Pretzel Logic*, Becker and Fagen had decided to retire from live performance in order to focus their energy exclusively on writing and recording. They disbanded the original group, but continued under the Steely Dan name, using different session musicians for each new record. The duo had virtually disappeared from the public eye, but their hit songs continued to dominate the airwaves, and their mystique grew to legendary proportions because people had no idea what the duo looked like. Studio musicians jumped at the chance to record with Becker and Fagen. Their music was challenging and fun to play; their records were guaranteed hits; and Steely Dan was an impressive name to have on a resumé. Both men developed a reputation for being obsessive perfectionists in the studio, often spending days working on a single drum track until it met their exacting standards. They knew exactly what they wanted for each song, and they would go to whatever lengths were necessary to achieve it. But by all accounts, the finished product was always worth the extra effort. Their music increasingly took advantage of complex jazz harmonies, while their lyrics combined black humor with fictional portraits of modern urban life. The Steely Dan sound was instantly recognizable.

Although they had a completely original style, it is also easy to see what they learned from Duke Ellington: his sophisticated use of harmony, and his colorful commentaries on life in the big city. They also learned from his methods as a bandleader, his proven ability to get what he wanted from his musicians to achieve a specific desired effect. Becker and Fagen soon developed their own techniques for working with musicians in the studio that would give them the maximum results for their time and energy. They gave their musicians relatively little freedom compared to Ellington, but they knew how to communicate in such a way that would inspire the musicians to give their very best performances in even the most grueling sessions. This process had been perfected by Duke decades beforehand, and was now being adapted by Becker and Fagen to suit their own needs. Ellington's influence on these two highly individual artists was subtle but pervasive, not only in their music, but also in their methods. It is therefore no surprise that the one and only time Becker and Fagen decided to record someone else's music was for an Ellington piece. The duo had vowed never to record anything but their own original compositions, but for Duke they made a special exception. In celebration of his 75th birthday, Becker and Fagen planned to complete the recording in time to send Ellington a special copy on April 29, 1974. The piece they chose would show yet another way that Duke had influenced modern pop music.

"East St. Louis Toodle-oo" was first recorded by the Ellington orchestra on November 29, 1926. It featured the unmistakeable growl of Bubber Miley's muted trumpet, creating the special "wah-wah" effect that Ellington became famous for in his arrangements. Steely Dan decided to record a modernized version of "Toodle-oo," substituting electric guitar for the muted trumpet. They were not the first to create this sound on guitar. In the late sixties, Jimi Hendrix had first popularized the so-called wah-wah sound on guitar through the use of a special foot pedal. When Hendrix was a child, he had heard Ellington's original version of "East St. Louis Toodle-oo," and was fascinated with the use of plunger mutes by Miley and "Tricky Sam" Nanton to produce this unique sound. As Hendrix began playing guitar in the Army and the soul music circuit, he told his friends that one day he would find a way to make his guitar "talk" like the horns in Ellington's band. His friends thought he was crazy. But by 1967 he had brought the sound of wah-wah guitar to the forefront of rock technology, and soon there was a whole generation of electric guitarists who were making their instruments "talk" like Bubber Miley's trumpet. For Duke's seventy-fifth birthday, Becker and Fagen felt it was time to return the favor and give their fans an idea of where this wah-wah sound came from.

They tracked down three different recordings of "East St. Louis Toodle-oo" by the Ellington band, and combined elements of all three versions for their own interpretation. The Steely Dan version is actually quite faithful to the structure of the original recordings, despite the modern instrumentation. Walter Becker's electric wah-wah guitar recreates Bubber Miley's opening melody note for note. Jeff Baxter substitutes pedal steel for the original trombone solo by "Tricky Sam" Nanton. Donald Fagen plays a piano solo where the clarinet solo is heard on the original. Using a two-handed stride approach in the piano solo, Fagen pays homage to Duke's roots. Fagen then switches to alto saxophone and duets with Becker on guitar for the trumpet/trombone ensemble of the original version. Becker returns on wah-wah guitar for Miley's closing theme before Roger Nichols bangs the gong at the end. "Toodle-oo" was Walter Becker's first performance on electric guitar on a Steely Dan record, having played bass guitar on their previous recordings. This is also Donald Fagen's only recorded performance on saxophone anywhere in Steely Dan's seven album catalogue, having exclusively played keyboards. Just like their decision to record this cover song in the first place, here again Becker and Fagen made a special exception for Duke.

Donald Fagen was pleased with their tribute to the Maestro. When asked about their decision to record someone else's composition, he replied: "Without having a missionary attitude about it, we thought it would be interesting for the audience to realize that this kind of expression is not a new thing. In 1926 a trumpet player was doing with his lip what it takes a complicated set of electronics to do on an electric guitar. Walter had been putzing around with that song for years. We wanted to hear it with all the expertise of modern hi-fi." When asked why Fagen substituted stride piano for Rudy Jackson's clarinet solo, Becker replied: "The piano solo was an arrangement of three bad clarinet solos, with notes changed only where absolutely necessary. Duke didn't have a good clarinet player in that period; a few years later he hired Barney Bigard." Fagen also felt that a stride piano solo would be a more appropriate tribute to Ellington.

Becker and Fagen sent Ellington a special copy of their recording of "East St. Louis Toodle-oo" for his birthday on April 29. But unfortunately Ellington was already hospitalized by this time, with less than a month to live. Fagen says: "I would have been very flattered if he heard it, but I don't know if he did." Although no one can say whether Duke actually heard the recording in his hospital room or not, he was certainly very proud if he did. Steely Dan were among the most highly respected musicians in popular music at the time, right alongside Stevie Wonder. To have two such influential figures in modern music pay homage to Ellington in the mid-seventies was certainly a testament to his stature as one of the greatest composers of any genre. Even if Ellington never heard Steely Dan's tribute, their fans certainly did. And like Stevie's "Sir Duke," it was further testament to the idea that music need not be divided along racial, generational, or stylistic lines.

As with Stevie Wonder, Becker and Fagen paid tribute to Ellington on a deeper level by following his example in their own work. They stayed true to themselves, and broke new ground in music by merging their sophisticated harmonic approach with their literary approach to lyrics. Like Stevie, if they had tried to imitate Ellington, their tribute to Duke would have very little meaning. But even with their version of "Toodle-oo," they were not making Ellington music. They were making Steely Dan music. Becker and Fagen were not about to compromise anything in their quest to create something new, and this is precisely what places them among Ellington's most worthy descendents.

Fagen has said: "I think our songs were derived more instrumentally. Not to make a comparison in quality, but more in the way Duke Ellington would write. He wrote for the people in his band, the specific players. He wrote lines that he thought they could play well. And although we weren't writing for instrumental performers—we were writing for my voice—I think our background, because it comes mostly out of arranging and jazz, made us lean toward melodies that had that kind of structure: they're more chordally situated."

One of the best examples of this is their own composition, "The Caves of Altamira," written during their earlier years in New York. As with many of Ellington's greatest pieces, "Caves" was inspired by a foreign landscape, and vividly conveys a sense of place. There is an actual cave located in Northern Spain called Altamira, well known for many prehistoric paintings and engravings of animals on the roof and walls. There are images of bison, deer, horses, goats, and cattle. Fagen creates a narrative of a grown man who looks back on the days of his childhood when he would visit the cave, observe the animal images, and dream of the ancient world. The narrator then reflects on how modern man has permanently altered the environment. The key is F# minor7, with a chorus that alternates between D-major9 and A-major7, with other well placed diminished chords and minor sevenths. The horns and piano are integral to the arrangement in a style that is strongly reminiscent of Ellington.

As with all of their compositions, these unusual progressions are so skillfully woven into the rhythm and melody, that the listener is not consciously aware of it. All that we hear is the story being told with the lyrics and music. The structure of the music does not obstruct the song. Becker and Fagen would spend countless hours in the studio communicating their ideas to the finest session musicians in the world, perfecting every nuance of each song. As Fagen has said: "Because the cost of rehearsal time with studio players was (and is) high, we began to prepare fairly detailed charts before going into the studio, sometimes with the help of one of the musicians on the date. The players would run down the tune a few times and then we'd start recording. Sometimes a player would come in and tip off a great solo, other times if they were playing something which we didn't think was stylistically consistent with the song, or if they were just having trouble getting any idea, we might suggest a stylistic or melodic idea to get them started."

༺✧༻

This sounds almost exactly like the process that Ellington would undergo when he went into the studio. As Butch Ballard and Luther Henderson both point out, Ellington would often arrive with some basic thematic material charted out, and then the collaborative process would begin with the musicians. This required a clear communication between bandleader and ensemble, something which Ellington had mastered very early in his career. Out of necessity, Ellington created a method of interaction with his players that would become a role model for future artists. Ellington did what no composer had done before: perform his pieces in concert on a consistent basis with his own band. For the first time, a composer had also become a bandleader. Where previously the two were essentially separate roles performed by different people, Ellington was bringing the two disciplines together.

This is the basis of Ellington's influence on the influential composer/bandleaders in jazz and pop that are examined here. Each has been recognized as a pioneer in his own way, creating his own musical language, and certainly not imitating Ellington or anybody else. But it's the *example* that Duke set for all future artists to follow: his unique working methods, his strategies for getting what he wanted from his musicians, his business savvy, and his determination to keep moving forward, that inspired these younger artists to follow their own creative paths in the same spirit. In this way, Duke Ellington has had an even deeper impact than simply that of a great musician. He created a *blueprint* for a new kind of artist: the composer/bandleader.

It takes a special kind of artist to be a composer and bandleader. Most musicians cannot successfully combine the two roles. One must be a leader, and be able to inspire other musicians to manifest the leader's vision. The leader must be in control, while still allowing the individual musicians the freedom to bring their own unique contributions to the table. This is a very delicate Zen-like balancing act, requiring highly developed communication skills on the part of the leader. There must be an intuitive understanding of human relationships and the constant process of give-and-take. Too much control will stifle and inhibit the other musicians from making their own statements, and the chemistry of the group will be lost. On the other hand, not enough control creates a formless free-for-all atmosphere where the leader's vision gets lost. Duke Ellington embodies this uniquely American principle of democracy: leadership that is enriched and inspired by the group. The other artists examined here have come the closest to mastering this delicate process, and they have all continued this special tradition in different ways, but none as effectively as Duke Ellington.

Butch Ballard

BUTCH BALLARD IS A HAPPY MAN. Every day he thanks God for giving him the chance to live his dream by working with so many brilliant musicians throughout his career, including the greatest of them all—Duke Ellington. His profound sense of joy and gratitude is contagious, whether one encounters him in person or on the telephone. He is especially kind to younger musicians, and has an endless supply of wisdom and experience to share with them. I have had the honor and privilege of being one of those who has been touched by his generosity. When we sat down to conduct this interview, he shared with me a great deal of the knowledge he has acquired as a professional drummer over the years. My only regret is that the interview was too short. Butch is still a very busy man at the age of eighty, always on his way to the next gig. When you're a world-renowned musician in constant demand, there never seems to be enough time to talk.

This discussion contains valuable information from an insider who had the chance to work closely with Ellington and observe his methods. Butch describes the process of communication between Ellington and his musicians, on stage and in the recording studio. As Luther Henderson also points out, Ellington did not always rely on specific charts, which allowed for personal interaction between him and his players. We get a glimpse of how Duke would handle problems concerning his players with typical Ellington style and grace. Butch points out that Duke was a master communicator who knew how to get what he wanted, mostly by taking the high road and treating his musicians with respect. Butch tells us how Ellington survived a difficult period of his career, when bebop replaced swing as the most popular form of jazz, by staying on his own path without limiting himself to one style or another. We also hear Butch's interpretation of how Ellington's music ultimately transcends these categories by speaking to people of all cultures in a universal language.

Above all else, a clear picture emerges of a group of individuals working together to express the musical vision of their leader, and of a leader giving his players the opportunity to assume responsibility and take credit for being themselves. Such mutual respect and admiration created an environment that encouraged loyalty and commitment. This is why Ellington's band had the least amount of turnover between musicians. Not only were they treated as individuals, but they were constantly provided with new music that challenged their skills. The Ellingtonian sound derived from his strengths not only as a composer, but as a leader who inspired his players to give their best. This is not only a model for all composers and musicians, but for the rest of society as well. It is a democratic model that was, and in many ways still is, ahead of its time.

I was fortunate to interview Butch Ballard.

PL: I must say that it is a rare privilege to speak with an Ellingtonian, and a fellow drummer at that.

BB: Thank you very much.

PL: What was your first professional gig?

BB: With Herb Thornton's band, back in the late thirties. I also worked with a band in Philly ironically called The Duke's Orchestra that was made up of high school and college players. Then I got married in 1940, and moved to New York to be closer to the action.

My main influence became Shadow Wilson, and I ended up eventually taking his place in the Basie band. But one of the greatest swing drummers and showmen I had ever seen was Sonny Payne. He was a crowd pleaser, but could still swing the band. He knew the music so well, everything he played meant something. I had also become friends with J. C. Heard, Papa Jo Jones, Big Sid Catlett, Cozy Cole, Jimmy Crawford, and of course Sonny Greer. I knew them from working around the ballroom circuit.

PL: Before you played with Duke, you worked with Mercer Ellington?

BB: Yes, back in the mid-forties. I had known him long before I had a personal association with Duke, or even before I worked with Basie. I was around New York trying to get established, waiting to get my 802 card so I could get steady gigs. Back then a lot of the drummers I knew who were working in the City would throw me a bone every now and then. Some of Mercer's players knew me, and knew that I could read charts and play. That's how I got started with him.

PL: Were you doing Mercer's material, or any of Duke's material?

BB: We did a lot of Mercer's stuff, and he had a couple of guys in his band that were also writing. We had some wonderful charts. We mostly played one-nighters, and the band sounded great. Of course, it didn't sound like Duke. It was a completely different style. We didn't have anyone like Johnny Hodges, and I wasn't playing like Sonny Greer.

PL: You knew Sonny personally before you joined the Ellington band?

BB: Only as an acquaintance around the City, but of course I knew of him since I was a kid. After all, he was playing with the greatest band in the world.

PL: What was your first exposure to Ellington's music?

BB: I had known about Ellington all my life, from radio and records. It's hard to pinpoint exactly when I first became aware of him. Ever since I can remember, he was widely known as the greatest black composer and bandleader in the world. And his band had the best musicians in the world. When I was a kid, players like Hodges, Carney, Rex Stewart, and Barney Bigard were big stars. I would always catch the band here in Philadelphia at the Pearl Theatre, the Uptown Theatre, or the Lincoln Theatre. They would play three or four shows a day, and I would play hookey from school and go downtown to watch

Sonny Greer play drums. There were other influences too, of course. I would go to see Jimmy Crawford with Lunceford's band, and Jo Jones with Basie. Sid Catlett was with Armstrong's band at the time. And I ended up working with Louis Armstrong in 1946–47. I also played and recorded with Cootie Williams's band. One thing I am proud of is the fact that most of the bands I worked with, I had a chance to record with as well.

And of course I worked with Count Basie, which was a wonderful stroke of luck. Shadow Wilson was leaving to join Woody Herman in 1948, and Basie called me from California and asked me if I wanted to join the band. What could I say? Of course I wanted to! So he sent me a plane ticket out to the West Coast. We did extended engagements in California, then a series of one-nighters. Eventually we wound up back in New York, and Basie broke the band back from seventeen pieces to an octet. Clark Terry, Freddie Green, Jimmy Lewis, were all still in there. As soon as he did that, Ellington called me from Las Vegas and asked if I wanted to go to Europe with his band. I said to myself, "Man, it doesn't get any better than this."

He told me what to do to get prepared for the trip: go to New York, talk to his agent, get my passport together, and discuss payment. I went to Europe with the band in 1950. That's when Duke had people like Johnny Hodges, Harry Carney, Jimmy Hamilton, Don Byas, Juan Tizol, Lawrence Brown, Quentin Jackson, Ray Nance, Wendell Marshall, Kay Davis, Billy "Sweet Pea" Strayhorn, Sonny Greer, and myself. We left from New York and played on a ship for seven days. When I stepped out on that bandstand in Paris, it was one of the happiest days of my life. When I was on the same stage with all of those outstanding musicians, I could hardly believe myself. After admiring many of these players since I was a kid, finally getting the chance to play with them was the high point of my career.

PL: How would you describe Sonny Greer's individual style?

BB: Sonny was the only drummer who played the way he did. He had his own unique style. A lot of press rolls, closed choke-cymbal stuff, and a whole lot of 2/4. It wasn't straight ahead, ding digga-ding digga-ding, boom boom boom. None of that. You never heard Sonny play like that.

And when I went to Europe with the band in 1950, we had both of our drumkits set up on stage. He had his full kit on a special riser that was built for him. I was set up down on the stage right between Duke's piano and bassist Wendell Marshall. That sure was a treat. I would look behind me and see Sonny up there with all of his drums, gongs, bells, timpanis, woodblocks. His drumkit was the only one like that in the whole world.

PL: How would he incorporate all of those special percussion items into the music?

BB: Duke's music was always very colorful and vivid. Sonny would use different percussion for different segments, particularly endings and interludes—more so on the extended pieces than the shorter swing numbers. When they would perform excerpts from "Black Brown & Beige," for example, there would be places for timpani or gong. Straight ahead pieces like "Cotton Tail" wouldn't feature anything like that.

PL: When the two of you played together, what were the differences between Sonny's approach and your own?

BB: Our styles were completely different. I used a standard four-piece drumkit and played the swing pieces like "A-Train," just straight ahead jazz. I didn't do press rolls or anything like that, I just kept it swinging right along. Sonny would play on pieces like "Frankie and Johnny," and "Ring Dem Bells." Two different styles altogether. It would take half a day to really explain it in detail. But the two approaches fit the band perfectly. You have to remember that Duke's band was not a pure swing band like Basie. The Ellington sound was much more colorful and unique. But both styles of music are great. That's why the approach that Sonny and I took worked so well.

PL: So you didn't perform on any of the extended pieces?

BB: No, Sonny played on those. He had the elaborate setup for that. I stayed on stage during those pieces, but I would sit out and not play. When we got around to "A-Train," "Perdido," "Cotton Tail," "Diminuendo and Crescendo in Blue," then I would play and Sonny would sit out. We switched back and forth throughout the show. It was the first time I worked in a two-drummer situation, and it was fascinating.

PL: How would Ellington conduct the band?

BB: He would start each piece from the keyboard, like Basie. Then the band would begin, with the tempo already set. That's when he would walk out in front and conduct. He had a very visual style of conducting, especially for us drummers. He would use his whole body. When he wanted a drum roll, he would raise his fists and give you that roll! When he wanted a cymbal crash, he extended his arm and gave it to you. He would count the time with his hands. He would dance and sway with the music. Duke was always a joy to watch as a conductor—alive and exuberant, fully involved and animated. All that we had to do was pay attention and keep our eyes and ears open.

PL: How would he react if someone hit a sour note?

BB: He would maybe grunt a little but keep right on going. But that didn't happen too often. Those players didn't make too many mistakes. You're talking about some of the best musicians in the world. They were all professionals.

PL: How would he deal with tardiness? Was Duke a disciplinarian with someone who was late or perhaps had been drinking?

BB: Well, he was crafty. Duke was very streetwise and crafty. He knew what he wanted and how to get it from people. He would never call anyone dirty names or anything like that. He would just give that person a certain look. And then on stage he may choose not to feature that player at all that night . . . or better yet, he may feature the player in question even more! Always eloquent and charming when he spoke to the crowd, "And now we're going to feature. . . ." And suddenly that player would be up there front and center! That spotlight can have a very humbling effect on a musician, making him work harder, sweat harder. That was Duke's way of handling his players, by making them play! Unless he was *really* upset with someone, in which case he wouldn't let them play at all.

But like I said, these guys were all the best. And he made sure that the world knew who his musicians were. "And now we're going to feature Clark Terry." "And now we're going to feature our high note man Cat Anderson." "And now we're going to feature all-American baritone saxman Harry Carney." Then came my turn. "And now we're going to feature our first chair percussionist Butch Ballard on 'The Hawk Talks!' "

PL: Since you were using a smaller drumkit, how would you provide Duke with the colors and textures he was looking for?

BB: He usually didn't have specific things like that written down on his drum charts. I just listened and paid attention. He would explain things to you in such a way that you didn't need charts. He was a very clear communicator, and if you couldn't understand what he was trying to say, then you didn't belong there in the first place. Actually, Tizol and Strayhorn always made charts. Juan Tizol wrote a lot of things for the band, and he always gave me ideas.

PL: Tizol's contributions very often incorporated Latin sounds and rhythms. How would you accomodate that with a standard kit?

BB: I would capture that sound with the mallets and tom toms. "Blue-jean Beguine," "Seventh Veil," "Ko Ko," "Caravan," and a lot of things like that. I did those numbers with the band when Juan was there, and I used my regular four-piece set. I just used mallets on the toms. No cymbals, no sticks, just straight mallets. And when we were on the road, every night I would finish with my solo on "Caravan." After that there was nothing left to do except close with "A-Train" and pack it up. You're soaking wet and out of there.

PL: So there weren't always specific drum charts? Ellington's musical communication to you was primarily oral?

BB: That's right. He was a genius. He would clearly explain what he wanted, and if you listened to him and followed his directions then you couldn't go wrong. Working with Ellington was like going from high school to working on your Ph.D. Everything was a challenge. On pieces like "Diminuendo and Crescendo in Blue," where the tempos would vary, you really had to pay attention. So many of his pieces had significant dynamic changes. His well-mannered, diplomatic method of explaining things made all the difference.

Some of the other players like Clark Terry, Cat Anderson, and Willie Cook would also give me ideas of what was required. They would help me identify certain things that I should play that weren't written down, because drum charts were never very specific. They would show me certain riffs in a song that they wanted me to hit with them to build it up, but those riffs would never be on the chart, so they would have me write it in myself. That was another learning experience. When you're first learning a song off the chart, it's hard to read and play fluently unless you have experience doing that on a consistent basis. So I learned how to mark things with red crayon, places where I had to return to a previous section and things like that. It also helps if you can memorize a chart after you play it a few times, so you can eventually play from memory without having to read it. It's hard to listen to the other players and respond to what they're doing when you're glued to that piece of paper.

Clark and Cat and a few others would constantly remind me about those things—to *listen* to what was going on around me, to respond to what they were doing. And they had a unique system of communicating to me when they wanted me to use the brushes. If the horns were using their mutes, they had a hand signal that would tell me that it was a softer number, and that I should use the brushes. But I waited to get that signal, because in Duke's band you never assumed anything! And when the mutes came back out of the horns, it was usually time for me to grab the sticks again. Again, these are things you didn't see on the sheet music. Besides, when drummers are trying to read charts and play at the same time, it is very difficult to swing a seventeen-piece band. With a big band, you've got to keep it going. It's not the same as a trio or quartet.

Syncopation was never written down on the charts either. Duke's band didn't want too much syncopation from a drummer. Basie's

1. Duke and drummer Sonny Greer. "He would explain things to you in such a way that you didn't need charts"—Butch Ballard.

band was just the opposite—they *wanted* to hear syncopation. But Duke's players wanted to hear the drummer play more straight time, not get too busy. They wanted the horns to carry the music. A lot of drummers go overboard with their paradiddles and fills, and they're not swinging the band. You do need to have a drummer's instinct to shade and color things the right way, but *you have to swing.* I learned those things from the great drummers like Shadow Wilson and Sonny Payne. Those guys would really work the band, hit all the accents with the horns but still keep it swinging. Sonny Payne was a genius. He would sit on that bandstand and hit everything right on the money, without even looking at his drums. People paid attention to him! He would do the craziest solos and drive the crowd absolutely crazy, but he still kept it swinging.

PL: When you were in the studio recording with the band, how did Billy Strayhorn fit into the process?

BB: He was always there, watching what was happening. Sometimes he would play piano when we were rehearsing the chart, especially if it was his piece. When it was time to record, then Duke would sit down and play. Strayhorn would always be there in the control room, or with us on the floor. They were both great, and they both loved each other. Duke loved Strayhorn, and Strayhorn loved Duke. It was a mutual admiration society.

Many of the pieces we recorded we were already familiar with from live performance. For example, "Satin Doll" was the first recording I made with Ellington, at Capitol Studios in Burbank back in 1953. Sonny Greer was gone by this time; it was just me on the drums. By the time we went into the studio, we had already been playing "Satin Doll" for about a month during a string of one-nighters in places like Wyoming, North Dakota, and South Dakota. When we arrived in Hollywood to begin recording, we were all very familiar with "Satin Doll," so we had it all together. Doing all those one-nighters, I had no idea that he was planning for us to go into the studio to record the song. But we did, and that was my first recording with the band. We had the charts there, but we all knew the song well.

PL: What other records did you make with Ellington that stand out?

BB: Another interesting one was Duke's first piano record in 1953, originally titled *The Duke Plays Ellington.* That was just a trio with Ellington, Wendell Marshall on bass, and myself. We recorded it over two nights in the middle of an intense period of activity. The band was doing four shows a day at the Paramount Theatre in Los Angeles. Each night after the last show we would pack up all the music stands and books, put everything on the bus and go out to Burbank to record. One night Duke told us that he wanted to record as a trio with Wendell and myself. We weren't expecting it; it just happened. And he pulled out all kinds of things—a little of this and a little of that. Some things I had never heard before, some I had. But it came out beautifully.

PL: Did he ask you to do anything different for that record?

BB: He wanted mostly brushes and mallets on those pieces. I used the sticks too, depending on what he was looking for. Many of the pieces I was already familiar with, but some I had never heard before, so I would start off with the sticks and play straight, and if he wanted something specific he would just explain it to me. He had a wonderful way with words, and he could make you feel relaxed enough to give him what he wanted. "Monsieur Ballard," he would say in his soft voice, "how about using your mallets again here?" You always felt comfortable around him. But I still had to watch him like a hawk, because you never could tell what he would do.

What can I say? The greatest experiences of my life were with that man. He was a great person to work with. Always a gentleman. And around the ladies! Oh, he had a way with the ladies! We would be playing somewhere like the Blue Note in Chicago, and he would be on stage with his white tails on, and get on the microphone and introduce "Satin Doll" with that charming voice, "And now our next number is especially dedicated to all the dolls here this evening, and you know you are ALL satin dolls! We're going to do 'Satin Doll' for you ladies."

And when we were recording "Satin Doll" among other things at Capitol Studios out in Burbank, the studio was filled with movie stars. It was like a Who's Who at Duke's session. Those were great days. And when we were doing four shows a day at the Paramount before going to the studio every night, I would hardly get any sleep. I'd be so wiped out when I got back to the hotel with practically no time to rest, one foot in the bed, one foot on the floor! But those were exciting times.

PL: Give me an interesting story from your travels with the band.

BB: That's a tough one, there are so many. I'll never forget when we played through Canada after we left California. We started in Vancouver, and played in Montreal, Quebec, Toronto. We primarily played in ice skating rinks. We'd get there around six o'clock and the band would have enough time to eat dinner, put on the tuxedos and go to the show. When we got there it would be so freezing cold—after all, it *was* an ice skating rink—and they hadn't cranked up the heat yet. We would all be setting up with our coats, scarves, and gloves on! I'm setting up my drums with my winter clothes on, because I'm freezing up there! It was hilarious. Then we would have about an hour to kill before showtime. They would crank up the heat and cover the ice, and before you knew it they converted the place from an ice skating rink to a dance hall! I always thought it was amazing how they covered up all that ice and turned it into a ballroom.

I had a lot of fun touring with the band in Europe, because I had a chance to record over there with other artists. Duke could never record with anyone else because he was under contractual obligation, but the rest of us could. So Hodges, Don Byas, Shorty Baker, and myself were doing sessions with different people and having a ball over there. But after the tour was over, I began hearing that there had been a falling out between Duke and Sonny Greer. I never learned any of the details. I don't know what happened because I wasn't right there next to them. I knew that Sonny liked to drink. But when I was flown out to Europe to join the tour, Sonny was always the epitome of diplomacy and tact with me. He asked me how I was doing, and I told him I was scared to death! I said, "What am I gonna do, Greer?" He just smiled and said, "Don't worry, I'll show you." He was beautiful—a privilege to work with.

PL: How about when Louis Bellson joined the band?

BB: That was after I left the first time. I ended up working with Duke again later. You see, Duke really wanted a drummer who could play double bass drums. But that wasn't my style. I wasn't interested in that, and I told him so. I didn't like the idea of having to carry all that extra gear around, and I would've had to learn to play all over again. I don't know if you've ever played double bass drums, but it's a whole different thing. Nevertheless, that's what Duke wanted. He wanted to hear those big thunderous bass drum rolls for his endings, but I just didn't want to get into that. He asked me two or three times, and I always said no. That's why we parted ways for a while. But he always liked me personally, and admired my playing. So I ended up doing more work with him later on. He liked the fact that I was always swinging the band. You can hear that on all of the recordings I made with him. They're all straight ahead. No double bass drum, just straight 4/4. I wasn't trying to copy anybody's style.

PL: But Bellson played double bass drum?

BB: He certainly did. He is one of the best drummers in the world, and a dear friend of mine. He did his thing on "Skin Deep," and "The Hawk Talks." He wrote those tunes, and played the hell out of them.

PL: Sam Woodyard had a similar double bass approach?

BB: Yes, but there were other drummers in there as well—Jimmy Johnson, Dave Black. I just never liked that style of playing for myself, but those cats were all outstanding players.

PL: How about Rufus Jones?

BB: He could play the hell out of double bass drum too. He was with Duke for a good while, a tremendous soloist. Phenomenal soloist. I think he lives out in Las Vegas, and I don't even think he plays anymore! Can you imagine that, with all of his talent? But Rufus, Sam Woodyard, and Louis Bellson all had that double bass drum style that Duke loved.

PL: When you first joined the band in 1950, swing was taking a back seat to bebop, and many of the big bands were under financial pressure. Could you sense any frustration from this when you were with the band?

BB: During those years, the Ellington style was not as popular. Not until Newport in 1956, of course, which was a major breakthrough for him. Many people felt that Duke started doing things on piano that emulated Thelonious Monk, playing in more of the bebop style. But in reality, it was the other way around. It was Monk that had been emulating Duke. After all, Duke had been experimenting with harmony and phrasing long before Monk came around. It took bebop at least five to ten years to catch up with what he had been doing since the thirties. It's just that Duke always had such an individual style, that he chose not to get stuck in bebop. Consequently, his popularity decreased for a while because his music was no longer in the mainstream the way it had been before. The big bands were not as popular. But boy, did he bounce back at Newport!

Ellington came from the old school of the two-handed stride pianists: Willie "The Lion" Smith, Art Tatum, Fats Waller. Count Basie too. All the older guys did that, using both hands. Stride. But you didn't hear that anymore once bebop came in. Bebop records were also selling more, and swing was taking a back seat. But Ellington had the genius and, most importantly, the determination to rise above those things, and from the late fifties onward he regained his status.

PL: In conclusion, do you feel that Ellington's music will continue to find a new audience, particularly in North America? Or do you feel that European audiences respond more favorably to Ellington, and jazz as a whole?

BB: What a question! They respond a thousand times better than the Americans do! People in America, white or black, don't pay as much attention to jazz. But in Europe, everybody loves it. That's why the jazz musicians flock to Europe—and Japan! The Japanese take jazz very seriously. I have not yet been fortunate enough to play in Japan, although I would like to. I was supposed to go a few years back, but I couldn't make it because I was already doing something with Clark Terry. But I would love to go. The two main places I have never played are Japan and Africa, which would be special for me as a black musician. I would love to play both places, but that seems far fetched for me now.

It's hard for me to recall specifics about that first European tour that I did with Ellington, as far as which shows stood out above the others and things like that. But what I do remember vividly is that we were playing large theaters, and every show was completely sold out. Packed and jammed. The Europeans love jazz, and they know more about your records than the Americans do. They're very knowledgeable, and they can talk with you about things you've done. They read about jazz, and they know your history when you visit their country. They understand the music, their culture supports the music, and the people always buy tickets for the shows. Most people in America, both white and black, would rather hear rock and roll, dance music, rap, or country. Jazz is not given enough exposure in this country. You can hear jazz on the radio anytime in Europe. Here in Philadelphia we have *one* jazz station, which is mostly a classical station that only plays jazz at night. It's the same way in most cities, if they even play jazz at all. But we have plenty of rap stations, rock stations, country stations. That's because jazz does not sell. It simply does not sell to the masses here. But what is really interesting is that the white people in this country support jazz more than the blacks! I see more whites at jazz concerts than blacks. The blacks will go to see rap music, but they don't seem to support jazz as much. The rock musicians and rappers are millionaires, and the jazz players hardly make any money.

PL: And yet Duke Ellington has societies dedicated to his music across America and around the world.

BB: Yes he does, and I cannot think of too many other jazz composers, or black composers in general, who have that kind of worldwide following. I've done things with Ellington societies in California, Toronto, Chicago, Philadelphia, Washington, New York. There are people all over Europe, Asia, South America, who study his music. That is nothing less than a major accomplishment.

And it is because of his universal appeal. Duke's music speaks to people of all cultures. His music is in its own unique category, instantly recognizable, comparable to no one. You can tell from the first few notes that you're hearing the Duke Ellington Orchestra. And everyone can feel it and appreciate it, no matter who they are. Duke didn't care if you were black, white, yellow, or red. He loved everyone. That is why people will still be listening to Duke Ellington a thousand years from now. There was nothing he enjoyed more than making people smile, making them dance. His music is a positive force in the world that will never die as long as the human spirit lives.

Miles Davis

BEFORE ELLINGTON, A COMPOSER would write music that could be played by any conductor and orchestra with access to the written score. The composer did not have any particular individual player in mind as he or she wrote the music. Composers were also not known to perform regularly in public. The act of performing live and leading a band was a different function performed by different people. It was Ellington who broke away from convention and combined the roles of composer and bandleader for the first time. Nobody has really matched Ellington's ability to compose music that suited an individual player's style, but there is a select group of artists who followed in Ellington's footsteps as composers who also performed as bandleaders. Interestingly, more people in rock and soul music have followed this path than in the jazz world.

One could say that Count Basie, Gil Evans, and Art Blakey were composers and bandleaders, but their talents were more tilted toward the bandleader side. Charles Mingus, as we will see, was innovative as a composer, but not widely known as a bandleader. There are two jazz artists who seem to have built on Ellington's example, setting new standards for composers and bandleaders alike: Miles Davis and Sun Ra. Both were known for their composition, as well as their ability to work with large groups of musicians. In popular music, there is the unique case of the rock composer/bandleader Frank Zappa. But most notably, there is a powerful lineage of funk artists who have actually done the most to carry the Ellington tradition into today's music: James Brown, Sly Stone, George Clinton, and Prince. It is surprising, yet somewhat appropriate, that these pioneers of funk music are the closest link in modern music to Duke Ellington. After all, Ellington had no interest in being categorized as a jazz artist, and was always reaching for new means of expression.

Miles Davis quickly established himself not only as a composer and instrumentalist in his own right, but as a bandleader who had a special knack for finding new talent and providing a training ground for many of the most famous names in jazz. Like Duke, Miles was always changing and experimenting with his music, while maintaining a sense of grace and continuity. Also like Duke, Miles had little affection for the avant-garde movement in jazz, despite his constant experimentation. Miles remains the closest equivalent to Duke as an innovator in jazz who enjoyed great longevity and endless creative rebirth. But unlike Duke, Miles would often change his musicians and make a fresh start with a new band and a new sound that would fit what he was looking for at the time. In his post-bebop *Birth of the Cool* phase, which Miles always said was influenced by the music of Ellington and Strayhorn, he collaborated with Gil Evans and hired a band that included Gerry Mulligan, Lee Konitz, John Lewis, and Max Roach. When Miles wanted to head in a modal direction, he formed a septet that included John Coltrane, Cannonball Adderley, and Bill Evans. These artists all continued in their own paths after they left Miles—or rather, after Miles left them.

Then Miles moved in another new direction with his renowned sixties quintet, featuring Tony Williams, Ron Carter, Wayne Shorter, and Herbie Hancock. This band combined the modal style with a conservative approach to free jazz, and developed a very unique chemistry and sound, until Miles was ready for yet another phase—this time moving into an electrified jazz informed by the funk stylings of James Brown, Sly Stone, and Jimi Hendrix. Miles formed a new group of musicians that would include Chick Corea, Joe Zawinul, Jack De-Johnette, John McLaughlin, Dave Holland, Billy Cobham, Lenny White, Airto Moreira, and other players who would become well known in the jazz fusion world. Joe Zawinul and Wayne Shorter would form Weather Report. John McLaughlin and Billy Cobham would form the Mahavishnu Orchestra. Chick Corea and Lenny White would form Return to Forever. These groups became popular with rock and jazz listeners alike, helping break down more boundaries between the two musical forms. Although most rock or jazz purists despise what the fusion movement became, there is no denying that it opened up new doors for musicians in both genres. Miles Davis was the visionary artist who first saw the possibilities in bringing rock, funk, and jazz together.

As a bandleader, Miles allowed his players a great deal of room for individuality and experimentation. He realized, as Ellington did, that it was the players themselves who made the band what it could be. They were his main instrument. As he states in his autobiography: "You got to remember that the people in a band, the quality of the musicians, is

2. Miles Davis: "You've got to always be open to what's new."

what makes a band great. If you have talented, quality musicians who are willing to work hard, play hard, and do it *together*, then you can make a great band . . . To have a great band requires sacrifice and compromise from everyone; without it, nothing happens . . . Another one of the first things you've got to have in a great band is confidence in the other guys, that they can do whatever it is that has to be done . . . To be and stay a great musician you've got to always be open to what's new, what's happening at the moment. You have to be able to absorb it if you're going to continue to grow and communicate your music . . . I understood that we had to do something different. I knew that I was playing with some great young musicians that had their fingers on a different pulse."

Dizzy Gillespie once said: "If you look at Miles, look at the musicians who have been with him; Miles raises leaders, a lot of them." Miles himself admitted that each band that he had put together had something special that none of his other bands, or anyone else's bands, had captured. Miles says: "That was my gift, you know, having the ability to put certain guys together that would create a chemistry and then letting them go; letting them play what they knew, and above it. I didn't know exactly what they would sound like together when I first hooked up guys. But I think it's important to pick intelligent musicians because if they're intelligent and creative then the music can really fly."

Miles began to see the potential in the new directions taken in blues and funk music by James Brown, Sly Stone, and Jimi Hendrix. He began incorporating these sounds into his own music, and a new form of jazz was born—one that took advantage of electric instruments and funk rhythms. Miles saw this as a welcome change from the traditional jazz structure, and he embraced it as a way to expand his musical vocabulary. He knew that this music could reach out to the younger rock audience, and Miles began sharing the live concert bill with experimental rock acts like the Grateful Dead and Santana, both of whom had been heavily influenced by Miles. Soon the lines between jazz and popular music were beginning to dissolve. Along with his skills as a bandleader, it was his transcendence of boundaries and his constant search for new ideas that made Miles one of the most successful exemplars of Ellington's own approach to innovation and leadership.

Miles made no secret of his admiration for Duke Ellington. He is famous for saying, "All musicians should get together on one day and get down on their knees and thank Duke Ellington." When Ellington died in 1974, Miles recorded his own tribute to Duke, *Get up with It,* featuring the side-long composition "He Loved Him Madly." Miles combined his admiration for Duke with his interest in electronic composer Karlheinz Stockhausen and funk pioneer Sly Stone, who both showed how music could concentrate on textures of sound over various rhythmic pulses. Miles was criticized for abandoning his traditional sound and experimenting with electronic effects on trumpet such as the use of a wah-wah pedal. Such critics must have forgotten that Ellington *invented* the use of real-time wah-wah with his horns back in the twenties! The lukewarm reaction to "He Loved Him Madly," which was a very personal expression of gratitude from Miles, became a factor in his mid-seventies retirement from music.

Miles had earlier cited Ellington as a direct influence for his *Birth of the Cool*. Certainly his collaborator in the project, Gil Evans, had also learned a great deal from Ellington. Evans had his own unique ability to create diverse tone colors with an orchestra. Although Evans was never a prolific composer of his own music, his mastery of timbre made him one of the most gifted arrangers in twentieth-century music. Miles and Evans both frequently referred to Duke Ellington as one of the greatest musicians of all time. But Miles knew that the best way for him to honor Ellington was to do as Ellington had done: follow his own path.

The one time Miles and Duke met and interacted in person was in 1948, when Duke called Miles up to his Manhattan office to offer him a position in the Ellington orchestra. Miles was shocked and flattered that Duke Ellington had even heard of him and his playing, and even more stunned at Ellington's offer for Miles to join the band. But Miles respectfully declined and said that he was too committed to his own music, and Duke certainly understood that. Although it would have been fascinating for these two pioneers to join forces and record—as Duke did with John Coltrane, Charles Mingus, and others—we are indeed fortunate that Miles chose to go his own way, because he went on to become an innovator that opened many important doors in music. Duke Ellington wouldn't have wanted it any other way.

But before Miles passed away, he made clear that he wanted to be buried in the same cemetery where Ellington, Louis Armstrong, and King Oliver had been laid to rest. And when one finds time to visit Woodlawn Cemetery in a corner of the Bronx, one will find Miles Davis and Duke Ellington within proximity of one another—probably making music together at last.

Sun Ra

ANOTHER COMPOSER AND BANDLEADER who learned a great deal from Ellington, and applied it to his own universe, is Sun Ra. Born in Birmingham, Alabama as Herman Blount before changing his name, Sun Ra was one of the most eccentric and innovative figures in twentieth-century music. In the Forties, while still known as Herman Blount, he moved to Chicago to play piano with the Fletcher Henderson orchestra. During World War II he was imprisoned as a conscientious objector. Then he decided to reshape his identity into something otherworldly. He became Sun Ra, and began claiming that he was actually from the planet Saturn.

This didn't stop him from exercising total control over his artistic direction on Earth. He formed the largest orchestra in jazz, the Solar Arkestra, featuring sometimes as many as twenty-five to thirty musicians, and kept it together for over forty years. He founded his own record label: Saturn Records. He recorded over 1,000 compositions on over 120 LPs, many of which were issued on the Saturn label and sold primarily at his own live performances, until they became available through distribution agreements with other labels. He kept up with music technology, and introduced many acoustic and electric keyboards to jazz for the first time, including celeste, clavinet, clavioline, organ, and Moog synthesizer.

He would dress himself and the Arkestra in flamboyant Afrocentric costumes and outer space garments such as flowing capes, golden robes, space caps, dashikis, beads, scarves, boots, medallions, jewelry, crowns, sunglasses of every size, shape, and color. The costumes were often designed by Sun Ra himself. Many of the musicians would descend from the stage and walk through the audience while playing. Concerts would often climax with the entire Arkestra marching aroud the perimeter of the room, playing and chanting. Much of the time, the musicians spent as much time off stage during a performance as they did on. There was no doubt that Ra had a taste for the absurd, and sought to challenge the expectations of his audience whenever possible.

Sun Ra began experimenting with free jazz in the sixties, but not before he had combined the lush orchestral colors of Duke Ellington with the harmonic approach of beboppers like Dizzy Gillespie and Charlie Parker. Sun Ra and his Arkestra had developed the only big band approach to hard bop in jazz history. But Ra became increasingly obsessed with the notion of space travel, combined with a fascination for African spirituality, and wanted to break through the structural limitations of jazz. As he moved into the free jazz domain, Ra began weaving a more percussive, African-based fabric behind his featured soloists. The Arkestra became the first large free jazz ensemble, and the longest lasting. He would sometimes exclude brass instruments in favor of the darker sonorities of reeds such as oboes and bass clarinets, augmented with marimba, timpani, or any one of his many electric keyboards. The result was an earthy, primitive sound. This is one of the areas where Ra learned from Duke Ellington and applied it to his own vision. He shared Ellington's fascination with African culture, and free-masonry. He even taught a course at the University of California in Berkeley during the spring semester of 1971 called "The Black Man in the Cosmos." Many younger jazz musicians, including Anthony Braxton, attended the lectures. His topics covered the Bible and other religious and historical documents from Egypt and elsewhere, and how these documents could be reinterpreted in light of today's racial problems, pollution, and war.

He shared Ellington's desire to keep the same musicians in his band over a period of decades. Like Harry Carney and Johnny Hodges, many of the musicians in the Arkestra would remain in the band for the rest of their lives, such as John Gilmore and Marshall Allen. Indeed, like Ellington, Sun Ra's main instrument was his band. He would utilize their individual strengths for his compositions, and encourage them to play in their own unique way. He would sketch rough themes and ideas based on a given player's sound, and then develop the piece based on how the featured player interpreted his original idea. As with Duke, Sun Ra usually wrote music alone in the middle of the night. Then the arrangements would be corrected and embellished by the band during rehearsal, allowing each player to have a hand in the creative process. Ra would often start with a melody line for one of his soloists, and harmonies for the other instruments would branch out from there, sometimes improvised on the spot as the band developed the piece.

Like Miles Davis, Sun Ra had the chance to meet and talk with Duke Ellington only once. But Ra's meeting with Duke was under much different circumstances than Miles. In the late thirties Ellington had performed in Sun Ra's hometown of Birmingham. After the show, Ra went backstage to show Duke his own book of arrangements. Duke was very friendly and gracious, and even showed Ra some of his own arrangements. The two of them sat and talked for a couple of hours, comparing notes and discussing orchestration. Sun Ra noticed the use of dissonance in Duke's arrangements, but was impressed by the fact that it never actually *sounded* dissonant. The young Ra was greatly inspired by the meeting.

Duke Ellington, in his "jungle" phase and elsewhere, composed programmatic pieces steeped in African imagery like "Ko Ko," "Pyramid," "Afrique," and many others. Sun Ra followed suit with pieces like "Ancient Aiethopia," "Egyptian Fantasy," "Pharoah's Den," and many more of his own. Sun Ra also worshipped the sun itself, as many of his other titles reflect, like "Children of the Sun," and "Sun Song." Ellington shared this connection to the source of all life, and like Sun Ra, he equated it to his own people. As Duke once said: "We are children of the sun, and our race has a definite tradition of beauty and glory and vitality that is as rich and powerful as the sun itself. These traditions are ours to express, and will enrich our careers in proportion to the sincerity and faithfulness with which we interpret them."

"Ancient Aiethopia," from the 1958 LP *Jazz in Silhouette*, is particularly close to Ellington's African program music. But Sun Ra's approach is unique, using hand percussion and vocal chants to augment the band. Sun Ra's piano opens the piece, then The Arkestra states the theme over an Ellingtonian jungle rhythm. Flutes and baritone sax with brass and piano give the piece a darker sonority. A small gong is struck, then two flutes begin to improvise together over the insistent beat of the timpani. The effect is otherworldy. The flutes fade as the timpanis take the spotlight with a brief solo, before giving way to a free form trumpet solo that slowly glides over the bass line. Then Sun Ra takes over with a piano solo that is rich with dissonance and chordal clusters. The drums return to the forefront with wails and cries from the horns, and wordless vocal chants in the background. The Arkestra returns for the closing theme. What makes this piece so close to Ellington's African music is its sense of direction and structure despite the harmonic freedom and openness.

Although Sun Ra used many different electronic keyboard instruments to provide texture, his piano playing was rooted in stride, and he gave many solo piano recitals in that vein. Like Ellington, Sun Ra had a special attack on the piano that produced undertones, which combined with overtones to create quarter-tones. Only Ellington, Art Tatum, Fats Waller, and Earl Hines mastered this same technique. And although most live Arkestra performances featured Sun Ra's own explorations in hard bop, free jazz, or jazz combined with funk, many of his concerts were full-fledged tributes to Ellington or Fletcher Henderson. These performances showed a unique approach to big band jazz. In these instances, Sun Ra found himself the leader of the most unlikely yet distinctive repertory orchestra in jazz.

Sun Ra was certainly not a bandleader in the same sense as Ellington or Miles Davis. He became more like a patriarch to his musicians. After relocating the Arkestra to Philadelphia in the late sixties, he lived with the musicians in a communal setting, and imposed his own standards of living on the rest of the band. He saw music as a model for successful government, with big bands like the Arkestra as a microcosm of government, representing society and peaceful human relations. Sun Ra also believed in discipline combined with freedom, and felt that without proper order, everything fell apart. Since most of his musicians lived in the same house with him, he had a more direct and complex involvement in their lives than any other bandleader before or since. He expected the Arkestra members to abstain from drugs and alcohol, and also encouraged celibacy—values more suited for monks than jazz musicians. He prohibited bandmembers from discussing their living and working practices with members of the press unless he was there. He demanded long hours of rehearsal as a way of strengthening the resolve of his players and testing their commitment. If there was a problem with one of the players, he would often scold them like a schoolteacher, placing them under house arrest. Or while on the road, he would prohibit the player in question from performing on stage. Gigs and money were always tight. But it was not money which kept the Arkestra together, it was their commitment to the challenge and innovation of Sun Ra's music. His players knew that he was giving them an opportunity to express themselves in ways that they could not do elsewhere.

Sun Ra would communicate to his musicians in unusual ways, often resorting to paradox. When he wanted his players to break away from convention, he would confuse them with instructions like: "Play what you *don't* know. You're not a musician, you're a *tone scientist.*" Sun Ra was concerned with tones rather than notes. He wanted to explore areas of sound that had never been heard before. He wanted each C-note to sound different in timbre and intensity than every other C-note. He told his musicians that each tone had a way of fitting with any other tone, and that if they could achieve this, then "you can hear what Billy Strayhorn heard on that subway which led him to write 'Take the A-Train.' "

Although Sun Ra himself had always rejected drugs, he found himself being identified with a new generation of psychedelic rock performers in the sixties who had been inspired by Ra's unique approach to music, live performance, African and space age philosophy, and communal lifestyle. Bands like Pink Floyd were venturing into free improvisation and space imagery reminiscent of Ra with pieces like "Set the Controls for the Heart of the Sun," and "Interstellar Overdrive." The Grateful Dead followed suit, and experimented with modal and free improvisation on pieces that were similarly titled, like "Dark Star" and records such as *Anthem of the Sun.* But the most conspicuous heir to Sun Ra's reign in the world of space music and Afrocentric philosophy was George Clinton: vocalist, composer, and bandleader who had assembled a massive funk/rock orchestra known as Parliament/Funkadelic.

Musically, the only recognizable link between Sun Ra and George Clinton is the heavy use of electronic keyboards as a way to provide color and texture over an improvisational and polyrhythmic fabric. Although Clinton's music rarely borrowed directly from the free jazz vocabulary of Ra, his concept of a large band was closely derived from the Arkestra. Clinton would feature elaborate stage props, and would make his grand entrance by descending on stage in an artificial spaceship known as the Mothership. The Funkadelic orchestra, also numbering in the twenties at times, were decked out in outlandish space costumes and would constantly interact with the audience in a similar fashion as the Arkestra in live performance. Clinton would populate his concerts with characters in a grand drama where Earth needed to regain "The Funk" of which it had been robbed by malevolent forces. Characters like Dr. Funkenstein would come to repossess "The Funk" from Sir Nose D'Void of Funk, who lived in a realm known as the Zone of Zero Funkativity. In the end, "Funk" was again available to all, and Clinton would climb aboard the Mothership and ascend to the heavens. The Parliament/Funkadelic cosmology was as unique unto itself as that of the Solar Arkestra. When Clinton was asked about Sun Ra, he replied: "He's definitely out to lunch—same place I eat at."

The outlandish appearance and behavior of both Sun Ra and George Clinton, combined with their unorthodox world views, have made it nearly impossible for the legitimate music world to take either of them very seriously. This is unfortunate, because both artists have profoundly reshaped modern music as we know it today, without receiving proper credit. But we reach many important intersections here. George Clinton, and the P-Funk orchestra, is closely linked to Duke Ellington in another way that has nothing to do with Sun Ra, and we will soon see why.

As with Miles Davis, Sun Ra incorporated many different influences from Duke Ellington's approach to leadership and experimentation. Both Miles and Ra took Ellington's concept of a bandleader and expanded it to suit their own purposes, each in a different way. Miles believed in constant change, and was always reinventing his sound, working with a steady stream of new musicians who could provide him with what he was looking for at the time. But Miles gave almost unlimited freedom to his players to be who they wanted to be, which is closer to Ellington's approach. Miles understood that a band is only as good as the sum of its musicians, and he believed in giving his players a chance to find their own voices. Then the players would leave Miles and go on to follow their own paths in music. This is a similar approach that composer/bandleader Frank Zappa would take in rock. Zappa became famous for developing many talented young musicians who would go on to form their own bands. Zappa, who first introduced avant-garde concepts of composition and performance to rock, often cited Ellington as a major influence for his innovations as an artist and leader. Zappa also frequently cited Sun Ra.

Sun Ra, unlike Miles or Zappa, believed in keeping one band together for as long as possible, and sought to develop intimate relationships with his musicians by becoming a father figure to the Arkestra in a communal setting. Ra's instrument was the Arkestra, and the unique voices within it that he had come to know over the years. Although Ra's own keyboard playing often reflected Duke's influence, it was his concept of an orchestra as his foremost means of expression, and his desire to work with one intimate circle of musicians, that is Ra's closest link to Duke. Of course, like Miles, Sun Ra took what he learned from Ellington and applied many of the same methods in the tireless pursuit of his own individual path. In so doing, both Miles Davis and Sun Ra have created their own movements in modern music. Both were also able to cross over into the world of rock music in the sixties and seventies, not so much by performing rock or soul music themselves—although they both dabbled with funk—but by appealing to younger musicians of the rock generation with their relentless spirit of experimentation and their ability to transcend boundaries. This is ultimately where Ellington has had the most impact on these two leaders.

George Clinton's link to Duke Ellington comes from his placement in a small lineage of funk artists who have actually done more to preserve and renew the Ellington tradition than any jazz artist. Long before Miles Davis or Sun Ra began appealing to rock audiences in the late sixties, a funk bandleader was following in Ellington's footsteps with a completely new approach that would actually inspire Miles to follow *him*. By the early sixties, James Brown had virtually invented the style of music that would become known as funk, completely on his own terms and with considerable success. James Brown was the first in a lineage of funk bandleaders who would go on to include Sly Stone, George Clinton, and Prince. Each of these artists have expanded upon Duke Ellington's concept of leadership in their own unique way, creating a legacy of their own that has permanently changed the course of music as we know it. More so than any current composer or bandleader in jazz, it is in the work of these four pioneers that the most authentic traces of Duke Ellington's legacy are to be found in today's music. This journey begins with a man who has been called the Godfather of Soul, Mister Dynamite, Soul Brother Number One, and The Hardest Working Man in Show Business: James Brown.

James Brown

IN THE SIXTIES, black music was reaching its height of popularity between the Motown roster of artists and soul performers like Aretha Franklin. But James Brown had set out to revolutionize modern music completely with his new approach to rhythm, which would become known as funk. As jazz had done between the twenties and sixties, funk was now giving black artists greater freedom of expression, and James Brown was the undisputed father of this new movement. Born in South Carolina and growing up in Georgia, James had come from gospel roots. He took the raw energy and melodrama of the church and applied it to his own live performances. James Brown became one of the first black artists to have a theatrical approach to entertaining an audience. A stunningly original dancer, James would direct the band with his every movement, with specific dance steps that would give cues to the drummer and other bandmembers.

Above all else, James had the determination to succeed and was always searching for something that had never been done before. He became the voice of pride for black America with his lyrics and fiercely independent stance, with songs like "Say It Loud, I'm Black and Proud."

Investing his money in small black businesses, as well as radio stations, he became a role model for achieving success without compromising his values. Few artists had as much social or political influence. With the model of Duke Ellington, who had shown how one can be a charismatic live performer as well as a composer, and who had also shown how a black artist can break new ground and succeed on his own terms, James Brown had decided to be a leader and innovator in his own right, applying the big band concept to his vision of funk music.

Although Ellington had already been received at the White House, James Brown was the first black artist in popular music to be invited there. Like Ellington, James Brown combined his strong sense of Negro pride with a conservative patriotism, advocating education and capitalism for blacks. Brown refused to endorse violent protest, and the day after Martin Luther King was shot in 1968, Brown was broadcast from a live performance at Boston Garden in order to calm the rioting and looting. People stayed off the streets that day to hear James Brown perform. He spoke in Washington, D.C. He performed in Vietnam for American troops. He also toured in 1968 with the Count Basie orchestra as his support act. When he was accused of taking sides with white politicians, Brown disagreed. Similar to how Ellington felt, Brown realized the importance of moving ahead as an African-American artist. Just the mere fact that a Negro country boy from the South was invited to dinner at the White House was enough of a powerful message in Brown's eyes.

Brown created an entirely new musical language based on rhythm. Instruments that had previously been used for melody and harmony, such as horns, were now accentuating a propulsive, polyrhythmic beat. Every instrument emphasized the groove. His use of syncopation in the drums made his music irresistably danceable. While onstage, Brown reinvented the concept of a conductor with his dance steps. Every hand signal or foot movement was a signal for the drummer to do a rim shot, cymbal splash, or bass drum kick. Every move had a meaning: hit something here, break the beat down there, and he had an uncanny ability to be so attuned to what each instrument was doing while he was dancing and conducting the show. If any musician missed a cue or hit a wrong note, James had a system where he would fine that musician, and he would call it out right on the spot—without stopping the flow of the music. He would signal to the player in question that he had just docked them five dollars for the mistake, without once missing a dance step or lyric.

"Get It Together" is one of the most vivid examples of Brown's approach as a composer and bandleader. Based on Brown's trademark syncopated funk rhythm, it begins with Brown's famous "ooo weee" vocal wail, and suddenly the band is in the groove. Drums and bass lay the foundation, rhythm guitar scratches over the beat, and the horns blow and stretch their notes as background rhythmic accents to Brown's vocal exhortations. Suddenly Brown calls on Maceo Parker to do a tenor sax solo, and Brown eggs him on during the recording. The rest of the band maintains their rhythmic drive. Brown then brings the band slightly down in volume, with Maceo continuing to solo as Brown directs the others. He tells the horns to lay out, leaving only Maceo and the rhythm section. He does some call and response with the other musicians, and then instructs the band to "hit" him with one accent, then two, then three, then four. He calls on trombonist Levi Rasbury to stretch a note over the beat. He then instructs trumpeters Waymond Reed and Joe Dupars to follow suit, stretching their notes in harmony with the trombone, as the groove stays steady. He gets baritone saxman St. Clair Pinckney to add some lines to the mix.

One by one, we can hear how Brown is building a structure in the studio, describing right on the spot how he wants the instruments to sound. He's directing the band during the recording process, as a part of the song itself. When the elements come together, the polyrhythmic fabric of sound is textbook James Brown. Suddenly, after having the horns come in one by one, he instructs them to once again lay out, with Maceo again continuing to play alone over the driving rhythm section. Suddenly he tells drummer Jabo Starks and bassist Bernard Odum to follow his instructions, "Hit it and quit it." James yells "Hit it!" Suddenly the band kicks up the volume and the horns come back into the fabric. Then Brown yells "Quit it!" Immediately the band drops back down to just the rhythm section and Maceo Parker, only this time without the rhythm guitar. Eventually Brown brings the entire band up for the close of the song. Although Brown's music is not harmonically centered, we can hear the influence of Ellington in Brown's approach to shaping and building the structure in his music, one instrument at a time.

These new directions in rhythm introduced by James Brown had completely reshaped popular music. But James was by all accounts a disciplinarian, who demanded nothing less than total perfection from his players. James called all the shots, and his musicians did not have the liberty to express their own ideas. Although the musicians in Brown's band were justly recognized for their excellence, they were not given the freedom that Ellington's musicians were given. Like Duke, James would feature many of his players on stage, but unlike Duke, James never constructed a piece with the sound of any specific player

3. James Brown: The Godfather of Soul gets on the good foot to conduct the band.

in mind. His musicians played to suit *his* vision. By the late sixties, a new composer and bandleader would emerge from the San Francisco Bay Area that would take Brown's rhythmic innovations one step further to include the musicians as a part of the main attraction.

Sly Stone

SLY STONE WAS FOLLOWING THE ELLINGTONIAN TRADITION of breaking down barriers: between black and white, male and female, and between many different forms of music. As a disc jockey in the Bay Area in the mid-sixties, Sly Stone was absorbing the sounds of white rock artists as well as black. San Francisco was the center of the flower power movement, hippie culture, and psychedelic rock. Sly wanted to merge these elements with rhythm and blues, and the funk approach of James Brown. In 1966 he formed Sly and the Family Stone, and released their debut record appropriately titled *A Whole New Thing*.

Their first hit single, "Dance to the Music," took a similar approach to James Brown's "Get it Together," only this time, band members would introduce their own parts, rather than be announced by the leader. The full band opens the piece, with a driving drum and bass line, horns, organ, guitar, and screaming vocals. Suddenly guitarist Freddie Stone breaks the music down by calling on the drummer to play the beat on his own: "All we need is a drummer, for people who only need a beat!" As drummer Errico hammers the groove along, Freddie then introduces himself: "I'm gonna add a little guitar and make it easy to move your feet!" Freddie jumps in with solo guitar lines over the drums. Then legendary bass man Larry Graham sings in his low baritone voice: "I'm gonna add some bottom so that the dancing just won't hide!" Graham then lays down some of the heaviest thumpingest electric bass lines ever heard. Then Sly comes in: "You might like to hear my organ, I said Ride Sally Ride!" Sly lays down a wall of sound on organ, and the musical fabric is almost complete, with the horns right behind. The listener is immediately aware that this is a *band* with diverse personalities.

This really *was* a "whole new thing." Visually, the band was a departure from James Brown and the big band tradition, in that the players didn't wear uniforms, but appeared as a diverse group of individuals. Sly was every bit as perfectionist as Brown, but he was much more open and flexible. He allowed his players to experiment on their instruments and try new things on their own. As a result, Larry Graham would completely redefine the role of bass guitar in modern music, with his trademark style of thumping, slapping, and plucking. Graham would simultaneously slap or pluck a melodic counterpart to his bottom end thumping. Graham became a pioneer for a new approach to bass guitar, and Sly created the environment where Graham's ideas could develop and take shape.

Another departure from James Brown was Sly's mass appeal to a white audience, combining the social and political messages of the youth culture with a funk groove. It was a magic formula that combined rhythm and blues with jazz, blues, funk, pop, and rock. Like Ellington, Sly refused to acknowledge musical boundaries, and the Family Stone were able to execute all of Sly's rhythmic and melodic innovations. Although Sly was a multi-instrumentalist, his band was his main instrument. His band was also a microcosm of America itself, featuring male and female musicians, black and white. One of Sly's song titles, "Everybody Is a Star," perfectly encapsulated this message. Everybody in his band, or in his audience for that matter, was somebody that mattered. Sly had managed to take Ellington's concept of a band composed of individuals that broke through boundaries, and adapt it to his own music and time. Sly had helped merge the peace movement with the Civil Rights movement through his refusal to think along racial lines. Sly sang the slogan, "Don't call me Nigger, Whitey! Don't call me Whitey, Nigger!"

౽౷౸౹౺

This was the beginning of an era when black musicians began expressing their frustrations with urban life in a more direct way, addressing the problems of drug abuse, poverty, unemployment, and crime. Marvin Gaye and Stevie Wonder had broken away from Motown's traditional apolitical stance with their new music. Curtis Mayfield recorded his soundtrack to the blaxploitation film about a heroin dealer *Superfly*. It was a more aggressive approach compared to Ellington's social statements like "My People," "Deep South Suite," "New World A-Comin'," or "Black Brown & Beige." But again, it was Ellington who first opened the door for this kind of open expression. One could say that Duke's approach remains the most radical, because his statements on the African-American condition still stand as major works of twentieth-century music that will continue to be performed everywhere from Chicago's Regal Theatre to Carnegie Hall.

No matter how complex his musical structures, Ellington always returned to the basic rhythm of the jungle, the drum. He never stopped writing music that people could dance to. His understanding of the power of rhythm, applied in the context of a large band, opened the door for James Brown's reinvention of groove in his own large band. Brown intensified the rhythm in his music by putting the main emphasis on the first beat of each measure: on the one, as he would say. This would become the basis for funk, placing the first beat of each measure on top. James Brown's orchestra was the driving force behind this new beat. But the band decided to walk out on James because he wasn't giving them enough credit on his records. Brown was notoriously stubborn and self-sufficient, and was not about to meet the demands of his musicians. In fact, streetwise as Brown was, he had already been preparing a new band to replace his old one. Among the new musicians was a young bassist from Cincinnati named William "Bootsy" Collins, his brother Catfish on guitar, and longtime friend Frank "Kash" Waddy on drums.

Bootsy took the evolution of the bass guitar one step further from Larry Graham's innovations with Sly and the Family Stone. Bootsy, Catfish, and Kash would be featured on lengthy instrumental jams in Brown's show. Bootsy gave Brown a much needed change in direction, and was able to experiment with more freedom than any previous musician under Brown's leadership. The combination of both artists significantly raised the energy level of the music, and gave it an even more rhythmic foundation than before. This was a stripped down configuration of Brown's band, unlike his previous ensemble. The rhythm section would be featured in longer extended jams. Brown's music had made a shift to a more aggressive sound, but Bootsy and his partners were anxious to experiment on their own terms. They soon decided to move in their own direction away from James Brown. They had learned a great deal from Brown's professional discipline, but were now ready to push the envelope further than James would tolerate.

They formed their own group called Houseguests, combining their funk sound with an outlandish visual approach influenced by British rock. People immediately compared them to a large band from Detroit named Funkadelic, who had merged the funk sound of James Brown and Sly Stone with Jimi Hendrix–inspired psychedelic rock, flamboyant costumes similar to Sun Ra's Arkestra, and a sense of mischief and

4. Sly Stone: Sly takes the everyday people higher at Woodstock.

satire inspired by Frank Zappa's Mothers of Invention. They were appealing to an entirely different audience among blacks. Funkadelic was masterminded by composer/bandleader George Clinton. Bootsy decided to track down Funkadelic, and soon met Clinton. The two immediately sensed a strong musical and spiritual affinity with one another, and began working together right away. Bootsy and his band knew that they would have the freedom to do what they wanted to do with George Clinton. For Clinton, who was moving back toward Ellington's approach as a bandleader who thrived on individual expression in a large band context, it was another opportunity for him to surround himself with musical excellence.

George Clinton

GEORGE CLINTON, BORN IN NORTH CAROLINA, had started making music in Newark, New Jersey. He had moved to Detroit with a doo-wop vocal group called the Parliaments, who had a minor hit with "I Wanna Testify" in the mid-sixties. But Motown was putting too much emphasis on its bigger name acts like the Temptations and Smokey Robinson's Miracles. The Parliaments were forced to go in their own direction. Sly and the Family Stone had already begun changing the face of black popular music. Now the emphasis was on an entire band as a performing unit, rather than a vocal act with studio backing. Sly had focused the attention on everyone in the group: the guitars, drums, keyboards, bass, and horns. The approach was beginning to move toward jazz, where individual musicians were respected and acknowledged. Clinton began recruiting the best musicians he could find in Detroit, while playing the club and ballrom circuit with rock bands such as the Stooges and MC5. These bands played loud and heavy guitar rock with large amplifiers. Clinton decided to try something new for his music by incorporating this heavily amplified rock sound into his funk approach. It was the first time that a black band was seen with Marshall guitar amplifiers on stage. New barriers between black and white music were being broken—even beyond Sly Stone's vision.

Clinton's visual presentation was just as innovative. Their elaborate stage presentation, outrageous costumes, and science-fiction leanings drew heavily from Sun Ra and his Arkestra. Suddenly young blacks who had never heard of Sun Ra were seeing Funkadelic in concert, absorbing the sights and sounds of the live spectacle. Their album covers featured cartoon art that placed the band in a sci-fi context. All of this was very new for blacks, and Funkadelic soared in popularity as they continued to push the envelope. Bootsy Collins passed on to Clinton what he learned from his experiences with James Brown, and Funkadelic further developed the consistent rhythmic emphasis on the one— giving their groove a monolithic power. When the accent remained on the one, whatever melody line was played would sound much larger. By always staying on the one, the rhythm would sink deep into the listener's subconsciousness. Then the guitars and keyboards would layer different textures and colors over this propulsive beat, while Clinton would add his vocal arrangements. George Clinton pioneered this new sound, which became known as P-Funk.

George Clinton was the opposite extreme from James Brown as a bandleader. George actively encouraged everybody to experiment as much as possible, leaving the playing field wide open for new ideas that he could incorporate into his own vision. On stage, he was charismatic and outlandish, bringing a new energy to funk and rock music. George's gift was being able to inspire everyone and harness their enthusiasm. Maximum freedom was the key. James Brown had freed the music from its melodic and harmonic constraints. George freed everybody from all constraints. There were no limitations on what his musicians could do. But somehow, everything seemed to enhance his vision, and George had an arsenal of the best musicians in the business.

Everyone in the P-Funk orchestra were the elite among funk musicians. Even Maceo Parker and Fred Wesley from the James Brown orchestra had joined with Clinton on horns. Classically trained keyboardist Bernie Worrell, who studied at the New England Conservatory in Boston as well as at Juilliard in New York, was another driving force in the band, as was Bootsy Collins on bass, and Eddie Hazel on guitar. All of the finest players wanted to work with George Clinton, because they knew they would be appreciated for what they could do. But when even these outstanding musicians went their own way, their solo efforts were not as convincing as their contributions within the P-Funk context, similar to the solo work by Ellington's players. With such an array of talent, a P-Funk performance was like no other. With the European harmonic approach and synthesized sounds of Bernie Worrell on keyboards, the matchless horn arrangements of Fred Wesley and Maceo Parker, the psychedelic guitar of Eddie Hazel and Michael Hampton, the thunderous bass of Bootsy Collins and Bill Nelson, and the propulsive rhythms of drummers Tiki Fulwood, Jerome Brailey, and Frank Waddy, P-Funk became a modern orchestra.

To this day, with the highest caliber musicians and singers in his band, George Clinton provides the audience with a musical experience that is the closest remaining link to the Ellington orchestra. Far from recreating anything resembling Ellington music, Clinton has created something new. Although Clinton is working within a rock and funk context, his musicians are given the room to improvise and express themselves freely, often moving toward the electrified jazz of Miles Davis and Herbie Hancock. Certainly, P-Funk is a far cry from the traditional appearance of a big band. There are no uniforms, as in the Ellington or James Brown ensembles. On the contrary, outlandish costumes are the norm, going back to Sun Ra's theatrical approach.

When one sees a P-Funk concert, one immediately recognizes that this is an ensemble in every sense. There is a leader, surrounded by the finest musicians who each get a chance to express themselves within the framework of the leader's music. There are points in the show where the entire band is featured as one large collective force, with sometimes as many as thirty or forty people on stage at one time. At other points, each player is featured, either individually or in sections. Clinton provides the structure, and determines who is featured when. Then the musicians are set free to do their own thing. Behind the visual antics and costumes, the P-Funk musicians are the best in their field, from the horns and guitars, to the singers, to the rhythm section. One cannot help but be in awe at the abundance of musical excellence on the stage. There are always new discoveries being made within the context of the music. No two P-Funk concerts sound exactly the same. The music develops and changes night after night. It is this emphasis on freedom of expression in a large band context, balanced by Clinton's cohesive vision and thirst for experimentation, that makes P-Funk the modern-day counterpart to the Ellington orchestra.

❧

It may seem that the development of funk in modern music is far removed from the world of Duke Ellington or jazz. But funk, as it was defined by James Brown through Sly Sone and George Clinton, is actually a return to the source of all music, African or otherwise—the drum. Ellington understood the importance of drums, which were the first musical instruments known to man. Ellington was always finding ways to incorporate African jungle-based rhythms into his concept of big band jazz, and Latin rhythms as well. From his earliest pieces like

5. George Clinton: The Godfather of Funk asks, "Who says a funk band can't play jazz?" (© 1996 Sony Music.)

"The Mooche" to his latest pieces like "Afrique," Duke's music had its own funk. Duke's music rocked. And Duke had a whole lot of soul!

As Ellington himself wrote: "Recently I was asked whether I felt that jazz had moved a great distance away from its folk origins. With the present state of rock and roll music, I don't know how anyone can even consider asking such a question! Rock and roll is the most raucous form of jazz, beyond a doubt; it maintains a link with the folk origins, and I believe that no other *form of jazz* has ever been accepted so enthusiastically by so many . . . I'm not trying to imply by this that rock and roll shows any single trend, or indicates the only direction in which things are moving. It is simply one aspect of many.

"I have written a number of rock and roll things myself, but am saving them for possible use in a show. As far as my own music in general is concerned, I would categorize it as Negro music. It represents what I absorbed as a child and have grown up with among the people around me who were musicians.

"There have been many rebellions concerning our music through the years. As far back as 1933, when I said I was playing Negro music, some critics complained, " 'Sophisticated Lady' is not Negro music." But the fact remains that "Sophisticated Lady" is Negro music—it's the Negro I know, and my interpretation.

"No matter how many controversies may rage about the direction in which our music, or jazz in general, is going, the music will continue to develop along natural lines. Some of it may become more complex, and some of it will remain simple. There will always be some kind of folk music around, be it rock and roll or western or hillbilly music."

Duke believed in giving his players the freedom to be themselves, albeit within the structures that he created in his compositions. Tracing the evolution from James Brown's role as a bandleader, down through Sly Stone and George Clinton, we can see that Clinton remains a link to the approach to leadership that Ellington had taken.

Soon Clinton's brand of funk, as inherited from Brown and Stone, would impact nearly every form of popular music, from disco in the seventies to the emergence of hip hop and rap in the eighties. Hip hop music has even further stripped down the rhythmic approach and returned to an African tradition where the human voice itself becomes a rhythmic instrument. Rap music has given the voice a percussive quality with its steady rhyming beat, usually backed only by a drum machine and sampled material from a turntable. The overwhelming majority of sampled music that is used on rap records comes from either James Brown or George Clinton, largely due to the rhythmic emphasis both artists have placed on the one. Brown and Clinton remain the most heavily sampled artists in rap. Once marginalized by popular radio and video stations like MTV, rap music has exploded beyond all expectations, and now dominates the popular music industry, because it has crossed over racial lines into the mainstream. None of this would have been possible without George Clinton, James Brown, or the man who first opened the door for these leaders, Duke Ellington.

⌒
Frank "Kash" Waddy
⌣

ONE PERSON WHO IS ESPECIALLY QUALIFIED to discuss the evolution of the composer/bandleader from Ellington down through the forefathers of funk is drummer/vocalist Frank "Kash" Waddy, who has the unique perspective of having worked with James Brown and George Clinton, as well as having a close friendship with Sly Stone. Frank's lifelong friend and partner, bassist Bootsy Collins, helped redefine the role of bass guitar in modern music in ways that were as radical as Jimmy Blanton's approach to the instrument in the context of the Ellington band. Frank and Bootsy both met James Brown in their hometown of Cincinnati, Ohio.

ᘒᙏᙏᘗ

PL: Frank, you and Bootsy had been playing together as a rhythm section in Cincinnati since you were both very young. How did the two of you get your start with James Brown?

FW: James based his entire King Records operation right there in Cincinnati. He had a business office, recording studio, and pressing plant all in one place. Bootsy and I would stop by the studio every day after school and get on their nerves, until they finally let us in to do some things. The rest is history, as they say. We started recording there on a regular basis, with many artists that we never knew about. We recorded with Arthur Prysock, but we didn't even who he was at the time. It was a learning experience. The producer showed me things on drums that I still use today. Our young minds were like sponges back then. Anyway, we met James when he would come to the sessions.

PL: When did James hire you and Bootsy to play in his own band?

FW: His previous band had just walked out on him the day that we were flown in to do our first gig. Maceo Parker and many of the others had some differences with James, and they quit on him right before a gig. But it turns out that James had been preparing us for the position for quite a while, and we just didn't realize it.

PL: Some of those players stayed. Jabo Starks stayed on drums. So you doubled with Jabo on drums?

FW: Jabo was still there, so we had both drummers there. Then Clyde Stubblefield joined, and we had three drummers! Playing between those two was a learning experience, because their styles were totally different. Jabo's forte was to play very clean, very straight ahead. Clyde was like fire, he just burned! I was right in the middle, I got all of it. Clyde could play clean too, but that was really Jabo's strength. Jabo was *clean*. But Jabo couldn't explode the way Clyde did. As a youngster, Clyde was more of an influence on me. Jabo was a much more disciplined player, and I didn't think I was ready for that. But I realize now that I learned a lot from Jabo's discipline, even if I wasn't aware of it then.

PL: Butch Ballard talks about the same thing. He played double drums with Sonny Greer in the Ellington band. Sonny would play the more complex material, while Butch would stick with the straight ahead swing.

So would you say that James Brown was the first big band situation you worked in, with someone like James conducting the band?

FW: Actually, we were the smallest band James ever had. Before us, it was the James Brown Orchestra, but we were called the JB's. Many people forget that. We were basically a rhythm section for James. There was only a two-man horn section, but a three-man rhythm section. Jabo was also there, so we had two drummers. At some point we added a third horn. But it was big time show business, that's what was big about it. Before we started working with James, we were making fifteen dollars a night for the whole band! We carried ourselves and all of our equipment in a Dodge station wagon.

The night before we played with James, we worked in a local bar for the same fifteen dollar salary. The next day Bobby Byrd rounded us up, put us in a limo and airplane for the first time, and flew us to Columbus, Georgia. That's where James was scheduled to do a show when his old band pulled a power play and walked out on him. James had us flown in to take their places. Of course, we didn't know what was really going on behind the scenes at the time. We got there a little late, and the venue was packed with people. They took us from the limo straight to the stage. James knew that we could play the material. We were huddled up there, like scared kids. James would call off each tune, and the key it was in. "Black and Proud" in F-sharp. We did the whole show like that, and it went very well. After the show we went to see him in his dressing room, and he was raving on and on about us. We each started making four hundred dollars a week. That was a big change, to say the least. We had brand new uniforms, three sets of clothes with shoes. We got brand new equipment. We traveled on a Trailways bus. It was like a fairy tale to us.

PL: Similar to Ellington, James would feature different players on stage. James would call on Maceo, St. Clair, and others. The audiences would then get to know who these players were.

FW: That's right. He utilized his people. He didn't work with other outfits, so he utilized his camp. He would call on Maceo or someone else to play, because at some point in the show he needed a break. And the audience also needed a break from James, to make James more exciting for the audience. That way, he would come back into the show and get everybody going again. He also had the female vocalists like Vicki Anderson and others.

PL: His band had a very consistent sound that was instantly recognizable as James Brown. How would he communicate to his players exactly what he was looking for?

FW: The first thing we had to do with James was learn his language. James was never technically trained. He didn't know music theory. But you could write a book on his natural theory of music. What made James such a phenomenon was his natural ability. And whatever he wanted was it. One time he described to me a drum roll he wanted to hear that he called a "compound triplet." But his idea of a compound triplet was something that he invented on his own. When he asked me to do a compound triplet, I did it based on my formal concept of compound triplets. But he said, "No, that's not it." So I asked Jabo to show me what James was talking about. Jabo showed me, and it was something that I never would have called a compound triplet! So I realized that the first thing I had to do was learn his jargon. I had to be able to communicate with him.

PL: It's exactly the same way with Ellington. He wouldn't always have specific charts for every instrument, but he would have a theme. He would walk into a session or rehearsal, and communicate to the players in his own way about what he wanted. They would discuss it, and come up with ideas. Because like James Brown, Duke was never formally trained.

FW: Speaking of that, what blows my mind is Buddy Rich! I studied him when I was a kid, and it took me a few years before I realized that he couldn't read music! And he was a bandleader! The technique and theory he was using to conduct that band from behind his drumkit just blows me away, especially when I realize that he was completely self taught.

PL: When you look at the evolution from Duke down through modern bandleaders like James, Sly Stone, George Clinton, or Prince, it seems that they were all self taught and communicated things in their own unique way. But they also had very high standards for their music. Would you say James Brown was a disciplinarian?

FW: No question about it. But that's what Bootsy and I learned from James: professional discipline. So when we left James and got together with George Clinton, that's what we brought to George's music. Because George never cared much for discipline.

PL: How would James react if he heard something that he didn't like?

FW: At one point, James had a fining system that he incorporated into his stage show. If he heard someone hit a sour note, he would flick his hand open and shut while he was dancing. Every time he opened his hand, it meant five dollars. The player who screwed up would get docked five dollars. James would do it with his hand backwards. He wouldn't even turn around, he would just flick his hand back at the player while he was still dancing. So to the audience, it looked like something cool. But to the player, it was money being taken from his paycheck. He did that for years before we played with him. But we were young, and all we cared about was playing music and having a good time. The other musicians took him too seriously. I mean, we idolized his undeniable skills as a musician and leader, but when it came to power trips, we just laughed it off.

The first time he tried to fine any one of us was Bootsy's brother, Catfish, who was on guitar. He tried it on Catfish while we were doing a show. I think it was up to thirty-five dollars or something, he had flicked his hand open about seven times or so. But when he finally turned around and looked back at us, we were CRACKING UP! We were holding our sides, right there on stage! We were laughing at Catfish for getting fined in the first place, and we were laughing at James because that whole business was just funny to us. He realized right away that we weren't the ones to fall for that. He knew it wasn't going to work with us, and that was the end of it; it never happened again. At least not when I was there.

PL: That must have humbled him quite a bit, because he was used to holding his musicians accountable for their actions.

FW: Of course. I mean, he's James Brown! We'd be smiling, and he'd walk up to us and say, "What are you guys always grinning for? What are you so happy about?" All we knew was that we were playing music, and that we should be happy for that.

PL: You also knew that you were in one of the tightest bands around.

FW: Of course. And we also brought something to the table ourselves.

PL: Speaking of bringing something of your own, how much freedom of expression did he allow you guys compared to the amount of freedom you would get with George Clinton?

FW: James gave us more freedom than he had given to his previous bands, because he wanted a new direction for his music, and he wanted to hear what we could do. We always wanted to play, so we would jam a lot. He would let us do instrumental segments in the show. We learned a lot from working with James. We took what we learned from James and applied it in a different way with Clinton.

PL: James was much closer to the big band tradition, even visually. All of his players wore uniforms.

FW: That's true, and he still does that today. He's always been old-fashioned in that way. The dancers and singers are dressed up in one set of uniforms, the players in another. That was really big at the time, and James wanted that discipline. If anyone was going to look different, it was going to be him and nobody else. It was just a standard way of doing things from the big band days.

PL: The band who left James before you and Bootsy got there had problems with him because he wasn't crediting the musicians on his records. This reminds me of Motown Records in the sixties. They had a spectacular house band for recording, including James Jamerson on bass, and Benny Benjamin on drums. But nobody found out who those players were until much later. James was the same way?

FW: Well, you have to remember that James was old, old school. He came from the country. And he was *always* right. If anyone ever had the guts to tell him he was wrong about something, he would say, "I'm never wrong. I'm James Brown." It was funny. I knew when I first got there, even as a youngster, that there was something funny about this picture. Everything revolved around James. *But* at the same time, I'm eternally grateful from the knowledge I obtained from working with James. It's my frame of reference forever.

After we left James, we were working on our own in a group called Houseguests. We started dressing up and taking a more visual approach. When we worked on the road, people would come up to us and tell us that we reminded them of Funkadelic. We kept hearing about this group Funkadelic. Finally we were playing in Detroit, and a friend of ours brought George to see us, and the rest is history. We became part of Funkadelic immediately. The difference was like night and day. We went from the regimented, disciplined environment with James, to something a little bit closer to Ellington, because George wanted us to be ourselves. He didn't care what we did, as long as we could play what he wanted to hear. Of course, by then we were smart enough not to go crazy with that freedom. We knew that there had to be some discipline in there as well, so that's what we brought from our work with James. We wanted the freedom too, because we were still young, wild, and crazy. We were into Jimi Hendrix, Howlin Wolf, and Muddy Waters. And Sly Stone too, of course.

PL: Ellington always made sure that he credited his orchestra. There was never any question who his players were, unlike Motown or many of the soul performers back in the sixties.

FW: Well, Ellington was more intelligent in a classy kind of way. James was raw, straight from the country, from the street. And James was never a very handsome or debonair type of singer like some of the other soul crooners like Sam Cooke, Otis Redding, or Jackie Wilson. Those guys were all suave gentlemen. They were tasteful, they had a developed personality. James was a country boy. He wasn't very pretty; he wasn't outwardly intelligent with his demeanor; he wasn't a smooth talker. But you can't even try to say that James Brown is not *intelligent,* because his natural ability as a composer and bandleader is phenomenal! He basically invented funk as we know it today. All that anyone has to do is look at his track record. James was a genius! It just goes to show that you can never judge a book by its cover, because as far as book knowledge goes, he was never very educated. It was all natural ability. He was also determined to succeed. When all the other singers either died off or retired, James kept going no matter what. And he's still going! He hasn't even thought about slowing down.

PL: Ellington was never formally educated either, but he was very democratic in his dealings with the orchestra. When Ellington had a problem with one of his players, he had a different way of dealing with it. He would call that player out for more solos, and put him on the spot, instead of cursing anybody out or sending him home.

FW: Well, with Ellington you're talking about a different kind of intellect. Ellington had to think an entirely different way with the players he was using. He wanted to hire players who had a certain sound that he needed. That was very important to him. George Clinton is the same way with P-Funk. Ellington may not have been formally trained, but he had street smarts. Duke was very slick, very polished. He wasn't a country boy like James, by any means. Duke had a different exposure to a different audience, working in different surroundings. He was a city boy. And remember that in his genre of music, the jazz genre, everybody was always respected as individuals. That's how it was approached, then and now. But in the soul genre, the focus was always on the main star, the front man. The other players were just seen as the backup band, including Motown. That's how it was done. It's starting to change gradually, not drastically. It's not like everyone is getting the credit they deserve today; it's just not happening.

PL: How did things change with Sly Stone, and then George Clinton? Sly seemed to be the link between James and George.

FW: Sly was very smooth. George learned a lot from Sly and idolized him, no question about it. Sly taught George how to conduct a band using cues with everything you had: your fingers, your feet, your eyes. You can cue a band so many different ways. But Sly also learned that from James. James had a very precise method of conducting, right down to very subtle yet specific dance moves that would cue the musicians to do certain things. James directed the band with his dancing, and the audience never knew it. If the bandleader is locked in with the drummer, he can do anything. And vice versa, if a good drummer can lock in with the front man good enough to know where the music's going, if the front man gives a wrong cue, the drummer will know and hit the right thing anyway.

Sly was the link between James and George, no question. Sly was very shrewd. He knew how to have mass appeal. He could incorporate the right ingredients to go mainstream, even visually. He mixed male and female, white and black, in his band The Family Stone. That was way ahead of its time in the sixties. He had Cynthia, the female horn player, that was something different. He had the hot shot white drummer, Greg Errico. He had Larry Graham on bass. Plus, he let those guys expand on the direction he was taking. He allowed them to be different. This was more like Duke. Sly was smart enough to know that he wanted to surround himself with excellence. He could've kept the focus completely on himself, and instead of "Sly and the Family Stone," it could have just been "Sly" with the other players simply known as Sly's backup band. But he didn't go that way. That was the departure from what James was doing, and it was moving a little bit closer back to Ellington.

Sly would let Larry Graham do things on bass guitar that had never been done before. Larry reinvented the bass guitar with his playing technique, and people acknowledged that. Sly also let his brother Freddie Stone do some different things on guitar. And of course his horn section was very unique as well. But at the same time,

Sly didn't give the players as much freedom as George. He gave them as much freedom as was possible during that time period. That's why he was the link.

Something else that linked Sly to George Clinton was his emphasis on the visual appearance of his band. He didn't have anybody wearing uniforms like James or the other big bands; everybody looked different. He really wanted to make the group a part of the act, not just musically, but visually. He put a lot of thought into how he put that group together. It wasn't just a group of talented cats who could play. Sly also went for a certain look, a diversified look. In reality, he was thinking ahead of his time. He was thinking about the visual impact just as much as the musical impact, and today that's what it's all about in the video era with MTV and everything else. Sly was tuned into that aspect of things even then. And of course, George wanted everyone in P-Funk to look different as well. George was definitely going for a visual appeal of his own. He learned a lot of that from Sly.

But unlike George, Sly took all of the weight of being the front man upon himself. It was many years before George really took it upon himself to be a visible bandleader. He avoided it for a long time. But Sly assumed that role from the very beginning. Everybody knew who Sly was, because he promoted himself in that way.

Sly was like a big brother to me, and we're still very tight. Some of the things he's written just knock me out. Back when he was struggling through one of his big ego periods, he wrote a lyric that goes: "Looking through a glass, couldn't see past my name." That just blew me away! His mind, his approach to songwriting, is one of a kind. People shouldn't write him off, either. One day you'll wake up and hear Sly on the radio, and you won't even know how it happened.

PL: Why do you think Sly dropped out of the scene the way he did?

FW: Lots of reasons. Much of it was improper business management and promotion. He was being taken advantage of all the time. Promoters would have him double booked, scheduled to play in two or three different cities on the same night, in different states even. The promoters didn't care because they were getting the advance money. Then when Sly wouldn't be there, the promoters would walk away with all the money. The fans would riot, and Sly would take all the heat and bad press for it. And the worst part about it is that Sly didn't even know it was happening! Those are the things that made him realize that he really didn't have any control over his finances or his career, and finally he just said enough was enough. And I can understand why. When you're so big that you're getting booked in places and you don't even know it, and the promoters are running with the money, it's not worth it. People would blame Sly for not showing up, and they didn't realize that it was the promoter's fault.

But this is something that you see with all of these guys, with Duke Ellington, with James Brown, with Sly, and also with George. These guys are all pioneers. They took risks, tried new things. There was no model for what they were doing. It's an experiment, something that hasn't been done before. And when you're the pioneer, the results of the experiment fall on you, good or bad. It's easy to be a follower, because you can watch the pioneer, and try not to make the same mistakes that the pioneer made. But when you're a leader and an innovator, like the people we're talking about here, you've got nobody to fall back on but yourself. People very often don't realize that, but that's the way it is. Leaders make mistakes, because they take chances. Everybody else can afford to sit back and watch what happens. Then they know what *not* to do. And Sly being a pioneer, he was taken advantage of a great deal, and it really hurt him.

PL: What was your own experience with Sly?

FW: Apart from just being a brother to him, I was the one who got him back into performing after he had dropped out of the scene for a while. This was in the late seventies by this time, and Bootsy and I had already been with George Clinton for a while. I was really pleased about the way it worked out, because Sly had gotten so far removed from the music scene in the mid-seventies that he didn't really know how to get back into it. But I hooked him up with George, and of course George was thrilled. They did a piece together called "Funk Gets Stronger." There was another interesting song called "Hydraulic Pump," that had a lot of good people involved: Bobby Womack, Sly, George, myself, and many others. He was getting involved in recording again, which was great. When I hooked Sly up with George, and he got back into playing, a whole lot of stuff started coming out. We did a tour together called The Greatest Funk on Earth. It was just a great experience for everybody.

PL: So how does George operate as a bandleader? How does he communicate to the band what he wants? Because George doesn't play any musical instruments, he's strictly a vocalist.

FW: That's right. Well, one way to know what George wants is simply by knowing him, knowing his rhythm. I can feel where he's coming from. He doesn't have to sit me down and write me out a chart, you know what I mean? It's just like Duke and his men, right? George doesn't have to make me a chart, he just communicates with me. As a musician, if I agree to work with someone, the first thing I do is my homework, to figure out who I'm working with and how I need to interact with them on a personal level. That takes some of the weight off of the leader. That's what I try to do, because I believe in being a valuable asset to whoever I work with. There's always players who are too busy fooling around, partying, or whatever. It was like that in Duke's band as well, and Duke would rely on the guys he knew that would always be focused and ready to do the job. George is the same way. George has a nucleus of players that are always on top of their game; they don't mess around. That's who he depends on every night.

PL: When George was first composing and developing his pieces in the studio, how would he get what he was looking for?

FW: He would give us a blueprint, and then let us do our thing. That's what he was looking for—he wanted to hear what we could do with his concept. He was one of the few bandleaders to do that. Most leaders try to control everything. George wanted us to do what we felt.

George would also incorporate many things he heard from us. When we first started with George, we would play an instrumental set before he came out on stage. Many of the concepts and patterns we came up with for those jams would end up being worked into songs later on. "Cosmic Slop," "Take it to the Stage," and many other pieces originated from these jams we did. George would hear something he liked, and he would run with it. George was a genius because he would get a whole *group* of geniuses together, and he would let them do what they could do. Then he would scan everyone thoroughly, and he would find out what made a person tick, and where they would fit into his plan. He saw where his players were going, and if it made sense, then that's the direction he would take.

And when it came to discipline, he was about as strict as Ellington, if that means anything. George would never yell and scream at people. Sometimes George would put a player on the spot on stage, the way Ellington did. But if someone was really unable to deliver what they were supposed to deliver for whatever reason, George might have them sit out for the whole show, dock them some pay, and then forget about it. He wouldn't send the guy home, or get physical with him. George never did anything like that.

PL: How was George able to persuade such a large group of talented players to come and work with him in the first place? Was it just the exposure, or did he have something else to offer the players in P-Funk?

FW: Well you see, George is a genius with people. He's got phenomenal leadership and organizational skills. It's very simple how he did it: he let people do what they wanted to do! He didn't put any boundaries or limits on what they could do. So what he did in most cases was the smart thing. He heard something he liked, and he encouraged it, and nourished it. George also made *sure* that if nothing else, he was the *craziest*, most out-of-this-world character you could ever work with. That was a big part of his appeal to these players. They gravitated to George's personality, his biorhythms. And he inspired them with his spirit. When you see George on stage, you know exactly what I mean.

PL: Where do you see Prince in this evolution? Prince has acknowledged George's influence, as well as that of James Brown and Sly Stone. Prince seems to be the heir to this lineage of composer/ bandleader figures in modern music. Miles Davis went so far as to call Prince a modern day Duke Ellington. But I think that Prince has an approach that is more similar to James Brown, because he demands specific results from his musicians—probably due to the fact that he is a multi-instrumentalist himself, and has very clear ideas about how each instrument should sound.

FW: Prince used to come and see us with George all the time when he was younger, so there's a definite influence there. But a big difference I've noticed is that, unlike George, or Ellington for that matter, Prince has never kept one band together for very long. He's changed his musicians many times, and it seems that his players don't get the chance to develop their own unique sound. He gets a good group together, and then maybe a year or two later, he hires new guys. And it usually takes at least a year or two for a band to really start to click as a unit. The one exception that I am aware of was his first big band, The Revolution, with Wendy and Lisa. You see, people knew Wendy and Lisa because Prince worked with them for several years, and they had enough time to establish themselves as a group with an identity.

I mean, Prince does credit his musicians. You see their names on his records and things, but he just doesn't keep any one band together long enough. That's the difference between his approach and George's approach, or certainly Duke's approach. Prince will work with a group of players until he feels he's ready for a change, and then he gets a new band. He totally calls the shots in that respect. And it keeps the focus solely on him, rather than the sound of his band. This is where I see things changing, going back to James Brown's way of doing things, or Motown. There just isn't as much emphasis being put on bands anymore, it's going back to the focus being mostly on the front man, the leader. People aren't aware of the musicians in the group as much. And that's really a shame, because that's what people like Sly and the Family Stone, George Clinton with Parliament/Funkadelic, and the Duke Ellington Orchestra were all about. It was about bringing different individual voices together, and letting everybody shine. I hope we don't lose that.

Prince

PRINCE WAS ACTUALLY DESCRIBED by Miles Davis as a modern counterpart to Ellington: "Prince is from the school of James Brown, and I love James Brown because of all the great rhythms he plays. But Prince has some Marvin Gaye and Jimi Hendrix and Sly Stone in him, even Little Richard. He's a mixture of all those guys and Duke Ellington. He plays guitar and piano and plays them very well. But it's the church thing that I hear in his music that makes him special. He's the music of the people who go out after ten or eleven at night. For me, he can be the new Duke Ellington of our time if he just keeps at it."

There are certainly many similarities between Duke and Prince, outside of their royal bearing. Born Prince Rogers Nelson in Minneapolis in 1958, Prince grew up in a musical family, and was constantly encouraged to pursue music. He was signed to Warner Brothers at age seventeen, and given complete creative control over the production of his music—which was completely unprecedented for such a young artist. Since then, Prince has developed into a singular talent in modern music.

Perhaps one of the main reasons why Miles felt this way about Prince is because, like Ellington, Prince is what one would consider a *complete* musician. There is Prince the studio musician, and Prince the live performer/bandleader. In the studio, he is a multi-instrumentalist, playing fluent piano, guitar, bass, and drums. He is a composer, lyricist, and vocalist, and his songs are just as rooted in harmony and melody as they are in rhythm. He produces, arranges, and engineers his own records—usually performing all instruments and voices on the record himself through the process of overdubbing. This makes Prince's records a direct expression of his artistic vision. On stage, he is a bandleader, live performer, and dancer in the tradition of James Brown. He has assembled many different large ensembles to perform his music live, and has been able to adapt his one-man studio concept to the stage through his skills as a bandleader, giving other musicians the chance to interpret his music in a concert format. Like his precursors, Prince only recruits the best musicians for his live presentation. He demands perfection.

One need only listen to the live track from the 1987 LP *Sign o' the Times*, "It's Gonna Be a Beautiful Night," to hear his full control over a large ensemble. Very similar to Brown's "Get It Together," and Sly's "Dance to the Music," Prince establishes the groove one instrument at a time, directing every nuance and building an entire structure from the drums up. Like his funk predecessors, he creates a complex rhythmic structure around the unwavering emphasis on the one.

Also like Ellington, Prince's music seeks to combine the spiritual with the sensual, the ethereal with the earthy. Sex has always been a major theme in Prince's work. His lyrics and stage shows overflow with explicit erotic imagery to the point of excess, but there is also a strong spiritual quality to his music, and the contradictory nature of these two themes has been his primary artistic focus. While Prince's lyrics and live performances are filled with graphic sexual references, he is also firmly anti-drug and communicates a message of spiritual strength and self-reliance. His performances are highly theatrical and combine the sacred with the profane, much along the same lines as Marvin Gaye's music. But as Ellington himself once said in an interview with *Ebony* magazine: "I say sex is no sin. The sooner more people find that out, the better off we'll all be. We need to start discussing sex, and need to start enjoying it more. I want to tell you what I think the sex act is. I think it is like a lovely piece of music, conceived quietly in the background of mutual affection and understanding, made possible by instincts which lean toward each other as naturally as the sunflower slowly turning its lovely face to the sun." Certainly Ellington was a well known romantic, and would often use his relationships as a gateway toward a higher inspiration. Prince took this to new extremes, and would recreate his erotic fantasies on stage, then elevate the sexual aspect of his performance to an act of religious devotion to God.

Although Prince has not composed a complete sacred work like Ellington, his religious songs are scattered throughout his entire catalogue. His gospel-tinged vocal piece, simply titled "God," finds Prince delivering a stunning vocal performance, stretching and wailing his voice beyond his normal limitations, backed only by his keyboard. Similar to Ellington's "In the Beginning God," the opening lyric reads: "In the beginning there was God/He made the earth and the heavens." Other pieces like "The Holy River," "I Wish You Heaven," "Soul Sanctuary," and "Saviour," all deal with this seeming contradiction between sexual relationships and divine inspiration. "And God Created Woman" sings: "And we were naked and did not care/There's a time to take and a time to share/Two in love, all around and all aware/Flesh of my flesh/And God created Woman." In "Lovesexy," he describes "the feeling you get when you fall in love, not with a girl or boy, but with the heavens above."

Although Prince incorporated many different styles into his music, ranging from the Beatles, Bob Dylan, Jimi Hendrix, Joni Mitchell, Carlos Santana, and Little Richard, his main influence has always been the funk innovations of James Brown, Sly Stone, and George Clinton. His approach to leading a band was more like Brown from a musical standpoint, because Prince demands precision from his players. From a visual standpoint, however, Prince continued in the tradition of Sly Stone, with a fully integrated band composed of women and men, white and black. Prince's first major performing band, The Revolution, featured three female musicians who would have considerable musical impact on Prince for several years: Lisa Coleman on keyboards, Wendy Melvoin on guitar, and Sheila E on drums, all of whom went on to develop solo careers after The Revolution was dissolved by Prince.

After a series of records in the late seventies and early eighties, Prince finally achieved massive commercial success with the help of video exposure on MTV. Black music had been shut out of the mainstream since the mid-seventies, but for the first time since Stevie Wonder, a young black artist made music that appealed to whites as well as blacks, combining funk with disco, rock, blues, and gospel, playing many instruments and producing his own records. Prince brought back the concept of the individual musician who could do it all.

Prince disbanded The Revolution in 1986, and wanted to return to a pure funk approach, as opposed to the eclectic pop sound that had given him mainstream appeal. He formed a band called the New Power Generation. Alan Light of *Vibe* magazine wrote: "The NPG are funkier than any of his previous groups. Watching him cue them, stop on a dime, introduce a new groove, veer off by triggering another sample, you can only think of James Brown burnishing his bands to razor-sharp precision, fining them for missing a single note."

At times, Prince would feature between fifteen to twenty musicians and singers on stage at the same time, resembling the extravaganza of a George Clinton show. The primary difference is that a P-Funk performance emphasized the individual talents of the players themselves, with Clinton as the galvanizing force. With Prince, most aspects of the show

6. Prince: "He can be the new Duke Ellington of our time if he just keeps at it"—Miles Davis.

were choreographed, returning to the James Brown or Frank Zappa approach of complete control over the creative process. This was where Prince diverged from Ellington's path as a bandleader: there was not as much open collaboration between Prince, Brown, or Zappa, and their musicians.

One way is not better than the other. As engineer Susan Rogers said: "Prince has an incredible talent for recognizing strengths and weaknesses. He has marvellous natural leadership, is very good at knowing just how to push you to get the best out of you, and he knew when to stop, in most cases. Singers and musicians would rise to levels they hadn't thought possible."

But Prince has also revived the concept of the self-contained musician, the multi-instrumentalist, the well-rounded artist. In the nineties, Prince became criticized as an "eccentric" artist trapped within the confines of his "genius," but the fact remains that he is known around the world as a great musician in many respects. No one can deny that Prince is the real deal: he can write songs, produce records, and play all of his own instruments—then go on stage, move like James Brown, sing like Al Green, and conduct like Duke Ellington. Greg Tate says: "Prince is the link between the younger generation who are into hip hop, and the tradition of black popular music. He's an encyclopedia of black music, he's the way in: he embodies James Brown, Jimi Hendrix, and Duke Ellington."

So with Prince we come full circle in the funk lineage. In popular music, we have returned to the conservatism of the James Brown and Motown era, where the main star was the focus as opposed to the musicians. But at the same time, we have returned to the concept of one musician who can do it all: compose, perform, produce, conduct. Duke Ellington, by being multi-talented and able to balance all of these functions effortlessly, was the first complete embodiment of this type of individual artist in music. Now Prince has brought this concept up to date in popular music, by assuming the identity of The Artist. So, while Prince's approach has closed the door on the type of musical democracy instituted by Ellington, he has once again opened the door for young musicians to diversify their strengths and follow their own paths in modern music. A host of multi-instrumentalist singer/songwriters have already followed in Prince's wake, ranging from funk rocker Lenny Kravitz to techno wizard Trent Reznor of Nine Inch Nails. Goodbye to the ensemble. Hello to the Artist.

Frank Zappa

FRANK ZAPPA WAS AN ENTIRELY DIFFERENT type of artist—truly rock's most direct musical link to Duke Ellington as a composer, bandleader, instrumentalist, and businessman. He was rock's most avant-garde composer whose music incorporated elements of free jazz; modern composers like Ellington, Varese, Stravinsky, and Stockhausen; late fifties doo wop; guitar-dominated jazz–rock fusion of the seventies; and his own brand of social and political satire and outrageous humour. His lyrics were well known for their biting social commentary, as well as his complete sense of absurdity, and while Zappa never achieved pop superstardom due to the challenging implications of his music, he maintained a devoted following from the late sixties up until his death from prostate cancer in 1993. He was revered by musicians and audiences alike, and several of rock's most accomplished players began their careers in Zappa's many bands. He was the Miles Davis of rock, bringing new talent into his organization and providing them with challenging and rigorous training that would help them in their own careers. Zappa was also the most prolific artist in rock, with fifty-seven records released in his lifetime, mostly on his own independent label Barking Pumpkin Records, in the spirit of Sun Ra's Saturn label.

After college, Zappa composed film scores to raise money in the early sixties, and built his own low budget recording studio in the suburbs of Los Angeles. He had already developed a strong interest in serial music, musique concrète, and particularly the music of Edgar Varese. Zappa had attempted to compose some twelve-tone serial pieces of his own, but was unhappy with the results. He turned to his other musical love, which was doo-wop and rhythm and blues. He joined a local band in 1964 called The Soul Giants, which would eventually evolve into Zappa's own band, renamed the Mothers, performing Zappa's original compositions. The bandmembers were a motley collection of misfits and self-described "freaks," and were attracting a cult following in Los Angeles. The Mothers were signed to Verve Records and were forced to change their name from simply the Mothers to the Mothers of Invention.

Debuting in 1966 with the first two-record set in rock history, *Freak Out,* Zappa and the Mothers recorded a series of records in the late sixties that challenged virtually every convention in rock and popular music: scathing lyrics, montage editing techniques taken from musique concretè, and elements of serial music interspersed with the doo-wop vocal harmonies—an unusual combination to say the least. Nineteen sixty-eight was a landmark year for Zappa, with the release of three projects. *We're Only In it For the Money,* by the Mothers, was a scathing attack on the hippie flower power movement of the time, as well as the Establishment. The ever rebellious Zappa felt that the naive utopian stance of the hippie culture, combined with rampant drug abuse, had robbed the youth culture of a precious opportunity to implement actual social change. *Lumpy Gravy,* released by Zappa as a solo project, was a full length instrumental orchestral composition, featuring more of Zappa's montage editing. *Cruising with Ruben and the Jets* was a tongue-in-cheek tribute to fifties doo-wop. These three records, released within the space of a year, showed the unprecedented scope of Zappa's music.

But as the sixties drew to a close, Zappa and the Mothers also became known as the most technically proficient musicians in rock, reaching a level of accomplishment normally achieved only by jazz and classical players. Zappa's own innovative guitar playing was also coming to the fore. But by the end of the decade, Zappa disbanded the original Mothers, and was ready for a new approach to his music. Similar to Miles Davis and Prince, Zappa demanded the ultimate commitment from his musicians, and only recruited the best. Zappa, like Prince, was also vehemently opposed to drug use of any kind, and prohibited it among his musicians. Over the years, Zappa would assemble many new configurations of musicians under the Mothers's moniker. As the seventies evolved, Zappa began following an established formula, combining jazz–rock fusion with outlandish X-rated humor.

As a live performer, Zappa was a consummate bandleader and conductor. Many of Zappa's live shows would feature the band on instrumental material that was not featured on the records. Zappa's complex use of harmony, melody, and abruptly shifting time signatures was a constant challenge for his musicians to interpret on stage, but his players were provided with charts, and Zappa would conduct the band in the classical and big band tradition. He would often have an assistant in the band who would organize rehearsals before Zappa himself would attend and supervise the band's progress. This was completely unheard of for a rock band, but Zappa wanted to make it clear

7. Frank Zappa: The present-day rock composer whose spirit refuses to die.

that he was writing music that demanded this kind of serious concentration. His music was certainly a combination of high art with pop art, and Zappa would easily juxtapose a complex orchestral piece with flashes of adult humor.

Like Miles Davis, Zappa's many bands were breeding grounds for the most accomplished musicians in rock. Guitarists Steve Vai and Adrian Belew, violinist Jean-Luc Ponty, drummers Chad Wackerman, Terry Bozzio, and Vinne Colaiuta, keyboardists George Duke and Ian Underwood, bassist Scott Thunes, and many others became the most highly respected musicians of their field, largely due to their experience with Zappa. Unlike Ellington, Zappa never attempted to maintain one band. He wanted to change his sound continually and bounce his ideas off new players with a new approach, in order to prevent what he felt would be creative stagnation. But there are many similarities between Ellington and Zappa. First and foremost, Zappa respected Ellington's ability to function as a serious composer and live performer/ bandleader at the same time. Unlike James Brown and George Clinton, who were primarily vocalists, Zappa also admired Duke's skills as an instrumentalist—not a multi-instrumentalist like Prince, but someone who focused on one instrument. Zappa admired Ellington's innovations on piano, and followed suit with his unique approach to the guitar.

As was the case with Ellington, Zappa found it impossible to develop his music without building his own business operation around his career. As Ellington had done with Tempo Music, Zappa formed his own recording and publishing entity, Barking Pumpkin. He learned from Ellington that if he didn't take charge of his own business affairs, he would never have been able to produce such a substantial body of material in a capitalist society. But Zappa had a discouraging experience in 1969 when he discovered that Ellington was not always in complete control of his finances. In his autobiography *The Real Frank Zappa Book*, he writes:

In 1969, George Wein, impresario of the Newport Jazz Festival, decided it would be a tremendous idea to put the Mothers of Invention on a jazz tour of the East Coast. We wound up working in a package with Roland Kirk, Duke Ellington, and Gary Burton in Miami at the Jai-Alai Fronton, and at another gig in South Carolina. Before we went on, I saw Duke Ellington begging, *pleading*, for a ten-dollar advance. It was really depressing. After that show, I told the guys, "That's it—we're breaking the band up." We'd been together in one configuration or another for about five years at that point and suddenly *everything* looked utterly hopeless to me. If Duke Ellington had to beg some George Wein assistant back-stage for ten bucks, what was I doing with a ten-piece band trying to play rock and roll, or something that was almost rock and roll?

Needless to say, Zappa stuck to his guns and continued making music for another twenty-four years. He was also acutely aware that Ellington had found himself in a delicate situation at the time of the 1969 tour, but that did not change Zappa's realization that Ellington had long ago made his mark as an independent musician and businessman.

Zappa also took Ellington's concept of utilizing the sound of individual musicians, and applied it to his own compositions—not only with actual band performances, but also in a unique way through his montage cut-and-paste editing: Zappa would incorporate random recorded items from other musicians, and create compositions based on these "found" sound objects. He felt that Ellington had done the same in real-time with his bandmembers. But now with the aid of modern technology, Zappa could assemble different pieces of information and manipulate them in his own deliberate way as a part of the creative process.

Also like Ellington, Zappa composed, recorded, and performed at a relentless pace. Zappa's discography is almost as difficult to navigate as Ellington's because of its sheer immensity. But ultimately, Zappa's closest link to Duke Ellington is a desire to raise a "popular" art form to the level of "serious" art. Zappa displayed a quote from Varese on all of his early albums with the Mothers: "The present day composer refuses to die." Zappa wanted the public to know that he was a *serious* composer, and that it was possible for a rock musician to aspire to such a level. Ellington in the same way had wanted the jazz community to know that he was a serious composer as well, and went to great lengths to make sure that his music was perceived as concert music on a par with European classical music. His Carnegie Hall performances demonstrated this desire, and Ellington was again innovative beyond his years.

Ellington's Carnegie Hall performances of his extended works would not only have a powerful impact on Zappa, but on composer/guitarist Peter Townshend of The Who as well. In 1969, Townshend unveiled what was considered the first full length "rock opera" with The Who's *Tommy*. Townshend believed it was possible for a rock group to create its own classical music, and The Who followed Ellington's example by performing *Tommy* at the Metropolitan Opera House in New York, the equivalent of Carnegie Hall in terms of its prestige as a world famous opera house. As "Black Brown & Beige" opened the door for African-American jazz artists to perform at Carnegie Hall and other classical music venues around the world, Townshend applied the same principle to rock music with *Tommy* at the Met. Soon there would be concerts given in classical venues by "progressive rock" groups who blended rock music with elements of European classical music, including Emerson, Lake and Palmer, and The Moody Blues, although these groups strayed far from the pure rock sound of The Who. *Tommy* was hugely successful and set a precedent, released as a film in 1975, and finally transformed into a Broadway musical. Today, it is commonplace for rock artists to perform in classical music venues, often with full orchestras. None of this would have been conceivable before The Who's *Tommy*, which in turn would not likely have been conceivable before Ellington's performances at Carnegie Hall—which proved that there did not have to be a division between "serious" and "popular" music.

When Zappa's music was performed by the London Symphony Orchestra in 1983, it was released and marketed as a classical recording. When his music was conducted the following year by Pierre Boulez in Paris for IRCAM and released on EMI's classical label as *The Perfect Stranger*, Zappa had finally succeeded in placing himself within the tradition of Varese, Debussy, Stravinsky, and Boulez himself. But again, as with Prince and James Brown, Zappa was not as democratic a bandleader as Ellington. Whoever and whatever was required for Zappa to achieve his desired result was always his top priority.

There is a beautiful Zappa composition that is most reminiscent of Duke Ellington: a short instrumental piece from his 1969 LP *Hot Rats*, entitled "Little Umbrellas." With a rhythm section driven by upright bass and piano, the opening theme played on electric keyboard is modelled after the closing theme of "Black and Tan Fantasy." Zappa embellishes the main theme with clusters of notes that provide melodic dissonance in a way that is unique to Zappa. For the middle section, Zappa superimposes a complex keyboard melody over an ascending sequence of chords. The melody over these ascending chords is so unusual yet attractive that we don't immediately notice how simple the harmonic progression really is. Then the main theme returns, but this time with a full woodwind section. For all of Zappa's scathing satire and provocative melodies, "Little Umbrellas" is an exercise in simplicity and beauty, a melancholy piece that has a distinctly Ellingtonian flavor.

Charles Mingus

ALTHOUGH ALL OF THESE POWERFUL FIGURES in music have learned from Ellington's skills as a composer, bandleader, organizer, communicator, and innovator, it is likely that none will be remembered as a composer on the same level as Duke Ellington. Here Ellington is completely in his own category, and this is ultimately how he must be remembered: not just as a great leader and communicator, or even a great pianist or improvisor, but as a great composer—someone who could commit his ideas to paper and transform them through the process of orchestration. It is possible that Frank Zappa will be remembered as a composer more than a rock musician, but there is only one musician who came close to taking Ellington's approach to composition and applying it to his own musical language that will surely stand the test of time: Charles Mingus.

Mingus, like Ellington, composed music that always related to people—who they are, where they live, what they do. Also similar to Ellington, Mingus's music covers the widest possible emotional spectrum—from light to dark and everything in between. Mingus was known for his unpredictable behavior and volatile personality, which he channeled into his provocative and eclectic music. His compositions completely reflected the complicated person he was. They incoporated concepts in harmony, rhythm, and melody that had never been attempted by any composer, including Ellington. Mingus was also conscious of race relations in the United States, but was more outspoken than Ellington. He also rejected the term "jazz." Mingus was influenced by everything: world music, gospel, rhythm and blues, classical music, Charlie Parker, and Ellington. Mingus was able to incorporate all of these different elements into his own unique form of expression. Mingus did not make Ellington music. Mingus made Mingus music.

Although Mingus was primarily known as a bassist, he also played fluent piano, and primarily composed his music at the keyboard. While growing up, he always had trouble fitting in because of the light brown color of his skin, which made it difficult to find acceptance among blacks or whites. He threw himself into learning bass. He also began studying European composers of the time, such as Schoenberg and Stravinsky—something that was unheard of for a young jazz musician of his day. Even Ellington had never studied classical music. But when Mingus heard Duke Ellington, he knew that there was something more to "jazz" than meets the eye. He began studying Ellington's style of composition and arrangement, his approach to harmony, phrasing, and color. Ellington embodied everything as a composer and innovator that Mingus admired. And like Ellington, no matter how much he experimented with his compositions, Mingus always kept his swing.

In 1953, Mingus was actually given the chance to fill in for Wendell Marshall with the Ellington orchestra at the Apollo Theatre in Harlem. Before the show, Juan Tizol called Mingus and his bass into his dressing room to go over the changes to his piece "Caravan." Mingus was having trouble with Tizol's chart, and Tizol got frustrated and told Mingus that he couldn't read music. Mingus became infuriated, and the two men eventually had a physical altercation on the side of the stage. Tizol was hurt, and never made it to the bandstand to play. Mingus performed as if nothing had happened. Ellington finally realized after a few numbers that Tizol was missing, and once he had found out what happened, he paid Mingus a two-week salary, and dismissed him. But the two reunited in 1962 for their brilliant trio record with Max Roach, *Money Jungle*. Mingus is the featured soloist for the majority of the record, which stands as one the best efforts by all three artists.

Mingus also learned from one of Ellington's other important influences on other artists—his decision to control his own music with the establishment of his publishing company, Tempo Music. For the first time in the entertainment industry, black artists began taking charge of their own business. Like Sun Ra with his own label Saturn Records, and James Brown with King Records, Mingus established his own label, Debut Records. Mingus packaged and sold the records himself. Later he would establish Charles Mingus Enterprises.

He would rehearse his band whenever and wherever possible, instructing his musicians in new and unorthodox ways. He would take his music one phrase at a time, and commuicate his ideas to the musicians on piano or bass. This proved to be the most effective way, because had he shown the players his actual score, they would have hardly been able to understand it—so idiosyncratic was his method of writing music down on paper, and so unusual were his choices of parts for various instruments. Mingus would compose parts that a given instrument would not usually play. Similar to Stravinsky, Mingus thrived on hearing the sound of an instrument stretched beyond its normal parameters. It pushed the musicians to grow beyond their comfortable capacities as players.

Like Tom Whaley's relationship with Ellington, Mingus hired a trombonist named Jimmy Kneper to be a copyist for his manuscripts and arrangements. Mingus began work on an extended piece named "Epitaph," which he attempted to debut at New York's Town Hall, but there was not enough time for the band to rehearse, and the performance was a disaster. Similar to Ellington's resentment of the mixed reactions to "Black Brown & Beige," Mingus refused to discuss "Epitaph" at any great length, because it was one of the most painful disappointments of his life. Mingus would follow up the next year with a masterpiece, his extended work, "The Black Saint and the Sinner Lady," a piece which bears a relation to Ellington not only because of the ambitious nature of the composition, but also because of the voicing of each instrument, particularly the horns.

Personal and professional setbacks in the late sixties drove Mingus into an early retirement from music. Jazz had also been changing, and was forced to take a back seat to the growing popularity of rock music. But in 1969, there was a tribute to Ellington in Berkeley, California, to celebrate his seventieth birthday. Mingus was asked to participate, and the orchestra performed a Mingus piece called "The Clown." The experience inspired Mingus to return to the music scene. In January 1974, there would be another Ellington tribute with Mingus at Carnegie Hall. He performed "C Jam Blues" and "Perdido" in a jam session with Roland Kirk, Charles MacPherson, George Adams, John Handy, and other artists.

As the early seventies progressed, he continued the Ellingtonian tradition of performing his music in concert halls as opposed to clubs. He started to work with younger musicians, and his audience began growing to include younger listeners who recognized Mingus's unique contributions to music. Singer/songwriter Joni Mitchell began work on an album where she wrote lyrics for Mingus compositions. The record was simply called *Mingus*. But this new energy would be short lived. In the late seventies, Mingus was diagnosed with Lou Gehrig's disease. He did not have very long to live, and passed away in January 1979. His ashes were scattered in the Ganges River of India. Joni Mitchell's recording was released after his death.

Since his death, Mingus's music continues to be performed by repertory orchestras, much in the same vein as Duke Ellington. Ten years after his death, his magnum opus, "Epitaph," was finally resurrected and performed at Lincoln Center in 1989, conducted by Gunther Schuller. The concert featured many of the outstanding jazz musicians of the time, including Wynton Marsalis, Randy Brecker, and

Ellingtonian trombonist Britt Woodman—all of whom would also be involved in repertory performances of Ellington's music as well.

⌒

Gunther Schuller

⌣

GUNTHER SCHULLER HAS CHANGED the way the world listens to Duke Ellington. As a trained composer and performer, he has an experiential understanding of the unique qualities of Ellington's compositions. As an eloquent writer and speaker, he communicates this knowledge in clear language that everyone can understand. His lectures and articles closely examine Ellington's style of composition and arrangement, but his scholarly approach to the analysis of Ellington's music is tempered by his skills as an educator. Everyone from serious musicologists, to casual music lovers who are only beginning to discover the Duke, can learn something from Schuller's expertise on Ellington.

For example, I attended a lecture he gave in Chicago on the early works of Ellington. He concentrated on four pieces that showed four different aspects of Ellington's approach to composition—all four pieces composed before the arrival of Billy Strayhorn. The pieces were "Mood Indigo," "Daybreak Express," "Azure," and "Reminiscing in Tempo." He began with an analysis of "Mood Indigo," which he cited as the first jazz composition solely intended for concentrated listening, rather than dancing. He used an overhead projector to show specific measures from the score, as well as an audio recording of the piece that enabled us to hear what he was showing us on the screen.

He explained how Ellington inverted the traditional roles of clarinet, trombone, and trumpet for the theme of "Mood Indigo." In traditional jazz up to that point, the clarinet normally occupied the highest register, the trombone the lowest, with trumpet in the middle. Through a remarkable stroke of genius, Ellington simply turned this configuration upside down. He pushed the muted trombone up into its highest possible register, just underneath the muted trumpet. He then brought the clarinet down to the very bottom of its range. This combination produced a sound previously unheard in any form of music—an introspective sound that perfectly conveyed the feeling that

Ellington wanted to communicate in "Mood Indigo." Gunther gave the audience clear examples of how Ellington was able to achieve this effect. His lecture was specific enough to satisfy advanced musicologists, but clear and understandable enough for laypeople as well. Everybody learned something new about Duke Ellington that day—thanks to Gunther Schuller.

⌒〰〰〰〰⌒

PL: How did you first encounter Duke Ellington in person, and how did you develop an appreciation for his music to the point where you knew there was something special there not to be found elsewhere?

GS: There are two distinct questions here. As far as first hearing his music and becoming fascinated by it long before I met him (which was not so long, actually) I heard him on the radio, of course. He was broadcasting from the Kentucky Club . . . actually it was not the Kentucky Club. It was the Hurricane Club on Broadway. This was 1943. Practically every night he came on at 11:15. He had played for many years at the Kentucky Club, back in earlier days. His manager, Irving Mills, owned it, so Ellington's band was like the house band.

When I was twelve or thirteen I started buying classical and jazz records, so I also bought Ellington records. I was a young composer, and I was completely amazed at this music. Coming from a classical background through my parents, at first I didn't know anything about Ellington. Nor did anybody else among my peers.

PL: What were the first pieces that struck you as being unlike anything else you had heard in music before?

GS: *All* of those pieces! In 1940–41 he was creating all those great pieces: "Ko Ko," "Cotton Tail," "A-Train"—everything! They were hot off the presses at that time. Of course, he was playing "Mood Indigo" too, and other earlier pieces such as "Sophisticated Lady."

PL: And you had the sensitive ears to pick out the unique properties in those pieces that many listeners may have missed.

GS: Well, I think at seventeen I was a little better about that than I was earlier at fourteen. When I was seventeen I went to Cincinnati to play first horn in the symphony orchestra there. The symphony hall in Cincinnati was—and still is today—a huge, enormous brick building in the middle of which was a main hall that could seat about 3500 people. At one end of the building was a wrestling emporium, and at the other end was a nightclub, I think it was called Coconut Grove—a real generic name for nightclubs in those days. They were called the Cotton Club or the Coconut Grove or something like that. And during the first year that I was in Cincinnati in 1943—maybe it was in December—Ellington appeared at this club for a week. All I had to do was go from my backstage area through a side door straight into the club. I was totally overwhelmed by not just Ellington, but by the entire band and the things they were playing. Johnny Hodges had just recorded "Warm Valley."

PL: This was not long after the unveiling of "Black Brown & Beige" in New York at Carnegie Hall.

GS: Yes, which I unfortunately could not attend because I was in Cincinnati at the time. But at the Coconut Grove, I just stood there in front of the band—I didn't dance or anything. I just wanted to hear the music; I stood there for hours. During my two years in Cincinnati, Duke came back a few more times. I think the last time was in April 1945, just before I left Cincinnati and went back to New York. At that point I had begun to play some jazz on the french horn, which was something unheard of in those days.

By the way, there was a *hell* of a lot of great jazz in Cincinnati. I'm talking about clubs in alleys with piano trios and small combos. But beyond that, in the black ghetto there were at least ten clubs that featured the big bands. Duke, Lunceford, Basie, everybody; black bands. I must have never slept, because I was there all the time, while during the day I was playing with the symphony.

Anyway, I think it was during Ellington's second or third visit to Cincinnati when I met him. I had met him briefly once before, through Lawrence Brown. But in 1945 (I think it was) I got up the nerve to not only talk to him, but to bring my horn along. Hodges had just recorded "Mood to be Wooed." It fit very well on the french horn, except that I couldn't do all of those incredible slides and scoops that Hodges was so great at. On the french horn that's virtually impossible, with the particular valves that we have. Anyway, I played it for Ellington, and he was completely amazed. He started to tell me: "You know, I've always loved the french horn, but I could never find anybody to play it." Among the blacks there weren't any french horn players. The french horn wasn't used in jazz in those days. Blacks couldn't get into symphony orchestras, so why would they play a french horn? By the way, a couple of years later Duke said, "Why don't you join my band?" I said, "Duke, you've got to be kidding!" I mean, a white kid, a french horn player, in a black orchestra in 1945–46? I don't know to this day if he was kidding or if he was serious. Anyway, that's how I got to know him.

PL: Were you already composing music yourself by then?

GS: Oh yes, for at least seven years.

PL: And so the two of you had some conversations about composition where you could possibly exchange ideas?

GS: Not really. I was so respectful of him—after all, I was seventeen and he was already in his mid-forties—that I didn't talk much about my compositions. I talked about his music, but he didn't know any of my music. How could he?

PL: But you learned a lot from those interactions?

GS: Oh yes, but mostly from listening to his music.

PL: In retrospect, looking back over his entire body of work, if you had to select a few pieces that stand out as having had the most impact on twentieth-century music, not just jazz but on modern music as a whole, what Ellington pieces do you think have had the most impact and may continue to have the most impact in the next century?

GS: Well, the sad answer to that is that very little of his music has really had the kind of impact that it should have had. Yes, Gil Evans, Charlie Mingus, Thelonious Monk, a whole bunch of people fed on Ellington's music, but in the classical field hardly at all; they didn't know what he was doing. I was almost the only one. Now, fifty years later, a lot of people are aware of Ellington, but in those days he was severely underappreciated, except by black people. In the thirties, white people didn't know about Duke Ellington. Even when I was growing up in New York and listening to the radio, except for the broadcasts from the Hurricane Club, all the other jazz shows on the radio on WNEW for example, and all those kinds of stations, they all played white jazz. They all played Benny Goodman and Tommy Dorsey and those people. Once in a while they played Count Basie or Duke Ellington. And if they played Ellington, they would play "Sophisticated Lady," or one of his ballads. So he was rather—I won't say rejected—ignored by everybody except the black audience, who dug him like mad.

PL: Even the more ambitious pieces like "Reminiscing in Tempo?"

GS: Those pieces were *totally* rejected! Totally rejected! But some of the other pretty things like "Mood Indigo," "Solitude," "Sentimental Mood," and that type of song, were appreciated quite a lot, but again primarily by the black public. The white folks didn't know much about Duke's music. They didn't know about Count Basie either. They didn't know about Lunceford. They didn't know about Chick Webb, except when Ella Fitzgerald sang some hit songs. It was a very segregated world. But it all changed, of course, after World War II. So it's sad to say that Ellington's influence has been really minimal except on half a dozen major jazz people that one could mention, like Mingus and Gil Evans. Certainly, on the classical field he has had no influence.

PL: So his music has not influenced any other modern composers besides the jazz figures you mentioned. Do you feel that any twentieth-century composers influenced *him* in any concrete way? Many people talk about comparisons between him and Delius, when there is no evidence to suggest that he ever really listened to Delius.

GS: Right. He never knew about Delius, especially in the early years of his career.

PL: Or Schoenberg, Stravinsky, Debussy?

GS: Not at all. But Delius, after all, is tonal music, and supposedly Ellington *could* have heard that, except that he knew very little classical music until much, much later. The reason the Delius rumor got started was because when Ellington went to England in 1932, Delius had just died, and the harmonic language of Delius and Ellington seemed at that time very similar to some people. So some of the English composers assumed that he had taken it from Delius.

PL: It's interesting to think of how they both arrived at many of the same conclusions harmonically.

GS: It is very common in music history that in Europe and America, people who didn't know each other were doing things that were very similar. They were just in the air.

PL: Is it possible that through Ellington's extended works he began to make other twentieth-century music more accessible for people? Did more people, through Ellington, become more aware of modern classical music? In a sense, that's how it happened for me. Once I began to absorb his more elaborate pieces, I became more aware of that style of composition.

GS: Yes, I'm not saying it didn't happen to anybody. But in a country of 250 million, if it happened to ten thousand people it was a lot. The awareness of Duke's music by a broader segment of the population came much later, in the 1950s and 1960s, with your generation, for example. My answer to your question would have to be: no, because the segregation between jazz and classical music—which you can't feel as much today—is something I've experienced for fifty years. Things are just now coming together, where classical music and jazz are really merging in fascinating ways. Yes, I suppose when Ellington did "The Nutcracker Suite," some people, who had never heard "The Nutcracker Suite," went out and bought the original of Tchaikovsky. But I certainly don't think that happened to hundreds of thousands of people.

PL: Do you think that this present-day merging of jazz and classical music is partly due to Ellington's example? What about people today like Anthony Davis or Anthony Braxton?

8. Duke at the piano with manuscript: "He'd sit at the piano and put his fingers down . . . and out came these incredible things"—Gunther Schuller.

GS: I think that all came much more from people like Ralph Burns—who wrote for Woody—and then Ornette Coleman, Eric Dolphy, John Lewis, and Mingus in particular. Mingus has been one of the most powerful disseminators of Ellingtonian ideas through his music. And one of the reasons I say "no" is that Ellington never joined, for example, the bebop movement.

PL: That's truly amazing when one considers how pieces like "Cotton Tail" and "Main Stem" from 1940 are early examples of bebop before the genre even existed.

GS: Yes, they are early *examples* of bebop, but they were far ahead of their time. Once bebop came in, Duke admired Dizzy, admired Bird, admired Monk—but he did not join that crowd. He stayed apart. And he *always* stayed apart. He often said, "I am myself; I am not those guys. I don't need to do that."

PL: Is that one of the reasons why he didn't care too much for the label "jazz?"

GS: Well, there was much more to it than that. He just thought that what the press and most people were calling "jazz" had to be dance music, and had to be loud and brash and happy, and all that stuff.

PL: It couldn't be concert music.

GS: That's right, it couldn't be concert music. Besides, he knew that "jazz" was originally the term in New Orleans's Storyville red light district for fucking, and that's a fact. A lot of blacks resented that. But the term got so entrenched that there was no way anyone could stop it.

Beyond that, Ellington always thought the term "jazz" too confining, too restrictive. His musical vision went way beyond the standard view of jazz. So he was always apart. But at the same time, what the boppers did by 1950, and even the "cool jazz" musicians, he had already done in some ways with certain pieces like "Cotton Tail." So here he is doing "Cotton Tail" in 1940, bebop comes in really big in the late forties, and he has now gone way ahead again. So is he going to go backwards just because the boppers caught up with him? Of course not. But again, the main reason why he never had the big influence that I think he should have had if the world was right, is that his music has *always* been too unusual, too subtle, too elevated for mass tastes. So that even in the height of the swing era, why did they crown Benny Goodman the "King of Swing?"

PL: You got me on that one!

GS: Ellington did not take that very lightly. He knew that *he* was the King of Swing, or Basie. But not Benny Goodman. That's just another example of how relatively little he was appreciated in the mass culture.

The intelligentsia in Europe and here, *they* certainly appreciated Ellington. As did I. My parents tried to get me to stop listening to jazz. They thought it was a vulgar, degenerate, or unimportant music. So everything was against it. But for me it was clear: the minute I heard Ellington, I said to myself, "This is great music."

PL: I have read your pieces where you talk about the importance of preserving his music in live performance.

GS: Absolutely. If we don't do that, it will eventually die.

PL: John Cage placed a lot of emphasis on live performance as opposed to what he saw as fixing the music in the recording process. We all know that Ellington was active in both areas. Do you think he got as much out of recording as performing?

GS: He did, no question. Because when you record you really have to refine the performance to a very high level. Mistakes and other unexpected things can happen in a concert and nobody really gives a damn, but on a recording it's different. It's a different process, and it's a different way of knowing your own music. But Ellington learned from both. The important point now after eighty years of jazz—not just Duke Ellington, but all kinds of great jazz music—is that if we don't keep playing that music and just keep it in museums on recordings it will die. Do the kids today buy jazz records? No, they buy pop and rock records.

PL: And an ongoing tradition of live performance is a way to improve our understanding of his work.

GS: Yes, if it were to happen, but it isn't happening! Well . . . it's beginning to happen. Bill Russo has a repertory orchestra in Chicago. I did one with the Smithsonian, and I've done repertory orchestras at my school at the New England Conservatory for thirty years. I've been on this front line for a long long time. Wynton Marsalis has a kind of repertory band, but the number of these bands that exist in the entire country, you can still count on one hand. If we had *fifty* of these bands, playing full time like symphony orchestras, then it would make a big difference. But five little ones that hardly even get to record or play around and tour. Wynton now is making tours, but the Smithsonian band didn't get to tour except for a very small stretch. So what I'm saying is in order for the live performance to have the real effect it should have, there has to be more of this. But I've been attacked by black musicians, because many of them are against this repertory orchestra idea.

PL: Why?

GS: Because they say, "That's a Eurocentric approach, and you're treating it like classical music. This music belongs to us, it must be

Afrocentric." This is all bullshit as far as I'm concerned. I keep on going; I don't care what they say. I want only to help preserve this great music.

PL: It seems strange that some people would have that reaction, especially considering some of the extended works like "Black Brown & Beige," "Harlem," or "My People," that have much to say about the African-American experience. Isn't it odd that some people would not want these pieces to be a part of a continuous living and breathing experience?

GS: Well, don't try to get me to explain it, because I do not in any way understand it. I absolutely don't. They throw around these words like "Afrocentric," and I don't get it. I am simply trying to keep the music alive in some kind of an authentic and pure way. What's wrong with that?

PL: How do you think Duke himself would react to such criticisms?

GS: I think he would be delighted that people are respecting his music and keeping it alive. Jazz musicians can very often reinterpret their music in new ways, and he did that himself many times. In other words, I'm certainly not saying that now we must *always* and *only* do repertory jazz. I've always said that this is a new thing that we can do now, and in the meantime the jazz mainstream will go on developing. Everybody does their thing. Why not have both? And that's what Ellington would have said too, I'm sure.

PL: You just made an interesting point about new interpretations of a given piece. One of the things that always struck me about Ellington was how he was the first composer to my knowledge who composed with specific individual players in mind to perform different pieces. You don't see that as being an obstacle to new interpretations of his pieces, with new players that don't have those unique qualities that his players had?

GS: No, not really. Mind you, it's very hard to step into the shoes of a Harry Carney, or a Johnny Hodges, or a Cootie Williams. But that's not to say that it can't be done, or that it shouldn't be done. It can be done with respect, with love, and with a sense of authenticity to represent how great that sound and style was. That's what it's all about—to keep that alive. Not everybody can do that; not everybody wants to do it, and that's fine with me too! If you don't want to do it, then don't do it! But don't try to prevent other people from doing it, saying that it's wrong somehow. I even feel that there are certain pieces, like Coleman Hawkins's "Body and Soul," that are useless to try to recreate. It would be almost impossible, and secondly, what's the point? That was such a great individual contribution that it would be like plagiarism just to imitate that. But with Duke's music, we're talking about arrangements and compositions. It's a whole different thing.

PL: It's a very organic creation that should be re-experienced by new generations.

GS: That's right. And besides that, as I've said before, there are so many pieces by Ellington where there's no improvisation at all, where they were all written out, so why can't we play them—*as* compositions?

PL: Let's talk about "Black Brown & Beige" for a moment. Many people have mixed feelings about the original piece the way it was performed in 1943. One criticism from people like John Hammond was that the third movement, "Beige," was very hastily written and barely completed on time for the performance. How do you feel about how the third movement fits in with the rest of the piece? Do you also think it was not developed properly?

GS: There is no doubt about it. I know it, because friends of mine were at the rehearsals in the days before the concert. That last movement was thrown together in such a frantic hurry, and is clearly not on the level of even the first movement, let alone some of his other great pieces. I mean, it does have its moments. Ellington's music always has its moments. Harry Carney plays the clarinet in the last movement and something special happens. But as a composition the entire piece starts quite high, in the second movement there are weak joints and things that were thrown together, and the third movement gets even weaker. It's very sad.

PL: Did you ever speak with Duke about that?

GS: No, I never dared. He was aware of that, and I know he was hurt by the lukewarm reaction. But again, it was the circumstances of his crazy life that he never got to finish the piece! And so they went into the Nola studio in New York and tried to somehow patch it together, but they ran out of time.

PL: How did you feel about the various recorded interpretations of the piece that were incomplete?

GS: Well, I feel bad about that, because what Ellington should have done—and maybe, again, he didn't have the time—was say, "OK, that was the first performance. It wasn't that good. We didn't quite finish the piece, now let's have Strayhorn and I get together and remake the piece and record it again." But again, in the rush of his life, he never got around to that. When he finally did it again, many years later, it was better—the musicians were more modern and more adept at playing it—but it wasn't fixed up enough; and it was different anyway. He gave up on certain things in the piece that aren't even in the second version.

PL: Do you think it's possible that one of the reasons why he didn't go back and complete it is because of that initial frustration, and the initial mixed reaction? That's something that I've always wondered about.

GS: It could be, it absolutely could be. Duke was very sensitive, and he tried to laugh it off like anybody else, or have some cute remark about it. But it hurt him very deeply sometimes, to the point of saying, "Okay, the hell with that. I'll leave that, and I'm going to go on to something new." Some people work that way.

PL: I've heard the work you've done with Ornette Coleman, which I enjoy very much. In those and other pieces you've written, how do you feel that Duke has influenced you in your efforts as a composer? What, if anything, have you learned from Duke in your work?

GS: It's curious. My work is so different. I feel that rather than being influenced by Duke, I have always felt that his music was a kind of confirmation in certain areas of what I was doing, in a different way. In other words, I am a very strongly harmonic composer. There are composers who don't know anything about harmony, who don't like harmony, don't use harmony, or whatever. I can't do that. For me, harmony is one of the essentials of music. And it certainly was with Duke Ellington. That's his strongest suit.

PL: Schoenberg once said that Cage had absolutely no understanding of harmony.

GS: None whatsoever. But Schoenberg certainly did, and Schoenberg is my greatest influence. Schoenberg and Stravinsky. Now as to Ellington's influence, I have written Third Stream pieces, jazz-influenced pieces, but out of the 160 pieces I've written, there aren't more than twenty-five or thirty that are involved with jazz. The rest are all what we call twelve-tone or serial music. That doesn't relate to Ellington at all. But I've always drawn strength from the fact that here was this great man in the jazz field who had a similar passion for strong and beautiful harmonies.

PL: But I've also enjoyed those pieces where he did experiment with atonality like "Clothed Woman" and "Azure." As you've said before, "Azure" is certainly one of the first examples of atonality in jazz.

GS: Absolutely, and "Clothed Woman" goes even further out. A lot of his later piano playing goes into atonality a great deal. But on the other hand he didn't make a big issue of it. That's just something he could do. He didn't formulate it into a theory like Schoenberg did.

That was just Duke's ears having this incredible need to explore the outer extensions of the harmonies. He didn't know the word "bitonality." We classical composers use it, but to him it was just a certain sound on the piano.

PL: Strayhorn had more of an understanding of those concepts.

GS: Yes, because Strayhorn had studied the French composers who first started doing all of that. Strayhorn was a well-read and well-educated musician, having studied theory and harmony and that sort of thing. Ellington never bothered. He was just a totally pragmatic person. He learned everything at the piano.

PL: That brings me to the question of Duke having some skepticism about formal musical training, and how that training would hamper a musician's creativity. In the case of Strayhorn that certainly didn't seem to be an obstacle.

GS: Yes, he did have those feelings. And no, it was not the case for Strayhorn, because Duke saw and appreciated what Strayhorn could do. I don't really know how deeply Ellington believed that about training. In any case, he was certainly wrong if he did believe that. Because that's just silly. I mean, yes, in a bad composer, too much formal training will make a bad composer even worse. But in a great composer? Beethoven is one of the greatest composers and he had the best of formal training of his time. So to say that formal training is suspicious, because it will ruin you and deprive you of your musical freedom, is nonsense. That's where Ellington was really weak, because he just didn't know what classical composers could do. Later in his life, once he dug into that Tchaikovsky piece, he began to realize what formal training can do for a composer, but he himself never had it, never had a chance to enjoy it. He started working professionally when he was fourteen, and he practically didn't even go to school. So that was one other reason why he had a little bit of disdain for it, because he simply never had the privilege to enjoy it.

PL: Because he did not have access to formal training, what do you think inspired him to create some of the more innovative and original pieces of his early career like "Mood Indigo" and "Azure?" What could have led him to making those departures from the norm in composition and arrangement?

GS: Well, there is actually no answer to that. That's what we cover with words like genius and talent. I don't know. We do not know and perhaps will never know where exactly an artist's inspiration comes from. It can come, of course, from an outside source such as a literary source or a painting. That's understood. But specifically what makes a composer think of a new idea, something that's never been done before, we have no answer to that. That's the mystery of creation. And we cover it with words like genius and talent. But that's about as far as it goes. When he, not having studied music and music theory formally, started writing bitonal chords as early as "Mood Indigo," or maybe even earlier, I suppose he discovered them on the piano and liked them. I remember not only Duke doing that, but Dizzy would play the piano, hit a chord and say, "Wow! How about that!" And if he liked it, he wrote it down.

PL: Going back to your first interactions with Duke, I remember you mentioning how you would observe him doing just that: sitting at the piano and making new discoveries.

GS: I lived in a room right next to him in a theater in Cleveland for a whole week. He hardly slept at all, I think he went to bed around five in the morning or something. But he would just sit at the piano all night in his stocking cap and robe and just sort of play and improvise, play anything. Ruminating, I call it, at the piano. And every once in a while when I would hear the piano stop, I knew that he had just heard something that he liked and wrote it down. But sometimes it was, "I've got to write a piece for next week or tomorrow," and he would work consciously on a piece. But sometimes he'd just sit there, almost like in a dream or a trance. But he'd still stop and write things down when he liked what he heard. It's that same thing that I've just said, about how I'm sure that that's how he discovered these bitonal and polytonal harmonies. He'd sit at the piano and put his fingers down in various places and out came these incredible things, and he had the imagination and the talent to not reject those things. At that time in the thirties, other jazz composers, if their fingers went into the wrong place and you got a sort of dissonant chord, they'd cry "Oh shit, what's that!" Instead he would say, "I like that!" But selectively, of course. It isn't just that he wrote down anything that his fingers happened to play. And after a while, of course, he got wise to the system that underlies bitonality and polytonality. There is a logic to all of that. And most of the bitonal chords he used were related through the diminished fifth, which now is standard fare. I mean, every musician since bebop from the mid-forties just does that in their sleep. But what is important to remember is that when Ellington was doing this it was at least fifteen years ahead of everybody else.

PL: Were there things you observed him doing when he would be in rehearsals or recording sessions with the orchestra that struck you as being different and unusual?

GS: I don't know. I saw him fairly often in rehearsals, but something entirely different used to happen there. That's where the players in the band got involved with the final result. Someone like Johnny Hodges would want to try something different with phrasing in certain ways, maybe even change a note here or there—although that was rare. Maybe just the notes were written down, but there wasn't any phrasing yet. Now, I'm not saying that the band took over. But we all know that this was a collaborative thing very often between his players, or many of them, and himself. He always had the final word. I mean, he didn't just accept everything that anybody suggested to him.

PL: We talked a little about "Black Brown & Beige" and some of the problems that Duke encountered with that piece. What do you feel are some of his most sucessful extended works that have held up the best conceptually and historically? Which pieces by either Ellington or Strayhorn come the closest to classical structure?

GS: That is very difficult for me to answer at the moment, because I have not sufficiently listened to all of them recently. I mean, I have heard all of the extended pieces at one time or another, some of them in live performance. So for me to try to answer that at this time would be unfair to the pieces. In terms of the question of classical structure, I do not at all want to create the impression that he tried to write classical music. He had no interest in that subject. The fact that some of his things remind others of classical music, yes. But that wasn't him. Worst of all—and I have to be very careful about this— I've been accused many times of saying that *because* some things in Ellington's music remind us of things that classical composers did earlier, that I am saying therefore that those pieces are thus "better" because they come close to classical music. I *never* say that, but I've been accused of that. So I don't want to get into that at all. He was very independent, and because he was a genius he did a lot of things that classical composers did or had done, but he didn't know that! And he didn't care whether he had done it or not! That's the greatness of Ellington's genius.

I actually want to pursue this a little further, because this is exactly the sort of thing that certain black musicians get very militant about. There's been too much writing in the history of jazz by jazz historians, and particularly this guy Collier who got crucified—he and Wynton Marsalis had a big debate about this at one point. He was constantly making the accusation that Ellington wasn't really that good of a composer, and he didn't know his classical stuff, and all of that bullshit. I don't blame some musicians who criticize Collier for saying that, because what that implies is that black musicians are not good enough to write something as "good" as classical music. And that's a totally specious, phony, stupid argument. And of course, there are many fine black composers who write classical music, who don't write jazz.

So this is sort of like saying that blacks are wonderful dancers and shoe shine boys, but they can't write anything "serious." Such prejudices have been going on forever. Scott Joplin got crucified for that, because he had the nerve to want to write an opera. Black people are not supposed to write operas, are they? "They don't possibly have the talent for that." But these militant black intellectuals have attacked me without realizing that I am one of the people who has never said anything like that. Many times they put me in with everybody else, so I want to be extra careful that there is no impression here that I am saying that Ellington is great because he wrote something as "great" as classical music. That is the last thing I would say.

PL: You have performed hundreds of repertory concerts of his music. How do you structure these concerts? Do you have specific themes or time periods that you focus on?

GS: I've done so many things. I've done early things, middle period things, late things. I've done programs that went through the whole range of his music. I haven't done the Sacred Concerts, but I've done some of the later pieces like "Night Creature" and "Harlem," which are big orchestra pieces. But I've mostly concentrated on the period of music from roughly 1930 to 1950.

PL: Have you done "Black Brown & Beige?"

GS: No, I've done excerpts from it. I've not done the entire thing, because, as I've said, that third movement has got a lot of problems and I haven't really wanted to perform that. It also requires singers, and I mostly haven't worked with singers. But I do mix different periods of his work for some concerts. It can actually go back to 1926 or 1927, to some of the really early pieces like "East St. Louis Toodle-oo" or "Black and Tan Fantasie," up to about 1950. I do the 1953 "Rockin' in Rhythm," which is a rearrangement. His genius was continuous, and the quality of the work is very high and consistent.

PL: You haven't delved into the sixties with pieces like the "Far East Suite?" That's one of my personal favorites.

GS: No, although I have done excerpts. I've done "Isfahan." I've done some things from the Shakespeare suite "Such Sweet Thunder." But I've not done the whole suites.

PL: Actually, when I asked you about the extended works, two of the ones you mentioned, "Night Creature" and "Harlem," are two of the ones that I and many others view as being some of his more successful longer pieces.

GS: They certainly are. "Night Creature" is really terrific. But the one that everybody forgets is "Reminiscing in Tempo!" That's Ellington's first big extended work, a thirteen minute piece—a piece that is virtually perfect. It's a "variation" piece in one movement, that's based on one or two themes, and in that sense it's really unique in Ellington's work. He never did anything like that again.

PL: Have you performed that piece live?

GS: Oh, many, many times. But getting back to these concerts, there are never specific themes in mind when I put a show together. I have thought of that, because there are certain themes in Ellington's oeuvre, but I haven't done it that way. I've just picked the pieces that show his talent in the most varied way. The last one we did was just three weeks ago in Italy.

PL: In conclusion, now that we arrive at a new century and the centennial of Ellington's birth, what do you feel that young musicians and composers have to learn from Ellington's music?

GS: That is hard to answer. It's like asking what people can learn from Bach's music, or from Beethoven's music. I suppose what makes Ellington as great a composer as dozens of others that one could mention is that his music is inventive and creative on all fronts: melodic, harmonic, rhythmic, color, timbre—all of these things, with many pieces experimenting in forms as we've discussed. So what I think is so remarkable about Ellington, among many things, is that he was a *complete* musician. There wasn't any aspect of music that he didn't deal with. And I say that as something to be recognized and appreciated and learned from, because there are many musicians nowadays who, for example, have given up on chromatic harmony. They write modal stuff or tonal things, but they are harmonically weak, uninteresting, bland. They don't know, or don't even want to know about it. Well, you can learn a lot from Ellington just in the harmonic realm.

But having said that, you can't suddenly say to somebody, "Hey, if you check out all of Ellington's music, you're going to be a great composer. You'll be a genius." If somebody has talent, then yes, they will be. And if somebody has real talent, they may not have to learn it from Ellington. After all, Ellington did it himself without learning it from anybody else. So a young musician, if he has really big talent, will probably do it him or herself. But of course, we all have to begin somewhere when we start studying. I've studied every composer you could probably mention: Schoenberg, Stravinsky, Bartok, Beethoven, Brahms, Tchaikovsky, you name it. And jazz as well. It's a curious question, but the one answer I would give is that it's the comprehensiveness, the completeness of Ellington's vision—a well-rounded vision. Because there are certain musicians who are, let's say, very strong rhythmically, but they're weak melodically or harmonically. Perhaps they're just not interested in harmony. And that's okay. I'm not a dictator, and I don't say what people should do. But if we're going to look at the scene and analyze what someone has done, or what we might try to emulate, then the answer—in my book—is to emulate people like Ellington and Mingus who were such complete musicians. They advanced and experimented in every realm. They didn't pick only one thing that they happened to like.

PL: And Mingus, as you say, was one of the more powerful disseminators of Ellingtonian ideas?

GS: Well, I don't want to leave it like that. He was going much more in other directions, including classical. But once he discovered Ellington, of course, Ellington influenced him, and he learned a lot from Ellington. But just like Ellington, Mingus went ahead on his own. He certainly did not imitate Ellington. He just took certain lessons from Ellington like the ones I've just been talking about, like the sense of completeness. He went ahead on his own. His harmonic language is totally his own.

PL: So one of the main points you're making for a new musician to learn from Ellington is to have an understanding of all these different approaches—the rhythmic approach, the harmonic approach—and then to go on from there in your own individual style.

GS: Absolutely. That's the process and progress of music history. I would also add, in my humble opinion, that Ellington's absolute unique strengths were his sense of harmony and his sense of timbre, of *color* in the orchestra. There he was totally unique. He certainly was also very stong in rhythmic ideas and so on. But let's face it, so was Basie and a lot of other people. But nobody had any of the genius and sensitivity and invention and imagination that Ellington had in terms of timbre and color, or what we call sonority, and harmony, including in his own piano playing.

PL: One of the things that interests me is that many people draw parallels between Ellington and Gershwin. But it seems to me that Gershwin was not the kind of live performer that Ellington was. Ellington was able to have this balance of being such a prolific composer and recording artist, but also being a world-traveled bandleader and performer as well. It goes back to this sense of completeness you mention.

GS: Well, Gershwin did play in public, but he lived a short life and died at age thirty-eight. And he did perform many pieces live. But you're right, Gershwin did not have a band that traveled around the world with such consistency and longevity as Ellington's. Combining that with his staggering compositional output, his achievement is truly unparalleled. And among everything else he did, Ellington was also a wonderful conductor. *He really did everything.*

⌒ﻌﻌ৩

Duke Ellington has had an influence on all of the artists mentioned above who have followed in his footsteps as leaders and innovators in their own right. The music of these artists has completely transformed American culture, not only in jazz through Miles Davis, Sun Ra, Charles Mingus; but also in popular music through James Brown, Sly Stone, Frank Zappa, Stevie Wonder, Steely Dan, George Clinton, and Prince. But there is one thing that all of these artists have in common: they are all American, and they have all walked through the doors that Ellington opened for them.

But Duke Ellington has done more for music than as a great composer, bandleader, instrumentalist, and communicator. He will possibly be best remembered for merging two completely different musical traditions, African and European, and creating an entirely new musical language. Even on a social level, Ellington's compositions and performances helped break down racial barriers. Suddenly a Negro composer from a folk tradition was performing at Carnegie Hall. Through combining the primitive elements of African folk music, with the structure of European composition and orchestration, Ellington created music of a global nature. It is Afrocentric and Eurocentric simultaneously, to the point where such categorizations no longer apply. It is simply human music, the music of an individual artist breaking through established boundaries.

Ellington applied this principle to his music inspired by Asia, Australia, and Latin America as well. Ellington travelled around the world, absorbed everything around him, and incorporated it into something completely his own. His music is the music of the twentieth century: a global music, drawing from every tradition and culture. As technology advances, and people travel and communicate throughout the world with fewer limitations, this greater openness manifests itself in creative expression. Even political and religious boundaries have dissolved through music, and Ellington was at the forefront of this revolution, bringing his African-American music to people all over the world. Duke Ellington is ultimately one of the forefathers of "world music," which may well stand as his greatest achievement.

At this level, there is only one other person who could accurately be regarded as Ellington's equal in terms of his influence on twentieth century music. Only one artist has been able to transcend cultural boundaries, and create an entirely new global musical language, combined with a renewed emphasis on spiritual expression, with the same degree of worldwide success as Duke Ellington. His achievements run parallel to Ellington's in many ways, although like Ellington, he has completely followed his own path, and has been universally hailed as one of the greatest musicians of all time, and as "the Godfather of world music." His name is Ravi Shankar.

Ravi Shankar

RAVI SHANKAR WAS BORN APRIL 7, 1920, in Varanasi, India. In many respects, like Ellington's hometown of Washington D.C., this city embodies Shankar's entire culture. It is the oldest remaining city in the world, steeped in East Indian tradition. Ravi's family also had strong ties with Europe. His father, a successful landowner in Varanasi who had studied yoga and Hindu doctrine, left India to practice law in London, where Ravi's oldest brother Uday was also studying painting at the Royal College of Art. When Uday returned from college, he pursued a career in dance. Uday began performing in Indian ballets around Europe, and was soon attracting a large audience. Uday recruited his brothers to join his dance troupe, and by the age of ten Ravi was living and training in Paris as a dancer. Ravi also began studying various Indian musical instruments, including sitar, sarod, and tabla. He had also been exposed to Western music at this time, attending concerts by Toscanini, Paderewski, Casals, Andres Segovia, and child prodigy Yehudi Menuhin, who would eventually become one of Ravi's closest friends.

In 1932, the dance troupe traveled to New York City. Ravi was enamored with this cosmopolitan American city, and drawn to the Broadway shows and cinema houses. Meanwhile, the dance troupe were creating their own stir on Broadway, being hailed as one of the most exciting new developments in dance. Ellington would later draw inspiration from another such dance troupe for his piece "Depk," which he composed after his first Asian tour, and recorded as part of "The Far East Suite." Ravi had encountered the music of Duke Ellington at the

Cotton Club, as well as Count Basie, and Louis Armstrong, and he was fascinated with American jazz. Soon the dance troupe made their way to Hollywood, where Ravi met many movie stars. He was receiving one of the most liberal educations a young man could hope for, but it was only the beginning of his journey.

Ravi's father, having been involved in a controversial legal dispute, was beaten to death in London by unidentified assailants. Ravi was only fifteen, and the loss was devastating. As he came out of his mourning, he met the man who would become his musical instructor and guru: sarod master Ustad Allauddin Khan. Khan had joined the dance troupe as a featured musician. He treated Ravi like his own son. Within a year of his meeting Khan, Ravi's mother had also passed away. Ravi had decided to throw himself into the sitar, a stringed instrument capable of producing microtones and drones, used in Indian classical music. The sitar is essentially a lute with an elongated neck. It is usually tuned to C-sharp, although tunings can range between B and D, depending on the sitar. There are seven steel or bronze strings, and eleven sympathetic strings which are not played, but resonate throughout the hollow casing. Sometimes there is an extra gourd mounted at the bottom of the neck.

Ravi studied with Khan and became his disciple, and began referring to him as Baba. His training with Baba was extremely rigorous and demanding, and he was prohibited from smoking, drinking, or sexual promiscuity. Baba left the dance troupe in 1936 and returned to India, and Ravi was forced to decide between the high life he experienced as a young teenage boy in the dance troupe, and the rigorous training available to him on sitar with Baba. As Hitler rose to power and Europe was changing, Ravi knew that the time had come to pursue a deeper path, and he returned home to study full time with Baba. He lived an ascetic and reclusive lifestyle, and followed a disciplined daily regimen, including fourteen hours of practice on sitar every day, often until his hands bled.

After mastering the sitar through years of concentrated study, Ravi began developing himself as a composer. He challenged prejudices right away, composing film scores for many successful Indian films, although traditional musicians had been shunned in the Indian film world. Because of his world travels in his youth with the dance troupe, and his exposure to all forms of Western music, Ravi envisioned new ideas for Indian music. In 1948 he was appointed music director of All-India Radio, stationed in New Delhi. He continued to compose film scores, working with the famous Indian director Satyajit Ray on a trilogy: *Pather Panchali, Unvanquished,* and *The World of Apu.* These films were landmarks in Indian cinema, and are widely praised as the most influential to come from India.

Ravi developed a desire to take his country's music to the West, and combine the two worlds. He performed to enthusiastic audiences in the Soviet Union and throughout Europe. His film and ballet scores were greeted with greater success, and he began incorporating Western instruments. Ravi had discovered his mission in life. Not only would he educate Western audiences about the traditional Indian musical form known as raga, which was based completely on melody and rhythm as opposed to Western harmony, but he would also seek ways to merge elements of Indian raga with Western forms of composition and orchestration, thereby creating a new musical language. This is where Shankar and Ellington would take similar paths. Ellington was determined to do the same thing with his African musical heritage by merging it with the European tradition.

In 1952 Ravi began a lifelong friendship with American classical musician Yehudi Menuhin. Menuhin was completely enchanted by Indian music, and had expressed a desire to learn Eastern musical principles from Ravi. Menuhin was impressed with the fact that although Indian music did not use scores, its theory required a much greater amount of discipline than Western music. This is because once a player masters all of the different scales and rhythmic cycles, he or she must then learn how to transcend the formula and improvise in a meaningful and appropriate way for whatever raga is being performed. Yehudi gained a deep respect for Ravi, and the two eventually collaborated together for several concerts and recording projects that would bring their two worlds together. In 1967 their album *West Meets East* won a Grammy award for best chamber music recording. In that same year, the two performed for the United Nations Human Rights Day Concert in New York, which was also recorded. Ravi ended up recording two more albums in the *West Meets East* series, featuring Menuhin again, as well as flautist Jean-Pierre Rampal.

Ravi returned to America, and began performing to unanimous acclaim and excitement. In 1957, he began recording his first long playing records, beginning with World Pacific Records, founded by jazz enthusiast Richard Bock. Then Ravi went to Columbia and developed a close friendship with George Avakian, the same man who played a crucial role in Ellington's enormous comeback at the Newport Jazz Festival the previous year. Because Ravi spoke English and French, he was able to explain to Western audiences the unique characteristics of Indian music.

Jazz musicians were becoming more and more fascinated with Indian music, which is also improvisational. But Ravi was quick to point out that jazz improvisation was based on Western harmonies, as opposed to a melodic theme and specific rhythmic cycle such as a raga. Ragas remain in one key, based on a rhythmic cycle known as a tala, which could range from a simple four or sixteen beats, to seven or ten or fifteen. Nevertheless, jazz musicians continued to be inspired by this form of music, and Ravi found himself collaborating with Bud Shank, and Paul Horn. He developed friendships with Dizzy Gillespie, and especially John Coltrane, who wanted to study some of the key elements of Indian music for his own experimentation.

Ravi and Coltrane became particularly close. Ravi was impressed with Coltrane's decision to quit drugs and study Eastern spirituality, which was relatively unheard of for jazz musicians at that time. Coltrane was fascinated with the complexity of the rhythmic talas in Indian music, and the improvisational system. Above all, Coltrane was attracted to the tranquility and spiritual expression inherent in Indian music. He would soon incorporate many Indian elements into his own music. Pieces like "India," "Spiritual," and records like *A Love Supreme, Meditations*, and *Om*, reflected Coltrane's affinity for Eastern music. Coltrane even went so far as to name his own son after Ravi. As their friendship grew, Ravi became more impressed with Coltrane's humility, spirituality, and tireless dedication to his instrument. But Ravi was troubled by the turbulence of Coltrane's late-period free jazz. It affected Ravi very deeply when Coltrane died of cancer at the age of forty in 1967.

Minimalist composer Philip Glass became friends with Ravi at this time. Glass, like Menuhin and Coltrane, was interested in learning more about the Indian classical system. Glass was also intrigued by the fact that Ravi was not only a composer, but a live performer as well—another similarity to Duke Ellington. Aside from Ellington, most modern composers did not regularly perform in concert. Glass was unimpressed with the atonal experimentation of Stockhausen and Boulez. He began composing music that was completely stripped of harmony, and instead relied on a steady rhythmic pulse that would sustain a sparse melodic theme. Eventually this style of music would become known as minimalism, its main proponents being Glass, Terry Riley, and LaMonte Young. All of these composers have acknowledged their debt to Ravi Shankar.

Much of this was due to Ravi's influence on John Coltrane. Coltrane would use elements of minimalism in his music by taking a fixed group of tones and reconfiguring them in several different mathematical ways. Although Coltrane's style was rooted in the blues, he combined the blues with his new-found fascination for Indian classical music and Eastern modal music. Coltrane was also influenced by the fact that Indian music was motivated by a quest for spiritual enlightenment, rather than commercial success. Coltrane was expanding his music to reflect this sense of a search for spiritual identity—something that would actually open the door for Ellington later in the sixties when he composed the Sacred Concerts. Suddenly jazz was becoming more openly spiritual in nature. Coltrane's friendship with Ravi Shankar, with their jam sessions and discussions on the nature of music, deepened his understanding of ancient musical principles where specific sounds reflected specific states of consciousness in the musician and listener.

Modal music takes a set of tonal relationships and repeats them again and again. Because Indian music has such a heightened emphasis on intonation, these tones are repeated with such precision that each complete tone cycle always returns to the exact same place. This repetition of tones can often create a pattern of responses in the mind and body of the listener, inducing a meditative state. While the universe consists of different vibrations at different frequencies, the use of sound in music is the most direct and immediate vibration that humans can absorb. This is the basis for the minimalist movement, as well as Indian classical music. Ironically, this is also the basis for funk, where the rhythmic emphasis always returns to the one. James Brown was in many ways a minimalist in his own right, stripping his music down to its barest rhythmic essentials with his driving, insistent groove.

Many rock and avant-garde musicians who had been listening to John Coltrane were beginning to discover and appreciate the unique properties of Indian music, and Ravi Shankar developed a following among these young artists. David Crosby and Roger McGuinn, from the Byrds, had been inspired by Coltrane's "India," as well as Ravi Shankar. In 1965, they wrote a pop song called "Eight Miles High," one of the earliest examples of psychedelic rock. With an Indian-style drone in the background, the electric guitar plays a melody that quotes the Coltrane piece, with the guitar engineered to sound like a sitar. The song was a smash hit, and opened many doors for experimentation in rock. The Grateful Dead, with their open-ended piece "Dark Star," would take the sounds of John Coltrane and Ravi Shankar to an entirely new level. Jerry Garcia incorporated many elements of sitar and Indian raga into his unique approach to electric guitar, and "Dark Star" became the first fully developed rock expression of Eastern modal improvisation.

George Harrison, of the Beatles, had heard the Byrds's track "Eight Miles High," and asked Crosby about its arrangement. Crosby told

Harrison about Ravi Shankar. George had already heard a sitar when the Beatles were shooting their second feature film *Help!* He was fascinated with the sitar, purchased one in London, and became the first musician to play sitar on a rock recording with "Norwegian Wood," which became a hit for the Beatles with its unusual sound. George and Ravi met later in 1965, and George expressed a desire to study sitar under Ravi. Although Ravi had never heard of the Beatles, he agreed to accept George as his pupil, and the two became the best of friends. Suddenly Ravi was shocked to find himself with an enormous new audience of young rock fans. Soon he would become the spokesman for Indian culture around the world.

At the time, he received harsh criticism from Indian music purists who felt that Ravi was beginning to cheapen their sacred musical tradition by selling out to Western audiences, as well as promoting drug use. These criticisms deeply affected Ravi, because he felt that he was bringing Indian music to the rest of the world. Ravi strongly disapproved of the widespread drug abuse of the hippie generation in Europe and America. Young people mistakenly believed that Ravi and other Indian musicians had regularly taken drugs while performing. Ravi sought to dispel this false notion as much as possible, asking his audiences to refrain from drinking or smoking while he was on stage playing music.

Ravi was invited to perform at the two most influential rock festivals in history: Monterey Pop in 1967, and Woodstock in 1969. Both appearances were milestones for Ravi in terms of reaching a new audience. He had become the musical ambassador of the East, introducing a whole generation of Westerners to the unfamiliar sounds of Eastern music. This sparked a revolution. Westerners were not only becoming aware of Eastern music, but also of Eastern philosophy and religion. As Ravi's music spread throughout the rock and jazz community, people began delving into all aspects of Eastern culture as an alternative to conventional Western lifestyles. Although there was a minority of Americans who were already studying Eastern spirituality, the tidal wave of interest among the younger generation in the sixties was unprecedented. Ravi Shankar is largely responsible for this cultural development, because he was the first artist to make the music accessible for Westerners.

But Ravi was disturbed by the performances of rock acts like The Who and Jimi Hendrix at Monterey, both of whom had deliberately destroyed their instruments while performing. This went against Ravi's belief that all musical instruments are sacred objects to be treated with the utmost respect. He was also dismayed by the rampant drug abuse, as well as the lack of intimacy in performing for a crowd of thousands upon thousands of people. After Woodstock, Ravi decided to retire from performance at festivals, although he and George Harrison staged the first ever rock charity concert for Bangladesh in 1971 at Madison Square Garden. The concert raised money through record and film royalties, and won a Grammy award for Album of the Year. After backing away from the rock music scene, Ravi returned to regular appearances at classical music venues like Carnegie Hall, as well as many traditional venues in India, where he would perform ragas for four to five hours.

At this time, Ravi had also begun composing extended works that would combine the elements of traditional Indian raga with European symphonic music. He wrote a series of concertos for sitar and orchestra. The first one was conducted by Andre Previn for the London Symphony Orchestra in 1971, and the second was conducted by longtime friend Zubin Mehta for the New York Philharmonic in 1981. While these concertos contained Western elements of harmony and counterpoint, these did not obstruct the rhythmic or melodic purity of his native music. They are not easily classified either as Indian or European music. Like Duke Ellington's extended orchestral works, they are simply beyond category.

As Ravi turned his attention away from Europe and America for a while, he concentrated on his Asian performances. Many critics felt that Ravi had compromised the values of traditional Indian music for commercial success, misunderstanding his desire to break down as many cultural barriers as possible. But Ravi wanted to merge with other forms of Asian music, so he began a collaboration with Japanese musicians. *East Greets East* was released in 1978, featuring Ravi and several Indian musicians as well as many famous Japanese musicians such as Susumu Miyashita on koto, and Hozan Yamamoto on shakuhachi flute. Ravi had composed new music for the occasion, and it was another union of two cultures. Encouraged by his Japanese experiences, Ravi began performing in China as well. In 1981 Ravi was also aproached to compose the score for the Academy Award-winning film *Gandhi.*

Although he has suffered many heart complications over the last several years, Ravi Shankar continues to be an active composer and performer. He performed a series of concerts at the Russian Kremlin, and a live recording was released to universal acclaim. In 1989, Ravi finally teamed up with longtime friend and minimalist composer Philip Glass, for a collaborative effort named *Passages,* where each artist composed a piece to be arranged by the other. Ravi's most recent effort is a collaboration with George Harrison called *The Chants of India,* where Ravi adapts ancient Hindu Vedic chants to his own compositions. It was a triumphant return to Ravi's spiritual roots, similar in concept to Ellington's Sacred Concerts.

9. Ravi Shankar: The Godfather of World Music seeks divine inspiration. (Photo by David Redfern.)

⌒

Two Kindred Spirits

⌣

WHAT MAKES THIS INDIAN MUSICIAN Duke Ellington's only true peer in twentieth century music? There are many significant parallels and differences as well. One of the most important differences between the two is that Duke Ellington was never a formally trained musician in the traditional sense. He was self-taught and proud of it, always skeptical of strict adherence to rules and norms. Ravi Shankar, on the other hand, spent six years training at the feet of a master, practicing for fourteen hours a day. Ellington was a harmonic composer, whereas Ravi Shankar is a rhythmic and melodic composer in the Eastern tradition. Another important distinction between the two is that one of Ellington's great innovations is his role as a bandleader. Ravi has never worked with any ensemble long enough to be a bandleader in any sense of the word. He has performed with different musicians from all walks of life, and the only musicians who have stayed with him for any length of time are his Indian accompanists on tabla and tamboura. And even those shoes have been filled by many people during the course of Ravi's career. There is no Ravi Shankar Orchestra.

But there are many more similarities than differences between these two kindred spirits. The most significant is the ability both had to combine elements of different musical cultures, and to do so in a way that was accessible and commercially successful. Many artists have sought to bring different world musics together, but none have had more profound influence on the public than Ellington and Shankar. And in this undertaking, commercial success is the point. It's about breaking boundaries of race, religion, politics, and culture, and finding the widest possible audience, so that the music really *can* bring people together.

The African music that Ellington drew upon is a folk music, no different in concept from the folk traditions of Europe, or the Indian raga. It is music that expresses the sufferings and spiritual aspirations of the people. Ellington always said that his music could not be categorized as anything but Negro folk music. He once said in 1931:

> My men and my race are the inspiration of my work. I try to catch the
> character and mood and feeling of my people. The music of my race is

something more than the American idiom. It is the result of our transplantation to American soil and was our reaction, in plantation days, to the life we lived. What we could not say openly we expressed in music. The characteristic, melancholic music of my race has been forged from the very white heat of our sorrows and from our gropings. I think the music of my race is something that is going to live, something which posterity will honor in a higher sense than merely that of the music of the ballroom.

His series of performances at Carnegie Hall and other classical music venues, where he unveiled his extended works, paved the way for other artists to do the same. Ravi Shankar, coming from his Indian background, had also resolved to elevate the stature of his native musical tradition, in order to merge it with the Western classical tradition. Shankar regularly gave recitals at classical venues, and for royalty, much the same way as Ellington. Shankar traveled widely as India's foremost musical ambassador, bringing his native culture to other parts of the world. Ellington served the same function as America's musical ambassador in other regions of the globe. It was this enthusiastic acceptance of both artists by foreign audiences that ensured the opening of many new doors for modern music.

In essence, Ellington created a distinctly American musical language by combining his roots in African folk music with European methods of composition and orchestration. "Black Brown & Beige" is only one example of how European principles of musical structure were employed by Ellington to express African spirituality. Shankar went one step further, and combined East and West. By merging traditional Indian raga with Western classical and popular music, particularly with his concertos for sitar and orchestra, Shankar combined elements of Western harmony with Eastern melody to create a sound that had never been heard in music.

Both artists also refused to limit their experimentation to one area. In addition to his African roots, Ellington had an affinity for Latin rhythm and melody, going back to pieces like "Caravan," "Perdido," "Conga Brava," and "The Flaming Sword." In actuality, Ellington was the forefather of Latin jazz, even before the excursions into the genre by Dizzy Gillespie, Cal Tjader, and Mongo Santamaria. Ellington went further in his approach to Latin music when he toured South and Central America in 1968, and composed "The Latin American Suite." Here again he took the folk tradition of a different culture, and incorporated it into his own musical vocabulary, creating something that sounded like nothing else but Duke Ellington. He encountered Asian music with the same approach on "The Far East Suite." Pieces like "Isfahan" and "Agra" evoked the colors and sounds of the Middle East and India. As many other jazz artists, Ellington had a special affection for Japanese audiences and their ability to listen closely to the music. His "Ad Lib on Nippon," composed after his first voyage to Japan, is among the most stirring pieces in his entire catalogue, particularly his gorgeous piano solo.

When the Ellington orchestra finally visited Africa in 1966 for the World Festival of Negro Arts, it was one of the most moving experiences of his life, resulting in more new music, including "La Plus Belle Africaine." As always, Ellington did not imitate African music, but created something new out of his own experience. "Afro Eurasian Eclipse" was a synthesis of sounds rooted in Australian, Asian, and African music. It was a return to Ellington's primitive "jungle" sound that had characterized his Cotton Club period. Composed in 1971 and released posthumously in 1975, it showed Ellington coming full circle at the end of his life with one of his most visceral and ambitious works.

Shankar not only combined Indian raga with European orchestration with his concertos for sitar and orchestra, but he also composed a series of pieces merging Indian and Russian music, "Swar Milan (Musical Notes Meeting)," and actually performed the pieces in his appearance at the Kremlin. He combined Indian raga with traditional Japanese folk music for a performance at the Japan America Theatre in Los Angeles at the Rhythms of the World festival, composing a ninety-minute piece which began with Japanese themes that gradually shifted to Indian melodies. Musicians from both countries performed on the piece.

Shankar also merged his music with jazz through his collaborations with Bud Shank, jam sessions with John Coltrane, and a rhythmic piece that he arranged and conducted for his tabla player Alla Rakha and jazz drummer/bandleader Buddy Rich, humorously titled "Rich a la Rakha." When Shankar recorded *Passages* with Philip Glass, his influence on the minimalist movement had come full circle. The same happened with rock music when Ravi and George Harrison collaborated for a record that featured Western popular musicians as well as Indian musicians, *Shankar Family and Friends*. Ravi composed a pop song for the project called "I Am Missing You," featuring Harrison and Ringo Starr.

Another important similarity between Duke and Ravi was their ability to combine the activities of a composer and performer. Both musicians had an intimate relationship with their instrument, and a distinctive style that was instantly recognizable. Ellington didn't just play the piano, he *felt* the piano, with a touch so personal that his technical facility never obstructed the music. Ellington utilized the full range of the keyboard, and was able to command the widest range of color, tone, and dynamics. Effortlessly moving from sophisticated to primitive in approach, his emotional range of expression was unlimited, from the percussive attack that would be adopted by Cecil Taylor, to the two-handed stride approach that he learned from his original mentors. His emphasis on chords, and spaces *between* the chords, would greatly influence Thelonious Monk, as well as a host of other keyboardists. He could employ dissonance to subtle effect, as well as gorgeous harmonies. Above all, his touch was his own.

Shankar had a similar relationship with the sitar. He introduced many new approaches to the instrument, changing the way the sitar would be tuned and strung, based on specific moods or colors he was trying to convey in his music. Most modern sitarists have followed Ravi's system. Ravi had a unique style of plucking the strings with varying degrees of intensity that gave him an unmistakable sound, particularly with his use of vibrato and bending of strings. One of his primary innovations is giving greater emphasis to the bass strings of the sitar, similar to another Indian instrument called the surbahur. Ravi applied the deep resonating sound of the surbahur to his use of the bass strings on sitar, particularly during the slow introductory movement of a raga. This would become another one of his trademarks which would be applied by younger sitarists. Another invention of Shankar's was the hook system, where he dampens certain strings on the sitar by attaching hooks to specific frets, muting the strings that are not needed in a given section of a piece.

But the most important connection between Ellington and Shankar with regard to their instrumental approach is that they both had a wonderful habit of staying out of the way of the music, not allowing technique to obstruct direct musical communication. Both were so deeply connected to their instrument, that there was no sense of separation between the instrument and the performer.

Also similar to Duke, Ravi has received many honorary degrees for his innovations as a composer, instrumentalist, and educator: Doctor of Fine Arts at University of California in Santa Cruz, Doctor of Music from Colgate University, New England Conservatory, and Harvard University, among others in the United States, and several in India. These include doctorates from the University of Calcutta, University of Delhi, and Benares Hindu University. Ellington received honorary doctorates from Columbia, Yale, Howard, and many other universities, as well as having postage stamps issued in his honor in two African nations, Chad and Republic of Togo, with a postage stamp that would be issued in America after his death. Perhaps the most important of these honors for Ellington was when Emperor Haile Selassie of Ethiopia presented him with the Emperor's Star. Ellington was deeply touched by the recognition he received from his spiritual homeland of Africa.

Ellington and Shankar also shared the experience of having an audience with Queen Elizabeth II of Great Britain. Ellington had performed in Britain many times before, and had been introduced to other members of the Royal Family, but in 1958 he was introduced to the Queen at the Leeds Festival in Yorkshire. When he composed "The Queen's Suite," featuring one of Ellington's loveliest melodies, "Single Petal of a Rose," he pressed a single copy which was sent directly to Buckingham Palace. In 1990, Shankar performed for the Queen, Prince Charles, and Princess Diana, along with the President of India and his wife. Prince Charles had met Ravi on previous occasions when Ravi had performed at Westminster Abbey and the Royal Albert Hall. Ravi and his family received a private audience with the Queen and Royal Family after the performance.

A Spiritual Bond

BUT ULTIMATELY, THE MOST IMPORTANT connection between these two musicians is their emphasis on spiritual expression, especially their determination to bring this expression to the widest possible audience. Ravi Shankar was the first to bring Eastern spirituality to a mass Western audience. Ellington was certainly not the first African-American artist to express his spiritual beliefs in his music, but Ellington took it to the highest level with his Sacred Concerts, which continue to be performed in cathedrals and concert halls around the world.

Before Ellington's sacred music began to take shape, Mary Lou Williams and John Coltrane (who had been greatly influenced in this regard by Ravi Shankar) were the first jazz musicians to bring spiritual expression to the foreground of their music. But Mary Lou Williams had never received the exposure that Ellington enjoyed with his sacred music. Coltane's spiritual compositions came at a late stage of his career. He was already being criticized for his experiments with free jazz, which has never gained mainstream acceptance. Blues, gospel, and soul artists like Ray Charles were incorporating the music of the black church into popular music, while Sam Cooke and Aretha Franklin had recorded gospel music, but these did not receive nearly the same exposure or radio airplay as their pop recordings. Even Elvis Presley recorded a series of gospel records throughout his career, but was still unable to cross his religious music over into the mainstream. Ellington's sacred music performances made headlines, and enjoyed widespread television exposure, surpassing even Ellington's own expectations.

Ravi Shankar made it clear from the very beginning that his music was a form of spiritual expresson. For him, music is "Nada Brahma (Sound Is God)." As Duke Ellington did with the Sacred Concerts, Shankar has been inspired to return to his spiritual roots in the twilight of his life. At the age of seventy-six, Shankar began working on a series of compositions based on sacred Hindu chants. The pieces were recorded and produced by George Harrison, and released as *The Chants of India*. Ravi composed and conducted music to devotional chants dedicated to Hindu deities such as Krishna, Ganesha, and Saraswati. The record was greeted with unanimous acclaim. Shankar has said: "The spiritual element in Indian music is absolutely essential. We seek the purity of divine inspiration through our improvisation. The raga reflects the spiritual hopes of the people, the constant struggle for life. It is drawn out of the moods of the seasons, the prayers in our temples, for our music is not written down, it is passed from heart to heart."

Ellington had expressed his spiritual beliefs long before the Sacred Concerts, with "Come Sunday," and its double-time reincarnation as "David Danced Before the Lord." Then the First Sacred Concert brought "The Lord's Prayer," and "In the Beginning God," taken from the first four words in the King James Bible. The Sacred Concerts show Ellington's intimate knowledge of the Bible, with many lyrics and titles coming directly from scripture, such as the Second Concert finale, "Praise God and Dance," based on Psalm 150. There were showcases for the orchestra, such as Cootie Williams on the piece that Ellington dedicated to Father John Gensel, pastor of the jazz community: "The Shepherd Watches Over the Night Flock." There were many segments that featured the extraordinary voice of Alice Babs, particularly "Is God a Three-Letter Word for Love?" and her duet with Johnny Hodges, "Heaven." Ellington also performed a solo piano recital with the gorgeous "Meditation." Duke felt that he needed to make an offering to God on his own instrument, and the result was one of his most sublime performances as a pianist.

Ellington always distinguished his sacred music from "jazz mass," calling himself "God's messenger boy," and never regarded his sacred works as commercial ventures. They were his most personal statements, which he regarded as the greatest work he had ever done. Ellington once said: "I play a lot of places. I play nightclubs, gambling casinos, and the greatest concert halls in the world, for a living. But when I play sacred music, I play this for *me*. This is personal, this is not career. This is the most important thing in my life!" Shankar shared this feeling, and once said: "Music is not for selling; music is not made for a commercial purpose. Music is like worshipping, and through music you worship God. When I become attuned to my sitar, that is the route for me to touch the God within myself, and within my millions of listeners over the years."

There is something beautiful and powerful about these statements. The purest motivation for the creation of music is spiritual expression, whether based on the Bible or the Bhagavad Gita. What matters is the spirit *behind* the expression, the impulse to express one's deepest beliefs. All forms of sacred music are the same, regardless of what faith they express. Sacred music is *selfless* music. That is to say, the motivation behind spiritual music comes from one's innermost life essence, which is shared by all living creatures. As Ellington and Shankar have both said, it does not come from the desires of the individual self for personal gain. Sacred music is *self-transcendent*. If the feeling is genuine, it speaks the same language to everyone.

When an artist creates sacred music, he or she is reaching deep down inside themselves, and expressing the core essence of who they are. This takes courage, for the artist has now opened himself or herself completely to the listener. This is the most direct form of communication in music. The musician is searching for something higher for himself and the audience. It is the *search* that is most important, because through this search comes some form of liberation. When Ellington performed his Sacred Concerts for the world, he liberated himself by finally being able to express publicly what he had always believed in his heart privately.

With sacred music, an artist is also returning to the roots of musical expression. Music through the ages has always been either a form of worship, or spiritual communication between tribes. With Ellington's Third Sacred Concert, he had come full circle, returning to the roots of his spirituality instilled in him as a child. The Third Concert is his

10. Frantic last-minute rehearsals before the Third Sacred Concert at Westminster Abbey, October 24, 1973. "You can jive with secular music but you can't jive with the Almighty"—Duke Ellington. (Hulton Getty/Archive Photos)

most honest expression of faith. More so than his previous sacred music, it is a direct form of prayer to God. He was no longer simply serving as "God's messenger boy," he was now communicating openly with his Creator in pieces such as "My Love," and "The Majesty of God." These pieces were composed at a time in Ellington's life when he realized that he would soon face his own mortality. They showed how Ellington had run the full gamut of emotion in his career, composing every form of secular music, and finally returning to the ultimate devotional expression.

A Buddhist or Hindu could listen to the Sacred Concerts, and be moved by Ellington's devotion to God. The Buddhist or Hindu may not believe in the same God, but can still identify with Ellington's deep spiritual capacity. A Christian could listen to Shankar's ragas or sacred Hindu chants, and be just as moved, as long as the listener is open to the feeling behind the raga or chant. Prayer is prayer. Prayer is surrender to a higher power, whatever form that higher power may take. Prayer is a meditation, and the act of prayer through music is a special form of meditation and communication that speaks one language in many dialects. It is a language of spirit. Ellington opened the Third Sacred Concert at Westminster Abbey with these words: "I am honored, and at the moment I feel a little bit blessed to be exposed to so much beauty. Of course, the theme of this program is mainly love. The first statement is love, my love. The first statement will be 'The Lord's Prayer' on piano. Since it is the theme of our evening, it will not be the only one. There will be many 'Lord's Prayers' said, because every man prays in his own language, and there is no language that God does not understand."

Ellington's sacred music had allowed him to once again rise above the limitations of jazz, as he did with his 1943 performance at Carnegie Hall, where he proved that jazz could be concert music. The Sacred Concerts are an equally important breakthrough, demonstrating how jazz, long denounced in religious circles as a vulgar "devil's music," can rise to the level of the sacred. The fact that Ellington performed his Third Concert at Westminster Abbey in the 1970s is very significant in twentieth-century music. He showed us how to "Praise God and Dance," and how "Every Man Prays in His Own Language," by making jazz a vehicle for spiritual expression. Ellington combined elements of jazz with gospel for the Concerts, uniting his orchestra with a choir. In this way he brought secular and spiritual music together, and proved that every available musical device could be employed for the purpose of worship.

The most important word in Ellington's vocabulary was "love." It may have seemed like a joke on the surface, but when he ended each performance with a reminder to the audience that he loved them madly, it was his own way of showing his love for his listeners. He always expressed deep affection for his parents in his music, from "Reminiscing in Tempo," to "My Mother, My Father." He expressed love for his musicians by giving them the freedom to be themselves. He wrote in his notes for the Second Sacred Concert: "We shall keep this land if we all agree on the meaning of that unconditional word: LOVE." And in his Third Concert: "Of course, the theme of this program is mainly love." It is Duke Ellington's consistent emphasis on unconditional love— love of a spiritual nature—that will enable his music to communicate a universal message to people from all walks of life for a long time to come. To my mind, this is Duke Ellington's most important contribution. As Stevie Wonder would say, when people hear the message of love in Ellington's music, it doesn't matter what language they speak, "they can feel it all over."

New World A-Comin'

As WE MOVE INTO THE TWENTY-FIRST CENTURY and a new millennium, Duke Ellington's music—and what people can learn from it— will have more impact with time. Although some are skeptical as to how clearly Ellington's message will be understood, there is little doubt that history will be the final judge. We have not even begun to scratch the surface. Technology and further research will help take us deeper into his work. Ellington's legacy is being preserved in many ways but it is up to each person to discover the music for himself or herself. It is also up to people who have already been touched by Ellington's music to do their part in the promotion and preservation of this timeless body of work.

It begins with education. Thanks to the efforts of the Smithsonian, Ellington scores are becoming increasingly available free of charge for schools. Students can discover the richness and vitality of this music through close study and actual performance. Younger musicians get the chance to experience the possibilties of expression on their instruments through their exposure to Ellington, one of the most emotionally diverse composers in history. Andrea and Brian Pinkney have written and published the first children's book on Ellington, *Duke El-*

lington: The Piano Prince and His Orchestra, published by Hyperion Books for Children in New York, telling Duke's story with language and illustrations that young children can appreciate and understand. Select schools have given students an opportunity to express their feelings about Duke Ellington with poetry. For children who will never see Ellington in person, he is presented as a great artist and American icon.

There is obviously much more that needs to be done, but these are the beginnings of the important work required for Ellington to take his rightful place alongside the greatest composers in history. This is crucial, because Ellington helped give American music an identity of its own by becoming America's musical ambassador to the world. Ellington composed American music—not solely based on any European or African model, but on a synthesis of the two into a distinctly American language. Children of any nationality or ethnic origin can learn from this African-American composer who composed music for *all* Americans, and for people from all walks of life—music that speaks a universal language of human emotion. One thing is certain: jazz is now taught in schools, because Duke Ellington paved the way and showed that jazz was a uniquely American art form deserving academic study.

Ellington's music will continue to be performed by repertory orchestras around the world, as well as by jazz musicians and classical ensembles who reinterpret Ellington in their own way. Just as the classics of the European masters are performed in venues around the world by many different orchestras, Ellington will make his own inroads into the pantheon of the world's great music. This is because of the unique character and quality of Ellington's compositions, which cannot be found anywhere else. With the abundance of available material from the Ellington Archives at the Smithsonian—200,000 pages of sheet music, half of which remains unpublished and unperformed—more pieces from the Ellington ouevre will enter the cultural arena. Again, progress in this area has been gradual, but steady. Ellington's immense body of work is in the right hands, and will be the classical music of the twenty-first century. One thing is certain: jazz musicians regularly perform jazz compositions in the world's finest concert halls and churches, because Duke Ellington paved the way and showed that jazz could be considered as concert music.

People will also continue to get together in groups to share their mutual love of Ellington's music. Although there are millions of Ellington fans worldwide, and many Ellington appreciation societies, there has never been one official International Ellington Society to coordinate the activities of individual chapters and provide financial assistance. Each chapter is responsible for its own survival, and there are few ways for people from different chapters to communicate with one another. Morris Hodara of the New York chapter, the largest Ellington society in the world, believes that the time has come for Ellington people around the globe to come together under the guidance and protection of a true international organization devoted to the preservation of Ellington's music. Morris is a former president of the New York society, and continues to serve as editor of its newsletter.

Every month the Duke Ellington Society based in New York (officially known as TDES Inc.) sends its newsletter to over 600 members worldwide. Each newsletter contains feature articles on the latest events involving Ellington and former bandmembers, as well as CD reviews, the calendar of Society meetings and live concerts, letters from members, and even trivia questions. TDES hosts at least two Ellington concerts a year in New York. Annual "members' choice" meetings allow people to discuss their favorite Ellington recordings from specific time periods. TDES also invites many former bandmembers and Ellington scholars to give presentations. Anyone can subscribe to the newsletter and become a member of TDES for an annual $25 fee, or a lifetime fee of $500, by writing to TDES at Box 31 Church Street Station, New York, NY 10008-0031. One can also receive information from the TDES website at http://duke.fuse.net.

The International Duke Ellington Jazz Society, known as DEJS, was formed in 1959 by a Canadian pianist named Bill Ross who had settled in Los Angeles. After receiving Duke's blessing, Ross placed ads in *Down Beat,* and attracted Ellington collectors and fans from around the world. Within a short amount of time, chapters formed in New York, Washington, D.C., Toronto, Chicago, Vancouver, Minneapolis, Milwaukee, Pittsburgh, and various European cities. But none of these chapters incorporated or collected membership dues, and after Ross passed away in 1979, DEJS slowly began to fall apart due to the lack of proper organization. The only chapters that now remain as individual entities are Washington, D. C., Toronto, Chicago, and New York.

In the early eighties, Morris became president of the New York chapter, and immediately set about expanding the Society's operations. He increased the size and scope of the newsletter to include contributions from Ellington scholars like Jerry Valburn, and began organizing more live concerts of Ellington's music. He recruited a growing number of guest speakers and band alumni to appear at Society meetings, and initiated the annual "members' choice" meetings, where people discuss their favorite Ellington recordings from different time periods.

He registered scores of new members from every corner of the globe, and began collecting membership dues, helping to ensure the Society's financial stability. Finally in 1993, the Society incorporated as TDES Inc. But Morris remains concerned about the future. There is still no official connection between the various Ellington societies that remain in existence. Morris also feels it is crucial for the Society to help expose and educate younger people to the music and spirituality of Duke Ellington.

Morris Hodara

PL: ALONG WITH THE MEMBERS' CHOICE MEETINGS, and live performances with musicians, what are some of the other ways that the Society structures meetings? Different experts come and speak?

MH: Exactly. This is another thing that I tried to pioneer—didactic lectures on Ellington on various subjects. We had a discussion on the first Carnegie Hall concert. Jerry Valburn, and others including myself who were there, gave impressions on the importance of the event. We've also had different musicologists. Mark Tucker has been a guest at least three times. Gunther Schuller has never spoken at the Society during my time, but we would certainly welcome him. Phil Schaap has spoken numerous times. We do a lot of teaching that way, and these meetings are always well attended.

PL: Where do these meetings take place?

MH: St. Peter's Church in New York. Once a year we have a large concert. We try to make it as varied as possible so people can hear different aspects of Ellingtonia. We have at least one piano concert a year, and we've had all the great piano players. We also have one big band concert.

PL: The New York Chapter is the largest in the world?

MH: By far. We have members from all over the world, from New Zealand and Australia, even Finland. The Internet has been very interesting in this regard.

PL: Describe the role the Internet has played in representing Ellington.

MH: There is an Ellington chat group, and people from all over the world contribute to it. It's interesting. Most people ask about records, and who plays on what. As far as I'm concerned it hasn't really taken off and become a big thing yet, but it will.

PL: The Society has something on the Internet?

MH: We have some computer experts in the Society who handle our website. Every month we get five or six inquiries, and usually a couple of them join. The members don't come from the chat group, but from our own Internet page. We have people from around the world. We have a fellow from Japan who is actually an American, and we have a man with a Swedish name living in Israel who just joined. It's an interesting group of people.

PL: Before this was happening with the New York Chapter, how were different Ellington people from around the world communicating with one another?

MH: Mostly on a personal basis with telephone calls, mail, fax, Internet, and so on. Until only recently, most international communication was primarily between discographers and collectors like Jerry Valburn, Sjef Hoefsmit, and Steve Lasker. But once we had the conferences, we began to have a lot of live music. People started coming, and now we have a steady clientele of about 150 people who attend everything.

But what bothers me is that you have a meeting and something fascinating happens, 200 people hear it, and then it disappears. There's no journal or record kept. Everything is taped, but there's never any real effort to distribute the tapes. And that's not right.

PL: In the simplest terms, what is the function and purpose of the Society?

MH: Our specific purpose is to promote the music of Duke Ellington by all legal and proper means, to get as many people as possible to play it, listen to it, appreciate it, study it.

PL: How successful has the Society been over the years in achieving that goal?

MH: I don't know. I really can't say we've done a hell of a lot, except as a fan club. But the music is being preserved, that's the interesting part. There's no question that Ellington's music is getting played in colleges. That's very important. And now CDs are preserving and distributing every bit of Ellington's music. People hear it and buy it.

At the 1998 conference in Chicago, John Hasse gave a talk about what he calls the Ellington Canon. I think this idea of developing a canon is deadly, absolutely deadly. What is a canon? A canon is when someone says, "This is it. This is what you listen to." But I think we need to preserve not just a few basic pieces, but *all* of Ellington's music so that people can listen to it with no restrictions. Is someone going to eliminate large groups of pieces by Mozart or Beethoven simply because they're not played as much as other pieces? Of course not, you have all of Mozart and Beethoven out there. I just don't see why we need to do this with Ellington, and I hope that it never gets done.

PL: What will be necessary for the future success of the Society, and what can people do to further its goals?

MH: More than anything else, younger people from your generation have got to become active in the Society. And not just coming to meetings, but literally taking it over and becoming officers, organizing concerts, finding members, being active.

PL: Do these people have to be in New York? How about people in different places who communicate through the Internet?

MH: This is exactly why I promote the idea of an international organization! If we had an international Ellington Society, of course we could do it that way.

PL: Why do you think there has never been one?

MH: I don't know. The international conferences have become annual spectacles. We've always been lucky enough to find someone who will volunteer to handle it. This is where an international organization can make a difference, take direction with these meetings, and incorporate the Ellington Societies into them.

PL: So younger people first have to develop an understanding of Ellington's music, and then take the initiative to expand these activities.

MH: There are younger people involved on a certain level, but not nearly enough. Most Society members are from my age group who have been listening to Ellington all their lives. They grew up with it. But I believe that's getting ready to change. Beginning with Ellington's centennial birthday in 1999, there has been an unprecedented amount of activity and publicity focused on the life and music of Duke Ellington. More people who are just now becoming aware of Ellington are gaining a deeper understanding of his matchless contributions to twentieth-century culture. We will see how this new understanding manifests in the next century.

Recordings

WE ARE FORTUNATE THAT ELLINGTON lived in the twentieth century. As the most prolific composer and live performer in history, much of Ellington's music has been recorded in one form or another. The remainder is preserved in the Ellington Archives, available for future publication and release. Ellington's immense catalog of recorded works will become more accessible to the public as new information becomes available, previously unheard performances are discovered, and technology allows for more accurate sound reproduction. In addition to Jerry Valburn's research, there is a group of dedicated Ellington scholars and discographers around the world who have been diligent in their efforts to chronicle every phase of Ellington's career. Ellington's music is becoming increasingly accessible through every available medium, including the Internet. With the celebration of his 100th birthday, the heightened awareness of Ellington's contribution to twentieth-century music opened the door for a wealth of new releases in the digital domain, where they will be preserved for all time. The challenge is making sure that the digital technology can do justice to the sound of the original analog recordings.

The Ellington discography can be intimidating, because there is simply so much to choose from. But there are many guides on where to start. Along with several discographies, there are jazz record guidebooks such as Penguin, Music Hound, and All Music, where Ellington recordings are rated by critics. These can be helpful pointers for those who want to begin their Ellington collection. Our discussion with Jerry Valburn, the world's leading Ellington collector, answers many important questions concerning the essential recordings and which versions are worth seeking out for the best sound quality and performance. But first I will give some of my own recommendations.

ᖳᖯᖯᖰ

When people ask for suggestions on where to start, I almost always recommend *The Far East Suite,* which has been my favorite Ellington recording for several reasons. It is the record that established Ellington as a composer of world music in the highest sense: taking the impressions from his travels abroad and incorporating them into his and Strayhorn's own unique musical vocabulary. Ellington and Strayhorn use Eastern modes and scales in a way that is timeless, exotic, spiritual, and completely Ellingtonian. There are no Eastern instruments on the record, but the Asian flavor of the suite is conveyed through the traditional Western sound of the Ellington orchestra. Like Ravi Shankar's Concerto for Sitar and Orchestra, *The Far East Suite* is a merging of East and West. This seems especially significant, because Ellington had already pioneered the merging of African and European musical traditions, and here he takes it one step further. Because I have always considered Duke Ellington as a composer of *human* music without ethnic boundaries, it is his world music that inspires me the most, along with his sacred music.

The Far East Suite features one of the most exciting configurations of the Ellington orchestra. In the sixties, Ellington had one of the greatest reed sections in jazz history, all heard on this recording: Johnny Hodges, Harry Carney, Paul Gonsalves, Russell Procope, and Jimmy Hamilton. Hodges is featured on "Blue Pepper," an Eastern variation on the blues, and the exquisite "Isfahan." This piece is one of the most gorgeous creations of the Ellington–Strayhorn partnership, not only for the Hodges solo melody, but also for the sublime background arrangements which are just as important. Gonsalves is featured on the majestic "Mount Harissa," and the opening "Tourist Point of View," which sets the tone for the rest of the suite. Cat Anderson is also featured on high trumpet in this piece, as well as "Blue Pepper." One of Ellington's finest brass sections is here, including Anderson, Cootie Williams, Lawrence Brown, and Buster Cooper. Brown is the featured soloist on "Amad." Harry Carney's baritone is the perfect vehicle for "Agra," a musical portrait of the Taj Mahal and the people who built it. Jimmy Hamilton's clarinet becomes the "Bluebird of Delhi," based on the melody of a mynah that appeared outside Strayhorn's hotel window. Hamilton is also the closing soloist of the suite, for the grand finale "Ad Lib on Nippon."

The suite also features some of Ellington's finest piano work on record, with gorgeous runs during the lively and infectious "Depk," a piece inspired by a dance troupe probably not unlike the one that Ravi Shankar performed with in Europe and America as a youth. Duke's piano comes through clear and bright in the recording, his unmistakable touch evident throughout. Duke's opening statement on "Mount Harissa" is one of the most understated yet sublime of his career, spiritual in quality, painting a regal picture of an imposing mountain in Lebanon.

But Ellington's finest performance on the record comes with the suite's finale, "Ad Lib on Nippon." A concerto for piano and orchestra before yielding to Hamilton's clarinet, Ellington opens "Nippon" with a theme that has a distinct Oriental quality, flavored with delicate cymbal strokes and bass notes. Suddenly Ellington switches to the stride piano of his early days, and the band jumps in with a bright swing. After some furious interplay between piano and orchestra, Ellington brings the band to a standstill as he begins one of the loveliest, most introspective piano solos of his career. I have yet to hear an Ellington piano performance that moves me as deeply. Ellington conveys the beauty of the Japanese landscape. He pauses, and Jimmy Hamilton takes over with a soaring clarinet solo that leads into the final section, the orchestra returning with a breakneck tempo that takes the piece to its dramatic conclusion. If I had to choose a single favorite Duke Ellington composition, "Ad Lib on Nippon" would be a serious contender for the way that Ellington's piano and the orchestra are featured in many different contexts.

The Far East Suite shows the close relationship between Ellington and Strayhorn. Most of these pieces were composed by both men, whose contributions are so closely intertwined that it is virtually impossible to decipher who wrote what. Strayhorn is generally credited with the lion's share of "Isfahan," and "Bluebird of Delhi," and Ellington with "Ad Lib on Nippon" and "Blue Pepper," but there are elements of both composers in every piece, and it is safe to say that there is too much grey area to identify whether any of these pieces were solely written by one or the other. Because of their effortless blend of styles, this unique partnership is unlike any other in music history between two composers. Nowhere is this reciprocity more evident than in these pieces.

Because of the modernity of the suite, the superb recording quality (significantly improved on the CD reissue entitled "Special Mix"), the consistency of the performances and personnel, and the timeless global quality of the music, I have always felt that *The Far East Suite* is the ideal Ellington introduction for people from the rock generation who are also fans of modern jazz artists like John Coltrane, Miles Davis, and Sun Ra. *The Far East Suite* is the ideal doorway to Duke for such newcomers, because it ushers them into the world of Ellingtonia with something that they can appreciate and understand: the "concept album." Although Ellington had recorded albums in a suite format before, *The Far East Suite* is the most successful in terms of overall coherence. The entire record flows as one piece, similar to Coltrane's *A Love Supreme*, which also has an Eastern flavor. And because Eastern music and spirituality were becoming more acceptable and fashionable among Westerners after Ravi Shankar's appearance, *The Far East Suite* was exactly the kind of Ellington record that many people wanted to hear in 1967. Those who have listened to *The Far East Suite* at my recommendation have always come back with positive feedback and an eagerness to explore more of Ellington's music. I always advise first-time listeners to sit down and fully absorb "Ad Lib on Nippon," a piece that tells people much of what they need to know about Duke Ellington the composer, pianist, bandleader, arranger, producer, and master of the avant-garde.

One of the most impressive testimonials to the importance of *The Far East Suite* is the arrangement and performance of the entire suite by Dr. Anthony Brown and the Asian American Jazz Orchestra. Brown and the Orchestra, composed of musicians from Asia, Europe, and the United States, performed the suite at the 1999 Chicago Jazz Festival in celebration of Ellington's centennial birthday. The response was ecstatic, and the Orchestra subsequently issued a recorded version of *The Far East Suite*. The Asian American Jazz Orchestra's version is stunning for its faithfulness to the original arrangement, combined with a degree of experimentation in the use of Asian instruments to express Ellington's Eastern musical themes. This has gone a long way to show how Ellington's music—particularly his world music—lends itself to new interpretations from other orchestras and conductors. This will surely become a greater trend among musicians of the twenty-first century as Ellington continues to find his place among the greatest composers in music history.

❦

Another personal favorite is *The Latin American Suite* from 1968, which again finds Ellington adapting the colors and sounds of another culture to his own music, without falling into the trap of imitation. I love the entire suite, but my two favorites are "The Sleeping Lady and the Giant Who Watches Over Her," and "Latin American Sunshine." Both are alive with Latin exuberance, yet have a wistful quality, as if Ellington realizes that he had waited far too long in his career to visit the region. "The Sleeping Lady and the Giant," ostensibly about two mountains in Mexico—one large and one small—could almost be interpreted as representing Mexico and her relationship with the United States. "Latin American Sunshine" is one of Ellington's most unusual harmonic and melodic themes, and one of his most joyous compositions.

I am also a fan of *Afro-Eurasian Eclipse,* one of Ellington's late works, recorded in 1971 after the tour of Australia and the Far East. Ellington returns to jungle music here, with some of his most aggressive and primitive material. His piano work is highly percussive, an aspect of Duke's style that had already been incorporated by Cecil Taylor. Although some portions of the suite are not as memorable as others, my favorite is the opening movement, "Chinoiserie," featuring a humorous and charming spoken introduction by Ellington, as well as an evocative piano solo and some aggressive freestyle blowing from Harold Ashby on tenor. "Didjeridoo" and "Afrique" are also highlights, the former featuring this percussive pianistic approach, and the latter bringing Rufus Jones out front for some thunderous African drumming. "Gong" features gorgeous piano from Ellington on a mysterious Asian theme that is strongly reminiscent of "Ad Lib on Nippon." "Tang" is an ensemble piece that blends dissonance and melody with a straight ahead rock beat. Ellington's use of orchestral color is simply breathtaking.

Ellington's distinct African music is among my most favorite as well, including *Afro Bossa*. My favorites are the title track, otherwise known as "Bula," "Purple Gazelle," "Sempre Amore," "Silk Lace," and "Anju." The entire record features an unusual amount of hand percussion in various shapes, sizes, and colors. The effect is intoxicating, even if the extra percussion can seem overbearing at times. Another favorite is the piece Ellington composed for the Negro Arts Festival in Dakar, "La Plus Belle Africaine." The live performance of this piece, heard on *The English Concert* from 1970, is notable for its contrast in dynamics between the ensemble and Duke's piano. Ellington's recording with Max Roach and Charles Mingus of "La Fleurette Africaine" on *Money Jungle* is a masterpiece of simplicity and grandeur. Ellington would often perform this piece on solo piano in concert, sometimes renaming it "African Flower."

But the most beautiful and intriguing African composition in my mind remains the lovely suite dedicated to Togoland, "Togo Brava— Brava Togo." This is one of Ellington's greatest late period works, a gorgeous suite that features Norris Turney on flute for the gentle "Soul Soothing Beach," and Gonsalves on the "jungle" movement, "Naturel- lement." The third movement, "Amour, Amour," is one of the unher- alded gems of Ellington's later compositions, and must be placed alongside his finest melodies from any period.

I have always felt that Ellington's extended works are crucial listen- ing for anyone seeking an understanding of modern music. "Black Brown & Beige," as it was performed in its entirety at Carnegie Hall, available on the live Prestige recording from 1943, is certainly an all- time favorite that I frequently recommend. Despite the criticism of the piece as a whole, I have always found it to be one of Ellington's greatest works, certainly one of his most personal statements. Not even the most casual acquaintance with Ellington can dismiss this magnum opus. "Reminiscing in Tempo" is a piece that ranks with the greatest twentieth-century music. Along with the Third Sacred Concert and "Black Brown & Beige," it is another of his most personal statements, dedicated to his deceased mother. It gives us a rare glimpse into the private world of Ellington's emotions, as do the other two pieces men- tioned. It is also one of his most successful extended works from a structural standpoint, as Gunther Schuller points out in our discussion.

"Night Creature" is another important piece, as performed on *The Symphonic Ellington*. This is a three movement work arranged for a symphony orchestra augmenting the Ellingtonians. The entire work is among Duke's best, but my favorite is the second movement, "Stalking Monster," where Ellington himself opens and closes the piece. His simultaneous use of the lowest and highest registers of the piano, one of his stylistic trademarks, is in full effect here. The orchestra then develops the theme with several gorgeous variations, only to return to Ellington. His playing here is decidedly avant-garde. There is no question that Ellington was an innovator of the piano, utilizing the full range of the instrument to serve his compositional needs, without being gratuitous. Every note and chord has inevitability. "Night Creature" remains the best example of how Ellington may have further expanded the vocabulary for orchestral jazz, had he continued in this vein.

Despite the brilliance of these other works, I share the popular opinion that Ellington's single greatest extended work is "Harlem," in terms of its range of expression, its consistency and balance, and its use of his orchestra in every capacity. It is an American classic, a vivid picture of a particular community of people going through their daily rituals. In thirteen minutes, Ellington tells us many stories of the people in Harlem, their joys and sorrows. It is truly a one-movement symphony, as descriptive as Charles Ives, yet much more exciting rhythmically. It swings! It is beyond category in every way. My favorite recording of "Harlem" is with the full orchestra on *The Symphonic Ellington*. Another outstanding studio rendition is from *Ellington Uptown*, and two live versions: Seattle in 1952, and Paris in 1963.

For live recordings, my first choice has always been *The Great Paris Concert* from 1963, with most of the same unbeatable lineup featured on *The Far East Suite:* Hodges, Carney, Cootie, Hamilton, Procope, Anderson, Brown, Connors, Cooper, and Gonsalves. The 1963 concert also features Ray Nance and Sam Woodyard. There are outstanding performances of "Harlem," as well as "Rockin' in Rhythm," "Suite Thursday," "The Eighth Veil," and many showcases for Cootie Williams and Johnny Hodges. But above all, the tightness and brilliance of the entire ensemble comes through vividly on this recording. My second choice for live releases is the Jack Towers recording of the 1940 Fargo concert, the complete version of which is now available on Jazz Heritage. The fidelity is superb for its time, and the performances are world class, from a world class lineup. There are definitive renditions of many classic three-minute Ellington pieces, and it was Ray Nance's debut performance with the band.

Speaking of the three-minute compositions, there are so many miniature masterpieces from the Ellington book, it is hard to pick favorites. But I have always been the most moved by the 1930 RCA

Victor recording of "Mood Indigo." This version has everything that defines classic Duke Ellington. Other favorite short compositions are "Black and Tan Fantasy," "The Mooche," "Black Beauty," "Daybreak Express," "Solitude," "Sophisticated Lady," "Azure," "In a Sentimental Mood," "Jack the Bear," "Ko Ko," "Morning Glory," "Concerto for Cootie," "Cottontail," "Dusk," "Sepia Panorama," "Warm Valley," Duke's wonderful atonal piano piece "Clothed Woman," and "Satin Doll." These pieces are all available in various forms, apart from "Clothed Woman," which can only be presently found on the 1947 Carnegie Hall recording on Prestige.

The Strayhorn memorial LP, . . . *And His Mother Called Him Bill,* is another top choice, one of the finest studio projects in Ellington history. Recorded shortly after Billy Strayhorn's untimely death in 1967, the orchestra gives one of the most gripping performances in their history. Ellington's eulogy for Strayhorn is included in the liner notes, and the band is in top form, bringing new life to Strayhorn's greatest pieces. Johnny Hodges is particularly strong here, with his most visceral performance on "Blood Count," written by Strayhorn while on his deathbed. Quite uncharacteristic of the normally smooth Hodges, this is a raw expression of anguish. Another stunning performance from Hodges is on the lush and plaintive ballad "Day-dream," providing a melancholy and poignant contrast to the more volcanic "Blood Count." The entire orchestra shines as an ensemble on "Raincheck" and "All Day Long." Finally, the record closes with Ellington's impromptu solo piano performance of "Lotus Blossom," recorded as the session was coming to a close. Ellington's interpretation is filled with the sense of loss and longing that permeated the entire session. This record is among the most highly recommended.

Finally, I will make a strong case for the Third Sacred Concert as the most personal spiritual statement of Ellington's career, and one of the most beautiful pieces of twentieth-century music. It seems that by the time Ellington composed the Third, he was unconcerned whether it sounded like "jazz" or not. He was only interested in direct communication with God. As a result, the Third Sacred Concert is not only the purest spiritual expresson of Ellington's life, but perhaps his purest emotional expression as well. It takes on additional significance because Ellington was acutely aware that he was approaching the end of his life. The Third was fully intended to be his swan song, his final statement to the world. This is Ellington the private man, opening himself wide for the sake of communication with his Higher Power.

The Third Sacred Concert has never enjoyed the same popularity or widespread performance as the Second, which is unfortunate but understandable, because the Second Concert is more accessible and approachable as a composition. The Third is more introspective and challenging, and requires concentrated listening. The Third has also never been released in its entirety, but only in the edited form that Ellington approved. Nevertheless, the Third needs to be reappraised as one of Ellington's masterpieces, and hopefully its reissue in the RCA Victor *Complete Ellington* box set will help achieve that goal. "Is God a Three Letter Word for Love?" "The Majesty of God," "My Love," and "Every Man Prays in His Own Language," are all among the most touching pieces ever written by Ellington, musically and lyrically. Like Ravi Shankar, one of Duke Ellington's greatest contributions to twentieth-century music is bringing a renewed emphasis on spirituality to a mass audience. For those who would benefit from a great artist's expression of faith, I strongly recommend the Third Sacred Concert. Duke would certainly concur.

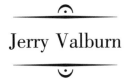

Jerry Valburn

THERE IS ONLY ONE DUKE ELLINGTON, and only one Jerry Valburn. Ellington created a body of work spanning half a century that is as immense in quantity as in quality. Jerry Valburn has dedicated his life to building and preserving the largest collection of Ellingtonia in the world. Ellington's music will forever touch the hearts of people around the globe, and Valburn's collection will continue to serve as the most complete document of Ellington's legacy. The Valburn Collection— presently consisting of almost 2,400 78s, over 4,000 LPs and 1,200 reels of tape, as well as hundreds of compact discs, acetates, transcriptions, and test pressings—permanently resides at the Library of Congress in Ellington's hometown, Washington, D.C. Anyone with a sincere interest in hearing anything from the Valburn Collection can do so free of charge simply by making an appointment. It is this kind of unlimited access to Ellington's music that has always motivated Jerry's burning desire to obtain everything related to Duke Ellington that he could get his hands on. Jerry not only wanted the most complete Ellington collection in the world, but he also wanted to share his knowledge with other Ellington listeners, always for the purpose of spreading the music. Jerry is not an average collector or Ellington scholar. He is truly "beyond category."

Not only did Jerry set out to obtain every single commercially issued Ellington recording released in America, but all existing foreign pressings as well—in all available formats: shellac 78s, vinyl LPs, cassettes, and compact discs. For example, one can find the 1941 RCA recording of "Take the A-Train" in the Valburn Collection many times over—depending on how many times it was released and in how many countries, including anthologies and compilations. Then there's the enormous wealth of non-commercially released live recordings, radio broadcasts, rehearsals, and unreleased studio outtakes. Many of the live concerts in the Valburn Collection were recorded by Jerry himself with the band's permission. By this time, Jerry had developed a career in broadcasting and studio engineering, and was able to apply his technical skills to his passion for Duke's music. With the help of his longtime friend and partner, engineer Jack Towers, Jerry has been able to repair and restore many crucial recordings that otherwise may never have seen the light of day, including the complete 1943 live performance of "Black Brown & Beige" that Valburn and Towers assembled from two concerts—New York and Boston.

Our discussion comes to a place where every Ellington enthusiast, from beginners to seasoned collectors, will have a special interest: Jerry Valburn, world's foremost Ellington collector, talks about his favorite Ellington recordings and why they have special meaning for him. Especially for those who are just beginning to discover Ellington, this is priceless information. Jerry cites which Ellington recordings have most successfully transferred to compact disc, as well as less successful remastering attempts that should be avoided by consumers. According to Jerry, compact discs are not always the most faithful reproductions of the music. Many do not approach the quality of the original shellac or vinyl sources, and it is important to know which ones to avoid. Jerry gives us some of the more obvious examples in current circulation.

Like everyone else, Jerry has his own personal Ellington favorites. But Jerry feels strongly that if one is to gain a proper understanding of Ellington, one must be willing to accept *all* phases of Ellington's career. Every stage of Ellington's development has something special to offer that cannot be found anywhere else in music, and Jerry cautions against prejudices that limit one's perspective. Ellington's music remained vital and unique from the twenties all the way to the seventies. Many Ellington followers remained partial to their favorite era featuring specific bandmembers or compositions, and would not open themselves to new directions taken by Duke in his music. The most notable examples were the mixed reactions to Ellington's extended works, particularly "Black Brown & Beige," and the Sacred Concerts. Jerry gives special mention to the Sacred Concerts as some of Ellington's greatest pieces that still have not received the recognition they deserve.

Above all else, Jerry's primary concern is that the legacy of Edward Kennedy "Duke" Ellington will endure alongside the world's other great composers, for as long as people listen to music. Jerry has spent most of his life in tireless pursuit of this dream. Because of his lifelong devotion to the music, and his commitment to its preservation, Jerry Valburn's dream is already becoming a reality.

ᏨᎳᎳᎧ

PL: What were your musical interests before you were exposed to Duke Ellington or jazz music in general?

JV: Essentially it was classical music. My parents were big symphony and opera buffs, and there was a theater in New York called the Hippodrome. One of the smaller opera companies would have grand opera there, and we got tickets and went quite a few times.

Later on I basically became a swing collector. I loved Artie Shaw. I loved some of the black bands of the time, including Ellington. Actually, it was when I was going to high school when one of my classmates who played in the school band took me to his home. His brother had a rather large collection of vintage jazz including quite a bit of Ellington, and I was really exposed to early Ellington at that time. "Bandana Babies" was one of the first Ellington things I'd ever heard. I was fascinated by Bubber Miley's solo. But the first record I ever bought when I started collecting as a kid was "Shout 'em Aunt Tillie."

PL: Did your early exposure to classical music help you develop an affinity for Duke Ellington's unique approach to orchestrated jazz?

JV: Ellington was essentially more sophisticated in his arrangements and in the way he presented even the pop tunes of the day. But I still enjoyed some upbeat swing, and of course he had the soloists in the band who could put these things over. That's why I eventually became *totally* infatuated with Ellington's music and decided, leaving the service after World War II, that even though there was a great deal of other music to appreciate at the time, I would probably concentrate on collecting Duke. What music would I want to take with me to a desert island? His music actually portrayed every era from the twenties onward. And of course, getting to meet him I was even more fascinated, because he came across as a warm individual who didn't try to hide anything—although I feel that with some of his answers he put

11. Duke at home. "He came across as a warm individual who didn't try to hide anything"—Jerry Valburn.

people on, which could be expected when he was bothered by lots of people every day of the week when he was working.

PL: You say that one of the first things you were taken with were the soloists. Who do you think were some of the key members of the early Ellington band?

JV: In the early Ellington band, "Tricky Sam" Nanton on trombone was among my most favorite. And I would say Otto Hardwick, because he had such an unusual and beautiful tone on the alto sax as compared to Johnny Hodges, who was also a very great and forceful sax player. And then of course Bubber Miley in the original band. Also Cootie Williams, Freddy Jenkins, and Arthur Whetsol, who all played in the same gutsy style.

PL: How about on clarinet?

JV: Barney Bigard. And it always amazed me that when Bigard left the band in 1942 and went out on his own, he no longer indulged himself in those beautiful dulcet New Orleans tones, but became a riff player. If you listen to his records that he made under his own name after '42, there are a lot of riffs.

PL: Not as much of that wood tone that he was known for.

JV: Right. There are so many wonderful things he did between 1927–42 during the days of his appearances with Duke.

PL: Which pieces were his best statements?

JV: Duke wrote a marvelous piece for him called "Clarinet Lament" in the thirties, and in the forties "Across the Track Blues." But there are so many other earlier pieces that would take quite a while to mention.

PL: The 1930 "Mood Indigo" is certainly one of his landmark pieces.

JV: Yes. Barney wrote that with Duke, and one of the amazing things was that in the 1970s when he was still alive, he was no longer getting royalties even though Ellington and other people were still playing it. Finally—I don't know if it was Stanley Dance or people that he knew at ASCAP—somebody interceded for him and he got quite a lump sum of back payment on royalties due.

PL: Many people point out that Fletcher Henderson, as the founding father of big band orchestration, had a tremendous influence on Duke. What do you think of Henderson's approach compared with Ellington?

JV: I think in the case of Ellington, the innovations were not only made by him but by the whole ensemble. They would go into a studio and he'd have something written out, and the guys would each offer something toward the final finished product. The Henderson band boasted some very great soloists for its day, but they played primarily black interpretations of pop tunes and some swingers, where Ellington was much smoother and could *certainly* play hot when he had to.

PL: One of the points that Gunther Schuller makes is that there were many bands that had strong rhythmic capabilities—Basie, of course— but that Ellington was totally unique in his use of different tonal colors in the orchestra.

JV: That is absolutely true.

PL: So when you first encountered Duke's music, what were some of the pieces that struck you as being unique?

JV: Strangely enough, I had not heard any of the extended pieces like "Creole Rhapsody" at that point. Those came along later. But I did get to hear the "St. Louis Blues" from 1932 with Crosby. I also heard the original and subsequent 1932 versions of "Creole Love Call." One of my favorite pieces, a great stride piano composition that Duke did a number of times, were his 1928 recordings of "Jubilee Stomp." That really fascinated me because it rocked. He made four separate versions: one for Brunswick, one for Victor, one for Okeh, and another one he made for the Dime Store labels. Every version is different in the structure, the actual arrangement, and the soloist, which makes it interesting. It's like having a cameo of four unique and individual performances of the same piece. It's fascinating to compare them side by side.

But generally speaking, I heard quite a bit of Duke mixed in with other things like Billie Holiday and some of the Goodman small groups. But Duke was just so much above all of this, he was certainly in a class by himself. When I was a schoolkid, naturally my parents would tell me to go to bed. But I had my own Emerson radio—before the era of portables—and I would sneak the radio, wires and all, under my blanket and listen to the broadcasts from the Cotton Club. These were the broadcasts from 1937–38, not the early classic broadcasts that were done from the original Cotton Club in Harlem. But it was wonderful to hear that band.

My first concert experience enjoying Duke and the whole band was in the Bronx at the Windsor Theatre. He was playing a few bookings at the Windsor and at the Flatbush Theatre in Brooklyn. He put on an hour and a half stage show which was magnificent. Ivie Anderson sang things like "Rose of the Rio Grande."

PL: When was this exactly?

JV: December 1940, a month after he had been recorded at Fargo, North Dakota by Jack Towers.

PL: Your impressions at first seeing the band?

JV: I was overwhelmed! Just to see these guys perform, and watch them pick up their instruments and blow, was so exciting. I was fifteen years old.

PL: So by this time you already knew many of these soloists quite intimately through the records.

JV: Of course. I remember going home after that performance and taking out a bunch of my Ellington records and playing them over again to compare them to the live presentations I heard at the show.

PL: And when you went home and played the records after the show, it helped reinforce the live experience?

JV: It most certainly did. I also met Duke briefly at the theater, but I didn't get a chance to talk to him. He was nice and he smiled and shook hands. But I really met him for the first time in 1944. I was working for the Post Office during the Christmas period, when they hired a lot of extra people in October and November. Among my special deliveries was one for Duke at the Capitol Theatre, where he was playing. I still remember the movie that was playing there, *Phantom of the Opera.*

The doorman stopped me and said, "You can't go in there." I said, "Yes I can, I'm a postal employee and I have something to deliver to Mr. Ellington for him to sign." So they let me in reluctantly. I went to his dressing room, and he was between shows. He chatted with me for a few minutes and Harry Carney stuck his head in the door, and it was the first time I ever had a chance to talk to Harry. But what fascinated me the most was "Tricky Sam" Nanton. I had heard him play these magnificent plunger solos and so forth, and he opens his mouth to talk to me and it's a high squeaky voice—the kind of voice you would get if you swallowed some helium! It was funny, but it was nice. Everybody there treated me warmly, as if I were a celebrity in their midst. It was a very friendly and happy feeling, because they were friendly and happy people. Very often when musicians live together and go on the road, they have feuds between them, and some play tricks on others. But these guys were super human beings, and they did a great deal to make anybody who came along feel really good, even though the person might only be going to see Duke.

PL: That's probably because they knew how incredibly fortunate they were to be doing what they were doing, and it only felt natural for them to spread some of that happiness around.

JV: I would say I agree with you. "Spread joy up to the maximum," as Johnny Mercer wrote.

PL: So the first recording that you actually obtained was "Shout 'em Aunt Tillie." How did you continue on from there?

JV: That was 1939. Whenever I had a little spare money, I would walk home from school to save the car fare. In those days you'd go down to Cortland Street, which was Radio Row in lower Manhattan where the Twin Towers are today. There were all of these stores down there that had tremendous piles of brand new and used records. You could buy the Bluebird label, which was basically a reissue of the Victor recordings. The small group recordings came out on them later. You could buy three for eighty-eight cents, which was cheap. You could buy Deccas at that price, you could buy Vocalion—which became Okeh—at that price. If you wanted to be grandiose and spend a little more, you could buy the Victors or the Columbias for forty-seven cents apiece.

PL: These were all 78 rpm records?

JV: These were all 78s. And it wasn't until after the war when I started corresponding with other collectors around the world that I made the resolve that I would try, in my lifetime, to collect every single known issue of Ellington's recordings from all over the world. And I came pretty close to finishing that.

PL: When did it become obvious to you, even before you began pursuing that particular goal, that you had such a special affinity for Duke that you were becoming a serious collector of his records? Was it before you went into the service?

JV: I would say so. And when I did go into the service, there was always music around us. The radio stations played a lot of pop tunes and we had a lot of AFRS programs such as "Jill's Jukebox" and "Swing Time," and a lot of people would request things like Duke Ellington and Jimmie Lunceford on those shows. So we were never deprived the opportunity of hearing the sounds that we loved so much. And it just carried over. When the war was over, we went right on collecting. But I would say that I was pretty well established during those war years as a primary Ellington collector. I loved other things like Bechet and Armstrong and Jelly Roll Morton, but they were no longer first in my heart or in my collection. They became secondary.

PL: How did you begin to meet other collectors and network with them?

JV: Very easily. There was a music magazine out of Virginia called *The Record Changer*. It was started during the war. People would buy and sell things in there, and their names were all listed. I had a subscription, and I would go through it and find people who were Ellington specialists, or who were selling Ellington, and I'd contact them. But the biggest contacts that I made came in the 1950s when I contacted people in England like John R. T. Davies, and then on to Sweden with Benny Aslund, and people I knew in France like Charles Delaunay—who later came and stayed in my home. These people really steered me right and exposed me to things that I didn't even know existed. I learned about these people from the magazine or when someone said, "You should get in touch with this person. He has a great collection, and may be able to share something with you."

PL: Did you ever send scouts to different places around the world who would obtain things for you?

JV: No, I had contacts, but I never sent scouts! [Laughs]

PL: But you did have a network of people around the world who would keep you informed and send you things that you didn't have?

JV: When Duke was playing in Europe, my guys would go to the concerts. They would either make arrangements to get professional copies from the PA system, or they'd make their own handheld recordings. Then they would send them over, and I would exchange material with these people on a one-to-one basis. I was always aware of Ellington's travels because I was on the mailing list from Ellington's New York office. When they sent out the monthly itinerary, I always got one. So I knew where they would be. That was very nice. And I still have some of his Christmas cards! He certainly had a tremendous way with words.

PL: When you were networking with these other collectors, when did it become apparent to you that you were building the world's largest Ellington collection?

JV: It wasn't immediately apparent because Benny Aslund in Sweden had one of the greatest collections in the world. But . . . at some point I passed him . . . [laughs] . . . and we slowly became very close friends. He concentrated on what he already had and was content to continue with his research. He wasn't interested in having every single issue of a given Ellington song, for example.

PL: When did you develop that interest?

JV: I developed that interest early on, as I mentioned about "Jubilee Stomp." I found it fascinating to put these things on the shelf, and I'd keep them by composition rather than record label if possible. It would be great when someone would come over to pull something out and say, "Listen to this, and then I'll show you the differences on the other versions." I'm not a musicologist, but I can read music and I really enjoyed it.

PL: You said that you came close to obtaining nearly everything. What have you missed?

JV: I know exactly what I've missed—Duke's first recordings in 1924. They were done on Blu Disc, a black company that survived for about six months until they were put out of business by Paramount Records. They were sold on newsstands and in cigar stores, and are among the rarest records in the world. I'm still missing an original. A collector in California has the record and won't part with it—but he made a transfer of it, pressed it as a 78, and used an original cover label on the record. I bought fifty copies from him to circulate among my friends.

PL: So it was a well-made duplication?

JV: It was a good duplication, considering that at the time he was the only one I knew who had it. I have since learned of a Swiss collector who has a copy, and he is not interested in parting with it under any circumstances.

PL: What's the title of this performance?

JV: This is Sonny and the D'Cns performing "Deacon Jazz" and "Oh How I Love My Darling." The other side is Jo Trent and the D'Cns. But we realize now that the D'Cns is not "deacons." It stands for District of Columbia. Most people have not picked up on that. We just realized this recently. But this shows you Ellington's association with Jo Trent, the music writer. One of those songs, "Deacon Jazz," was in the show that was produced in Germany called "Chocolate Kiddies." It was recorded in November 1924.

Apart from that I'm just missing a few obscure foreign issues from Europe, South America, and Japan that would make the collection completely complete.

PL: How difficult was it to obtain a lot of imports and bootlegs from foreign countries?

JV: It wasn't that hard because I was in the record business for myself at that time, except that I was only producing mail order so that I wouldn't be punished by the companies that own the copyright in the U.S.A. But in most cases in Europe, anything that's over fifty years old is in public domain. And a lot of this material indeed was. But there are some very late things that have come out from the 1950s and even the late 1960s, where enough time has not yet passed to have them in clearance for copyright. Those are definitely bootlegs, and nobody bothers to go after these people. But they're not too hard to obtain. One French label was very readily available in the United States called Trema Records. They have a batch of marvelous concerts of Duke and other people. When I was in Europe last year, there was a four-CD set they put out on Miles Davis that my buddies over here wanted because it's a very good period of Miles, but here in America the Davis estate told them, "It's okay that you release this in Europe, but we don't want to see this in America." Trema Records have pretty much disappeared from the United States since then, but they can be ordered from Europe.

PL: What's your favorite detective story, your best discovery?

JV: As far as original material I found in America, obviously there are detective stories involved as well as extreme rarities that nobody else in the world knew about. For example, with the Treasury Series, I was in New Jersey doing some junk shopping. I found the original 16-inch acetates that were cut by Armed Forces Radio to make the "Date With the Duke" radio shows. These were the actual broadcasts. They had a radio line going to the Armed Forces from ABC. Then they would edit, and they did this all on disc—which was incredible considering that this was before tape. They made up their own series of "Date With the Duke" transcriptions. There are seventy-nine altogether. I found a whole batch of these, and the price was right. It gave me the opportunity of going ahead and putting out the complete Ellington Treasury Series. Without them I would have been lost. I had most of the AFRS ones, and [laughs] there's a story there too.

A very big collector in England who had a few record labels was very tight on money, and he offered me some of these things. It was a package that ran me almost 700 dollars, and it was a bad time because we were having layoffs in the broadcasting industry. But I took the chance and the records arrived, but by mistake they were sent to Plainfield, New Jersey, instead of Plainview, New York! So I had to go down to customs to claim them. And I sweated a few bullets while the agent opened up this tremendous crate and started looking at these things. He was looking for drugs or jewelry, so he gave them to me, and I said that they were American in origin. I actually filed and got the duty back that I was supposed to pay on them. But what I was concerned about—and the Europeans didn't notice it—was that on the label of every one of these Armed Forces records, it says "Property of the U.S. Government." But the customs man missed it! So I wound up with all of them, and of course they are now at the Library of Congress with the other series of transcriptions that I owned.

PL: So once again they are indeed the property of the U.S. Government.

JV: That's right [laughs]. I was told by the Library that I could borrow back items to listen to or copy for myself, but anything that was on Armed Forces labels—once they're in the Library, that's it. Forget it. But that's okay, I transferred most of them to tape. So we still have the performances, and in the case of the "Date With the Duke" shows, we put out the complete Treasury Series. One of Ellington's close

friends who was also a jazz critic—and I won't mention names here—
told me when I started the project that I was insane to try to put out
a complete set. The total output of these turned out to be forty-eight
separate LPs! Jack Towers and I worked on this together. To give
people the full fifty-five minutes on each record, we did not use any
spiraling on the discs. We just went from one selection to the other
and made it all fit, and the quality was not affected.

In order to put the complete Treasury Series on CD, we've decided to release a double CD each month. The entire series should
be out within a couple of years after the first release, and will include
liner notes by me. Jack Towers did all the transfers to DAT, and right
now the DAT masters are at Storyville in Denmark. Karl Emil Knudsen has a license with the Ellington estate, so everything is completely
legitimate.

PL: How did you get involved in audio engineering?

JV: I started as a pre-med student, but the war was on and my heart
wasn't in it. I went into the service and took the aptitude tests, and
they found that I was supposedly gifted in electronics. So after I
finished my basic training they sent me to a place in Florida called
Boca Raton, and I went to radar school there. But when I got out of
the service and went back to college, I switched my major. I remained
in the School of Arts and Sciences because I had too many accumu-
lated credits, and I got a B.S. in Electrical Engineering. But when I
graduated, I decided not to sit at a draftsman's table. I was more
interested in entertainment. So I started at a small radio station in
Connecticut and made my way to Voice of America and then to the
networks in New York City, and this became my livelihood until I
retired.

With Voice of America I worked in the recording section where
we used to cut everything right off the air. That was fascinating. But I
did not do any actual live broadcasting until I went to ABC. This was
in 1950, and I worked all shifts, all kinds of great shows, and it was a
great experience for me. But I had many other jobs as well, and every
station I worked for had a very large record library. I would get
friendly with the librarian, and whenever stuff came in that they
weren't interested in, they said "Take it, it's yours." That really helped
me build my collection with some oddball things that I did not have.

PL: So your engineering experience was running parallel with your
collecting interest.

JV: Absolutely.

PL: So when you started to develop more sensitive ears to sound and
the technology of sound, you also developed more of an appreciation
as to how Ellington would be recorded in the studio?

JV: Oh, I did indeed. Because I realized, attending Ellington recording sessions and thinking about what must have happened many years before I even got interested, that Ellington would have made a very great musical sound engineer, because he would balance his own orchestra. He would go in and listen to it.

PL: How would he go about doing that?

JV: For example, at RCA he would have the engineer reset the mikes where he felt they would bring out the best of the sections, the soloists, and the rhythm section of course.

PL: How do you think he responded to the improved technology of the fifties and sixties with LPs?

JV: He went along with every change that benefited himself. When mikes got better, and when studios were not only built better but sounded better, he would take advantage of it. And it would reflect in his recordings. One thing that really disappointed me was the original *Money Jungle*. When it came out I thought the balance was horrific. But when Michael Cuscuna did the CD, he rebalanced the original channels, and it turned out to be a beautiful recording after that.

Duke was very impressed with sound, and when I went on the road with the band and recorded them in Cleveland, Tanglewood, and Connecticut at the Fairfield Jazz Festival, he always asked to hear the tapes, and he was very pleased with what I was able to get with only up to six microphones. When he was in England and they were getting ready to record *The Symphonic Ellington* with the various classical orchestras of Europe, he called me from London to have me make a copy of "Night Creature" that I had recorded in Cleveland back in 1956. I took it to the airport myself and had it sent over by courier to the Savoy Hotel where he was staying. Duke, Strayhorn, and Tom Whaley sat down and actually reorchestrated the entire "Night Creature" from that tape.

PL: After meeting Duke initially, how exactly did you go on to develop a working relationship with him where you would be recording his shows, rooming with Harry Carney, and things like that?

JV: First of all, Carney was very friendly and he would call and say "Hey, we're doing a concert. Why don't you and Barbara come?" He was always a very warm person. Some of my friends were very close with Ellington. One of my closest friends was Arthur Singer, the true Audubon twentieth-century artist. A gentle and unassuming man, he loved music and Ellington above all. He went to Duke's home when his father was alive, and he attended recording sessions from 1938 on. He had a great appreciation, and Johnny Hodges was his hero. So we would go to most of these things, and go backstage between halves of the concert or afterwards, and spend some time with Duke. And when the band was traveling in 1956, at Duke's suggestion, and Harry Carney also, I was asked to go along. I had a brand new Ampex 350-2, which was a seventy-five-pound portable machine. But I was young and strong in those days, so I took a mixer and some Telefunken mikes with that machine, and I made two or three trips with him that summer and made some recordings.

PL: What other kinds of equipment did you use in those days?

JV: I often used a Sony stereo microphone which was plugged into a professional Sony stereo recorder, and I made a hole in the side of an attaché case so that the mikes faced out wherever we were. This way I was able to get a pretty good balance from both speakers in the control room when I recorded them in the studio, and also when I'd go to some outdoor concerts like Central Park. I always got pretty decent recordings. Sometimes I was challenged by security going into a concert. They wanted to know what I had in the box, I said it was my thermos and lunch, and they let me through. And Duke was always appreciative. But we were staying up late with him in his dressing room after the evening concert or whatever, and somewhere along the line you could feel yourself being tuned out, because his mind was on something else. But he was a good listener when he wanted to be.

PL: Before you were asked to make that trip on the road, how did they first become aware that you were interested in recording the band?

JV: They knew that I was an engineer at NBC. One day Duke showed up as a guest on a show we were doing at the Waldorf Astoria, and he was very happy to see me. I brought a whole layout of album covers, pictures, and records, and they even had me guest on the show and talk with him. So they knew where to get hold of me, and I don't know whether it was he or Harry that initiated the call to see if I would like to go. But the minute I heard those words, "Would you like to go?" my mind was made up. It was hard, because I had two young children and vacation time was premium. But I had an understanding wife and two wonderful kids, and they said "Go ahead and do it." And I did, and I have no regrets that I made those trips.

PL: What are some of the fondest memories you have of those trips staying with Carney and being with the rest of the band?

JV: I roomed with Harry, and one time was very funny. We were having a few drinks toward the end of the evening, and there were about two inches of scotch left in the bottle. Harry said to me, "How about a taste?" I said, "No, Harry, I've had enough." He said, "Are you sure?" I said yes. He picked up the bottle and gulped it down like soda!

PL: Harry Carney, from what I understand, was a very easy going person. He and Duke spent a lot of time together.

JV: He was very easy going and quiet, but I'd like to point out that he was also a leader. Many times at a gig, Duke would be late coming out to the stage, so Carney would stomp out the theme. Sometimes they started with one of the old standards, like "Stompy Jones" or "Main Stem," and when Duke came out they finally went into "A-Train." Harry traveled with Duke in those days. He had a big Chrysler and Duke rode with him, and the guys rode on the bus. I'm not talking about the thirties now, this is the sixties and beyond.

PL: Carney had actually stayed with him the longest out of all of his musicians.

JV: Oh yes, he stayed the longest, and in fact he went on to play with Mercer Ellington after Duke died.

PL: What are some of your fondest memories of personally interacting with Duke?

JV: One was at the end of a Stockpile recording session now called the "Private Collection" they did at A & R studios in New York. Duke sat down and ordered coffee for everybody. He took the brown paper bag from the coffee, it was a little bit wet, and he took a pencil and wrote down a whole list of compositions. He said "I want you to go home and make a tape of these compositions and send it to CBC in Toronto, because I'm doing a special up there and I want them to know what it's going to sound like when we set up." I did indeed do that; the show was a great success, and I have a videotape copy in my collection.

PL: So by this time Duke knew that you were one of the leading if not *the* leading collector of his music. How did he respond to that? Was he amused or flattered?

JV: He was flattered but he also teased me at times. Once he said, "Over in my apartment I have the complete sessions we did in Paris with the violins. You haven't heard that." He didn't know that a friend of mine in Paris who worked for RTE over there had gotten the original tapes, made copies and had sent them to me. But I said, "Yes, Duke, I know about those, but I haven't heard them." That's what I told him. But he would also call me for information. For example, when they were doing the Reprise sessions, he called me to find out when he had first recorded "The Eighth Veil." He didn't remember, and I would refresh his memory. And one night he and Strayhorn called me about a song.

PL: "Raincheck."

JV: Yes, it was "Raincheck." They hummed the piece to me over the phone and said, "We know this song, but we can't remember the name of it." I recognized it and told them it was "Raincheck." Many of these calls would come very late at night. One time Barbara answered and said I was sleeping, but if it was okay with Duke I would get up early and call back around seven in the morning. And Duke said, "No, don't let him do that!" He went to bed around six and didn't want to be disturbed. But those were happy times.

PL: Obviously it didn't bother you too much when those calls came.

JV: No, it didn't bother me at all. The only one that was an embarrassment—and the New York Times picked up on this when my collection went to Washington—the phone rang one day and it was Duke, and my son answered. Duke said, "Where's your father?" My son said, "He's out walking Duke." And I never heard the end of it! We had a cocker spaniel . . . [laughs] . . . and the kids insisted that it be called Duke!

But he was a remarkable person whose mind was so sharp that he could come back with an immediate answer. I saw him at the Rainbow Grill the first year he played there in 1967. He played four sets, and he'd come out with his beautiful blue jacket—he loved the color blue—and he had a pair of gorgeous slippers. I was dancing and I leaned over and said, "Shades of the Cotton Club!" And he said immediately, "No, I had twelve people then!" This was the septet at the Grill, you see.

PL: Where was the Rainbow Grill?

JV: The Rainbow Grill is still there, it's on top of the RCA Building between 49th and 50th on Sixth Avenue. He played there every August for a number of years, and in 1973 he played at Christmas time as well—his last Christmas. What was great about that place was that CBS had broadcasts from the Grill, and I knew the engineer. I was working for Mutual Broadcasting at the time. They would leave the microphones open and CBS Master Control gave me a direct patch from the Grill to Mutual, and I was able to record all the talk and the music that was played before they went on the air, as well as the actual broadcasts.

PL: How many times, and in what periods, did you actually record Duke in concert yourself?

JV: Nineteen fifty-six was a very prominent year. I also recorded the studio sessions for Reprise with Fred Christie, and in addition to that I recorded Duke at Columbia University in 1964. Professional recordings, not a handheld cassette recorder from the audience. Basically that's about it. They did invite me to come along on one of the European trips in 1963, but I was working in a recording studio at the time and my boss said, "If you go, you may not have a job when you come back." So I apologized to Duke, who was concerned about the tour, because each country's government controlled the radio and TV stations. They were recording all of his concerts, and he had no say over what would be heard or not heard by the public. So they wanted me to go over and do the recording myself so they could bring back the tapes. Later, when they were in France in 1967, they hired a professional engineer who did all the recording for them. I would have loved to go in 1963, but I couldn't afford the possibility of coming back and not having a job, so I declined.

PL: Duke used to refer to you as his "Boswell." What was that?

JV: Boswell was the biographer of the great English writer Samuel Johnson. Ellington felt that I was his Boswell. He also appreciated a very nice and talented man named Brooks Kerr, a blind piano player who is about the age of my daughter. He didn't go blind until he was in his mid-twenties, so he traveled with the band. He could afford to do this, and he also has a tremendous knowledge of Ellington and the band, and he gave private parties in his home. He comes from a very wealthy family, and Ellington actually showed up and played at these parties.

PL: What was your last interaction with Duke before he passed away?

JV: My last interaction with Duke was in January 1974. He was very sick, but it was before he went into Presbyterian Hospital. I went with Arthur Singer to see him. We each brought our copies of his autobiography *Music is My Mistress* and he autographed them. He looked very tired and worn, but he was happy to see us. We wished him well, he kissed us on both cheeks, and we left.

PL: Had Dr. Arthur Logan passed away by that time? That had a traumatic effect on him.

JV: Oh yes, that was a great blow to Duke. Logan passed away in November 1973. He was a fine and wonderful man. He was good to Duke and Duke loved him, and it really broke Duke's heart. It also broke Duke's heart to lose Strayhorn and Hodges, two of his best people. Those to me are great losses, and I think what is most remarkable about Duke in the last years of his life was the actual religious music that he composed and was recording, like the Concert from Westminster Abbey.

PL: That's my next question. When you last saw him, was he still working on his Third Sacred Concert?

JV: I'm very disappointed about this. I have tapes in my own collection of what was broadcast in stereo on the BBC, and when RCA

Victor brought out the LP, they did not bring out the complete Concert as such. I understand from what has been told to me that they're coming out with the "various" Sacred Concerts, but they're coming out with both the Concerts that were done in New York at the Presbyterian Church in 1966. They're still going to keep the Concert in England as an edited performance! They're not going to come out with the whole thing!

PL: That's a pity.

JV: It's a shame, it really is. The Third is beautiful. A lot of it is very sad, but of course it's upbeat and very spirited about God. A guy who really appreciates this is guitarist Kenny Burrell. He thinks it's one of the most beautiful things that Duke ever did.

PL: I know Duke felt that way, but many people don't share that opinion.

JV: Well, it's unfortunate. I'll tell you something strange about Duke. Duke would come out and write a new composition and perform it, and many times when you first hear it, it doesn't hit home. It's not something you latch onto right away. But after you've heard it a few times, you realize how beautiful and important the particular composition is. It was that way, for example, when I first heard "Suite Thursday," but it has become one of my favorite extended Ellington works.

PL: One of the things I've noticed about the Second Sacred Concert is that despite the spiritual joy inherent in the piece, there does seem to be an underlying darkness that always seems ready to break the surface.

JV: Duke had a certain amount of that in his writing, but remember that the Second Concert that came out on Prestige is not the live recording. It's the studio recording. The one recorded for Duke at the Church was done in December of the previous year, and is much livelier. I think the very fact that Lena Horne was there really lifted everybody's spirits. But there are some sad things in those Concerts. There has to be, because God is a serious subject.

PL: Duke took that work very seriously. It's a disgrace that the Third Concert is not going to be heard in its entirety.

JV: It's a shame, unless the record company someday decides to reverse themselves. We'll have to wait and see what happens.

PL: And now for the magic question: what are some of your own personal favorite Ellington recordings?

JV: I think "Black Beauty" is an extraordinary composition. It's just the mood of the composition. It was done as a dedication to the memory of Florence Mills, a black actress who was on the Broadway stage and died at the time. He continued to play it through the years, and he rerecorded it in the mid-forties, and again in 1960. He also played it on the Treasury shows.

"Blue Belles of Harlem" is another extended piece that is very interesting. It was commissioned by Paul Whiteman. You can hear it on the 1943 Carnegie Hall recording on Prestige. I've been to Williams College in Williamstown, and I've examined the original manuscript that's there. It's an extraordinary piece of music. But basically from every period of Ellington's recording life, starting in the twenties and going right through to the seventies, there is always something that stands out.

PL: It seems appropriate that you picked the 1928 Victor "Black Beauty" as a favorite, because it's a perfect representation of the many different aspects of what Duke was doing. It has elaborate background orchestration, exuberant solos, wonderful rhythm section work featuring a fine bass solo as well as Duke's piano, and it swings. It even features unique percussion sounds from Sonny Greer. It's also a very well-balanced recording for 1928, with strong low and high end. I would say it's a shrewd and educated choice from someone who certainly knows.

JV: Thank you. One of the most interesting renditions that's in my collection is a broadcast from the Panther Room of the Hotel Sherman in 1940. They were on the air coast to coast, and he did it as a piano solo. You wind up with all of these things. "Black and Tan Fantasie," "Creole Love Call," and "The Mooche" are all standards. And the versions of "Take the A-Train" are still coming out of the cracks of the cement!

PL: What are your favorite versions of "A-Train?"

JV: One in particular is from Sweden in 1963. The band was playing in June at an amusement park named Grunalund. The guys were feeling no pain, and they were getting ready to come back, but they hadn't yet returned to the stand. Duke goes into "A-Train" and plays chorus after chorus until the guys come back, and as professional as they were, when they got back they picked up at the end of his twentieth chorus and went right into the melody.

PL: It must've been quite an entrance.

JV: I have it here.

PL: I still love the standard Bluebird version . . .

JV: That's a very fine version.

PL: . . . but another version I particularly like is from *Ellington Uptown*, with Louis Bellson and Betty Roche. It has a very exciting piano introduction, and climaxes with a fine Paul Gonsalves solo. That's a very well played and well recorded version.

JV: Yes, that is also outstanding.

PL: What are your favorite extended works? How do you feel about "Black Brown & Beige" the way it was originally performed at Carnegie Hall?

JV: I was there. After he performed it at Carnegie and Boston in 1943, Ellington never performed the entire work again.

PL: I thought he did another one in Cleveland.

JV: Cleveland probably also as well. What he did from that point on, starting with his return to Carnegie in December of 1943, was excerpts from the piece. Jack Towers and I have culled many different versions from the Treasury Series. They repeated various excerpts many times, and we chose what we consider the best performances—from the delivery of Ellington and the band, to the sound of the recording and the appropriate time. We assembled it as a piece, and it really sounds interesting. The one done with Mahalia Jackson for Columbia on the West Coast in the late fifties is a good one, and it's interesting to hear her sing.

PL: How do you feel about the complete live performance in its original form?

JV: Well, the whole ending of that piece is too flowery for me.

PL: Gunther Schuller mentions how the third movement was thrown together rather hastily when it was written.

JV: It was. Jack Towers and I were involved with that performance coming out. We had the original concert recordings and some of them were off speed.

PL: That's something I'm curious about. The "Black Brown & Beige" from the Prestige CD is not all from one performance. How was it patched together?

JV: They were recorded on glass based acetates, and the very first disc which had "Black" on it cracked and broke, so we used the one from Symphony Hall in Boston a week later. And Prestige is the kind of company that is honest enough to tell people this on the liner notes. "Black" is from Boston, "Brown & Beige" are from New York.

PL: What was your personal reaction when you first heard the piece?

JV: I didn't understand it, and a lot of people from my age group didn't understand it either.

PL: If "Black Brown & Beige" had an unfamiliar effect when you first heard it, what do you feel are some of the extended pieces that are most successful conceptually? How do you feel about "Night Creature?"

JV: "Night Creature" is marvelous.

PL: How many recorded versions of "Night Creature" exist today?

JV: There are only two. There's the one we did in Cleveland in 1956, and the one that was done in Stockholm, Milan, and Paris combined to make the version that came out on *The Symphonic Ellington*. Those are the only ones. The one from Cleveland is not commercially available at this time, but it will be soon. Once Karl Emil Knudsen gets to that point, we'll put it out. The only version people have heard is from the Reprise record. That originally came out on CD on the now unavailable Discovery label, and has been reissued by Mosaic along with the other Reprise records, including *Afro Bossa,* for *The Reprise Studio Recordings,* in commemoration of the Ellington centennial. *Afro Bossa* is an excellent recording, along with *The Symphonic Ellington*.

"New World A-Comin' " is a wonderful composition. Going down the line, I consider the Shakespearean suite "Such Sweet Thunder" as an extended work, although it's in different movements.

PL: "Harlem?"

JV: "Harlem" definitely, and it's something that he kept on the books right up to the very end. But something like the "Perfume Suite" never really moved me.

PL: How about the "Far East Suite?"

JV: "Far East Suite," yes. But again, that's not really an extended work. It's a grouping of pieces that are impressions of places in the Far East.

PL: That's one of my favorites, not only for the writing, but also because it's a very well balanced recording.

JV: Well, RCA pulled the original tapes and remastered it in 20-bit a couple of years ago. It's now called *Far East Suite Special Mix,* and they included some very nice alternate takes on there as well, which really makes it wonderful to listen to.

PL: The pieces themselves are absolutely sublime. "Isfahan" must be among the sweetest melodies from the Ellington–Strayhorn collaboration. It's also a spectacular Johnny Hodges performance.

JV: Oh, that's a marvelous piece. I have some concerts of that material that were done in Europe, and one of my favorites is the piece for Japan, "Ad Lib on Nippon." Duke does the most magnificent introduction to that from a concert in Paris in the sixties. It's just marvelous.

PL: The introduction he does on the record has a very spiritual quality.

JV: It does, but this is even better. It's really beautiful.

PL: Do any high quality live tapes exist of the Asian or Latin American tours?

JV: As far as Latin American shows, I was sent a batch of cassettes from Argentina that covered all the concerts down there. But these were handheld recordings, so they're not really high quality. I also have a couple from Chile. I have a few things from the 1963 Asian tour in my collection. Those are nice, they're professionally recorded and good performances. Let's hope they surface one day.

PL: What are your favorite vinyl LPs?

JV: Favorite vinyl LPs . . . we'll start with the 10-inchers. Of course, the one that Victor put out on Label X from the Rex Stewart and Ellington performances, titled *Rex Stewart,* is outstanding because not only did they bring out previously unissued pieces, but the sound quality is so good—even by today's standards.

There's the remake Duke did in 1945 of all his famous pieces. It's called *Duke Ellington's Greatest Hits.* That's one of my favorites. Victor at that time was competing with Columbia promoting their 45 RPM records, and they were putting everything on 12″ that belonged on 10″. But in Europe they released it on 10″. This has all the famous compositions starting with "Black and Tan" and "Mood Indigo," "Sophisticated Lady," and of course "Black Beauty." It's an excellent LP.

Then when you get to the 12-inchers, there's just so much. To this day, I still enjoy the sessions he did for Bethlehem—two albums, *Historically Speaking* and *Duke Ellington Presents.* Only Ellington himself can re-record his own work and do it so well. They're just marvelous. They have everything. They've come out on a whole batch of different CDs. They were done in 1956 just before he went back to Columbia. He did the sessions for Rosemary Clooney's *Blue Rose* album in January. Then he returned to Chicago for the Bethlehem sessions, went back to New York and signed a temporary contract with George Avakian at Columbia, and appeared at Newport.

The remixed *Ellington at Newport* was finally released for the centennial, and it sounds remarkable because Voice of America had their mikes right on, and the mix is vastly superior. Columbia was shut out, with their mikes all the way over to the sides, and when you hear Paul Gonsalves on the original recording, you're hearing more of the crowd reaction than the saxophone itself. But the new reissued version of Newport is excellent, despite some inaccuracies in the liner notes.

Also as far as LPs go, *Masterpieces by Ellington* and *Ellington Uptown* are two great recordings.

PL: Unfortunately, *Masterpieces* never made it to CD in this country.

JV: It's on CD in France.

PL: It's in *The Complete 1947–52 Duke Ellington* 5-disc collection.

JV: Not completely. They only took one piece from *Masterpieces* for that collection. That's been remixed. And they tell you in the liner notes where the other pieces from the original LP can be found. They even give the catalogue numbers on them.

PL: When *Money Jungle* was originally released on LP, there were only seven tracks. It was a very short record.

JV: For the CD, they added two alternates and four tracks that were never heard before. They also drastically improved the balance and mix.

Of course, the record he did with Coleman Hawkins, and the one with John Coltrane, are both good recordings. But among my most favorites are the one that I did called *Reflections in Ellington,* where I put the 1932 pieces into stereo, and *Ellington Indigos,* which was done at Columbia in 1957 with Irving Townsend and has all of those gorgeous arrangements of pieces like "Prelude to a Kiss," "Solitude," "Mood Indigo," and other non–Ellington standards like "Willow Weep for Me." The only problem is that "The Sky Fell Down" from the original LP was inexplicably left off the American CD.

Surprisingly enough, many people don't feel the way I do about the album that features "Under Paris Skies." It's called *Midnight in Paris,* and it's a gorgeous album. Now *Paris Blues* has come out on CD with a lot of previously unreleased material, including the sessions that were done in New York when the band returned from Europe.

The 1963 Paris concerts supervised by Delaunay are also outstanding examples of what could be done with live performances. They can be heard on *The Great Paris Concert.*

PL: How about the two volumes of *All Star Road Band?*

JV: I did the one from 1957 in Carroltown.

PL: That one sounds very nice, but the other volume from Chicago in 1964 has virtually no bass in the mix.

JV: After John Gill and Jack Towers delivered the masters, the engineers screwed up in their transfers. They re-equalized it, and I don't know what happened to the bass. We have the original tapes in our collection.

PL: Even when you turn the bass all the way up, you can barely hear it. It's a shame, because that performance from May 31, 1964 at the Holiday Ballroom in Chicago is one of my favorite live Ellington shows.

JV: It's a tremendous performance.

PL: How about *Afro Bossa?*

JV: *Afro Bossa* is interesting. Don't forget there are some older pieces in there, like "Pyramid," and "The Eighth Veil." One of the pieces is identical in format and composition to a piece that Herbie Fields wrote in 1945/46. If you've ever seen a TV show called "Mike Hammer" on A & E, they use that piece, "Autumn Nocturne." The other albums on Reprise are fairly good. I don't care for *Mary Poppins* that much, the same way that I don't care for *All-American in Jazz*, except for a few pieces.

The recently reissued Mosaic box set of the Reprise material is very good, although many of us are disappointed that *Serenade to Sweden*, the record Ellington made with Alice Babs in Europe, was not included. It was released in Germany on Reprise, and later on another label in Sweden. It has never been released in the United States, although it would have sold tremendously well. But apart from that exclusion, the Mosaic box set is important for people these days who did not obtain the original Reprise LPs when they first came out.

The only additional material included was something that I had released myself as a souvenir record for the 1994 Ellington conference: the piano summations for *Afro Bossa*. I was thanked on the credits. There were some alternate takes from *Violin Session* which were left off the Mosaic box as well. So it has its flaws. The Alice Babs record is a marvelous recording, but very difficult to find. I don't have the actual album myself, I only have the outtakes from the session. I'm not sure why it wasn't used for the box set. But I am going to contact Alice Babs and make a deal with her. I want to bring this material out with her permission, because it's in such demand here in the United States. I would only sell it mail order, so it would not interfere with Warner Brothers, who issued the Mosaic box.

But going down the line, I like some of the small group Fantasy recordings. "The Queen's Suite" is a magnificent piece. I had one of the original copies of it along with the Queen of England, and it's a beautiful piece of writing. I think you can hear the Strayhorn influence.

PL: That reminds me of how much I love the record they made after Strayhorn passed away: *And His Mother Called Him Bill*. That's a tremendous record.

JV: We actually screwed that up. I had taped the entire session in the control room with the professional portable recorder behind the console, facing the speakers. Then we thought the session was over. I'm walking out, and there's Duke playing the piano on "Lotus Blossom." You can hear the voices on the LP in the background. But when they came out with the CD, they cut out the high end so that you would only hear the piano. They tried to eliminate other background stuff. They also included on the CD the other version of "Lotus Blossom" that had never been issued before, the one from San Francisco.

PL: The one with Harry Carney.

JV: Yes. That was used in a baseball film called *Field of Dreams*. Many of Duke's pieces keep popping up like that. I just saw *Seven Years in Tibet*, and there's a scene in the film where they're playing the 1942 recording of "Perdido."

PL: So the original LP of the Strayhorn memorial had the impromptu piano version of "Lotus Blossom."

JV: Right. That's the one where you hear me in the background. It was the closing track on the LP.

PL: That record has some of the most passionate playing I've ever heard from the band. Johnny Hodges gives one of his most emotional performances on "Blood Count."

JV: Yes, and he did two versions, but they only used one.

PL: That's a shame.

JV: It is.

PL: Everything from those sessions should be made available.

JV: They should be. I agree with you.

PL: What do you think are some of the most successful or unsuccessful CD transfers? I know that many people were disappointed with RCA's remastering on *The Blanton-Webster Band*. That 1940–42 period is seen as being one of Ellington's peaks, but the CD quality is poor. There's no bass, and no high end either.

JV: And they clipped off notes, like the opening couple of notes of "A-Train." They also used an unissued take on "Hayfoot Strawfoot," and the wrong take on "Sepia Panorama." A lot of mistakes were made when that came out.

PL: With the importance of that period, it only seemed appropriate that they finally remastered those recordings, and came out with the RCA Victor box set for the centennial.

JV: In the eighties none of these labels gave a damn, they just reissued stuff. It was horrendous when Columbia only gave people thirty-six minutes of music on *First Time* with Count Basie. There were two unissued items from that session which were left off the original CD, and only came out on separate anthologies on LP: "One More Once," and "Blues in Hoss' Flat." But for the centennial reissues, Columbia finally went back and included those two tracks on the new remastered version of *First Time*, and they did a wonderful job. They also did a fine job on *Anatomy of a Murder*, because the original Columbia and Rykodisc versions had horrible echo on them.

PL: I was not completely satisfied with the Columbia reissue of *Such Sweet Thunder*. Along with the fact that they used an alternate ending to "Up and Down," eliminating Clark Terry's wonderful original coda on trumpet, the stereo mix is lacking in comparison to the mono.

JV: That was early stereo for them. That's why the original album was never released in stereo. I still have the mono CD. They've said that they might come out with a alternate reissue in mono, and with the correct performance on "Up and Down." But Columbia has been notoriously stingy about the time they spend on a particular record. RCA Victor has been much more generous. But Columbia has their three disc Ellington retrospective for the centennial, as well as *A Drum is a Woman*, both coming out. What's interesting about *Drum* is an interview that I have with Ellington and Strayhorn, where one of them made a remark about all of the extra material they wrote for that piece that was never used! It just makes you wonder how much material is around that we don't know about.

PL: My old Columbia import CD copy of *Drum* sounds like it was transferred from a vinyl record. The sound is good, but I can hear the slight clicks and pops of a record being played with a stylus.

JV: That's very possible. In many cases, Columbia International did not have access to the original masters. So they did the next best thing, which was simply get it out using what they had. There have been much worse cases. RCA put out a very cheap version of *In a Mellotone*, transferred from an old record, and it did not sound good at all. But all of that material is now available on the RCA Victor box set.

There's other important stuff as well. For years I had the Japanese version of the record that Ellington made with Coleman Hawkins, because it had "Mood Indigo," which came out separately on an Impulse anthology with other artists. But recently when they put it out on 20-bit, they did a beautiful remastering job and included the "Mood Indigo."

On the remake of *The Popular Duke Ellington*, which is a very fine recording, I wrote the liner notes and got paid for them, but they never used them because they ran into a legal problem. Mercer Ellington had licensed to Bob Thiele one of the tracks that they had recorded at that session but never issued on LP in this country. So as a result of that, they cancelled the CD which is shown in my book as such. Now the 20-bit remastered CD is out, but it doesn't have "Wings and Things," because that was issued on Doctor Jazz. But they did include the unissued "Caravan."

PL: So *The Blanton-Webster Band* remains the most unsuccessful CD transfer?

JV: Probably. But the most unsuccessful record ever produced and released, in my opinion, was the one he did with Teresa Brewer in

1973. That is a horrendous recording effort, and a waste because he could've done so many other things.

PL: What do you think are the best CD transfers to be released? *Far East Suite Special Mix* is a great one.

JV: *Far East Suite Special Mix* and *The Popular Duke Ellington.* They were very foolish, because I offered them the Seattle concert in stereo, the 1952 concert. I have it in stereo, and they didn't want to go the expense. So it remains at the Library of Congress.

PL: How do you feel about the Chronological CD series on the Classics label?

JV: I think they've done an excellent and honest job. What is equally as good is the series on Masters of Jazz/Media 7. In my opinion, the finest collection to come out for the Ellington centennial is their thirteen-disc box set. It is one of the most interesting and thoughtful compilations of Ellingtonia from all periods, and the transfers are excellent. The title and catalog number *Duke Ellington Anniversary* thirteen disc box, MJCD 1300. It is a must for anybody that collects Ellingtonia. I got Jack Towers a copy, and he was thrilled with it. And if he likes the way the transfers sound, that's good enough for me.

The discs are broken down by category. The discs are titled in order as follows: Ballads, Things Ain't What They Used to Be, Composer, Dance, Friends, Jungle, Ladies, New York, Pianist, Portraits, Soloists, Swing, and Vocal. On the final Vocal disc, there is a very rare recording that most people haven't heard. Duke does a demo in early 1937 at the soundstage of Republic Pictures in California, where he plays and sings "I Gotta Be a Rug Cutter." That alone is worth the price of admission.

PL: So they've gone through the Victor pieces that were on the *Blanton–Webster* collection?

JV: Oh yes, with much better transfers. They are much preferable, and they are very easily accessible because they have a good distributor in Oregon called Allegro. They get them into all the stores, the Tower chain and others, very efficiently and shortly after they're released.

The Victor box set is good, except for a couple of things. There is still some surface noise on the earliest recordings like "Creole Love Call," which is unfortunate. Just because the early recordings did not have the range, there is no reason why you can't use the restoration process to your advantage, and clean up surface noise without losing high end. Also, they left off the Louis Armstrong/Ellington masterpiece, "Long Long Journey." On the Pittsburgh piano concert, they left off "Sweet Loraine," because they said it wasn't Duke. But Duke was actually the secondary pianist on that track. They left it off the box set, and also the Bluebird reissue of that album, which is unfortunate.

They did not release the stereo version of the 1952 Seattle concert either. They stuck with the mono recording, and still did not release the complete performance, which by this time is rather frustrating. These things should come out! It's the same problem as the edited version of the Third Sacred Concert, although Ellington himself had edited it for release. But Ellington is gone, and we should be able to hear all of the music that he composed for the Concert. In most cases, artists are not the best people to judge their own work. We should be in a position to judge all of Ellington's work for ourselves, and it's not happening.

But the RCA Victor box is certainly an improvement over the *Blanton–Webster* collection, as well as the three disc *Black Brown & Beige* collection. Not only because of sound quality in most cases, but also because of better chronology, and alternate takes from certain LPs that are included in the box set. You can't get those alternate takes on any of the Classics issues, because they usually stick to original takes. The RCA box has all of that material, and actually the *Blanton–Webster* collection made the mistake of using four alternate takes, where they were only supposed to use official takes from the 78 releases. So everything on the box set from 1940 and afterward is good. The material before 1940 still has some problems with sound.

One of the reasons for the failing of the *Blanton–Webster* collection along with other releases of that time was the fact that RCA was using the No Noise system developed and produced by a group of computer experts. What they would do is take a digital master and put it into this system, which would transfer it overnight and take out all of the noise and clicks. Unfortunately, it also took out much of the music. I went to a demonstration at RCA in New York many years ago. They played something from a noisy shellac 78, and then they played what No Noise was able to do. It was fine except for one thing—you didn't hear the cymbals anymore! They completely disappeared. A computer is a machine, and many times what it detects as "noise" is not noise at all—like cymbals, or maybe sound effects like train sounds. No Noise takes those out also. But they now have a marvelous system developed in Europe. John R. T. Davies is using it there, as well as quite a few people here including Jack Towers. It's called the CEDAR system. It's very good.

PL: What are your favorite live recordings that have made it onto CD? You mentioned *The Great Paris Concert*.

JV: Yes, and of course Jack Towers's recording of Fargo 1940. That's one of the most wonderful of all. There are so many that it's hard to find specifics. I like most of the live performances.

PL: There were so many phases of Ellington's career that are completely different from one another. Each period of his work has its own merits. But many Ellington fans of a certain era would remain biased toward that particular period. Many of his followers would not be open to the new ideas and changes in personnel that he would introduce. This would manifest in different ways, from mixed reactions to newer pieces, to what sometimes amounted to open hostility toward new band members. For example, Paul Gonsalves was greeted with very little warmth when he first came into the band. It wasn't until he proved himself at Newport that people really began to appreciate him. There are many other examples. Certainly someone at your level of Ellingtonian scholarship would not have these prejudices. So how do you feel about this?

JV: That is very similar to the break that developed between collectors who went along with traditional and mainstream jazz, and those that went to bebop. There are indeed a number of collectors, including Ellington collectors, who only listen to things up to 1930. They don't give a damn beyond that. There are other collectors who will accept Ellington through the 1950s, not even the 1960s. And there are some collectors who will not even own a CD player, they don't want one! So you have all of these undisciplined characters, and each holds his own prejudices and tastes.

In all honesty, I also found certain things hard to accept at first. But I've always had an ear for listening. So the more I listened, and the more I heard the band, I realized that you don't stop with one period. You go right on through. What's sad for me is to hear the band in what turned out to be Duke's last year (1974). They were very raggedy. And they didn't do very much recording at that time apart from the session they did in California, *This One's For Blanton*, with Louis Bellson and the others. These guys were all leaders in their own right, but they felt so strongly about making that record with Duke that each one of them insisted on being paid only scale for their contributions.

PL: How about *Afro-Eurasian Eclipse* shortly before his death?

JV: *Afro-Eurasian Eclipse* is interesting. Obviously there isn't any of Strayhorn's influence there. It's strictly Ellington himself who put the pieces together based on his impressions of Australia and the Far East. However, when you talk about something like this, you often think in terms of something else. The other piece I'm thinking about is a very beautiful one called "Togo Brava—Brava Togo." That is a gorgeous piece of writing. I don't know whether Strayhorn had left any charts behind, or whether Duke did it all himself. It doesn't matter. It's just a marvelous piece of writing. And when it first came out, I had mixed feelings. But then as I listened and listened, I fell in line with what the importance of the piece was.

PL: Many times it's the same for me. Certain pieces that take time to grow on me actually seem to have the most longevity. *The Latin American Suite* is a good example for me. It's one of his happiest and most exotic records. "The Sleeping Lady and the Giant Who Watches Over Her," and "Latin American Sunshine" both have a spiritual exuberance. I think Duke had a wonderful time on that tour, the music certainly reflects it. I feel that Ellington wrote some of his best pieces in the sixties. But for many people, the Blanton–Webster period of 1940–42 is one of the essential peaks of Ellington's career.

JV: That's very unfair, because the thirties was a magnificent period, the so-called Blue period. The twenties was the Jungle period. Each of these periods has something to offer that is outstanding. But of course when you get a group of musicians together as Ellington had in the early forties, including Jimmy Blanton who was alive at the time, and Ben Webster who had joined just when they were going over to Victor to record after their last Columbia date—which he was also on—and the arrival of Strayhorn, all of this made for a completely unique and powerful combination of forces. Amazingly, when Stanley Dance wrote an article for a small English jazz magazine, he put down the Ellington band of the early and mid-forties as being too "flowery," getting away from what Ellington was supposed to be doing. Later, of course, Stanley reversed himself completely.

You've got to accept the things that Strayhorn did. He was a very fine musician, and of course he had a lot of classical influence in his writing. But certainly you don't want to take away from the greatness of Ellington.

PL: Describe your first meeting and most memorable interactions with Billy Strayhorn.

JV: I didn't meet Billy that many times. I met him at Newport with Duke in 1963. He had had a few drinks, and we didn't get a chance to talk very much. I saw him at the studio sessions. On *Afro Bossa* he played piano, but Duke would come down and put the last note on each piece, as I mentioned before. The only time I really had a chance to chat with him was in 1964 when I was recording Duke at Columbia University. Billy came early, and he was very relaxed. He was in the back near the stage, and I had a chance to talk with him for quite a while. Of course, he was ill at the time. We could see how serious it was, even though some people say that no one knew how serious Billy Strayhorn's health was at that time. That's not exactly true.

But I never had any really long conversations with him. He appeared as a guest of the Ellington society, and the most interesting thing he told us is that he held off showing "A-Train" to Ellington, because he thought it belonged with a band like Fletcher Henderson. It was not an Ellington type of piece. How wrong he was.

PL: What are some of your favorite Strayhorn pieces?

JV: As you've said, I feel that "Blood Count" is gorgeous. "Chelsea Bridge" is another one. "Something to Live For," the ballad itself— even with or without a vocal—is really a gorgeous piece of music. As far as "Lush Life" is concerned, I like it. But when it was performed in Paris, the people booed the singer off the stage. They didn't like the implications of homosexuality. It bothered them, and at the time I could understand that. Of course, today it's completely different. But that was then.

PL: "Day Dream" is probably my favorite of them all.

JV: That is gorgeous. In a sense, he was writing all of those little concertos for Johnny Hodges. "Passion Flower," of course. Johnny and Billy were tight. They respected each other, and they enjoyed what each was doing for the other.

PL: When you listen to how Hodges plays on the recording of "Blood Count," there is such an intensity and edge to it that is quite uncharacteristic of his usual style.

JV: It's also on Pablo's *The Greatest Jazz Concert in the World*, a Carnegie performance. Strayhorn was still in the hospital at the time. Ellington held the manuscript in front of Hodges, and Hodges played it just beautifully. I was there.

PL: How do you feel about the debates people have had about Strayhorn not getting enough credit for his work?

JV: I think that's nonsense. Duke gave Strayhorn as much credit as he deserved, and sometimes even more. They supposedly worked hand in hand like alter egos, and I would imagine that there was never any real competition between them. Duke may not have supported him in the style that Strayhorn wanted, based on what Strayhorn felt he was contributing to the Ellington organization. But I think he gets a lot of credit, and certainly on his numbers his estate still gets royalties, because they are his own compositions. With "Take the A-Train" alone, the Strayhorn estate is getting quite a bit of money every year. So that's my answer. I honestly feel that Strayhorn has not been unjustly or unfairly treated.

PL: One of the points Gunther Schuller makes is that Strayhorn was a brilliant twentieth-century composer, but a follower. He was not the fearless innovator that Ellington was when Ellington developed many ideas out of a clear blue sky, not having had any formal training.

JV: That is a very good point and very true.

PL: And how about the debate many people have had regarding the extended pieces. "Is this jazz or not?"

JV: Ellington hated the word "jazz," as we all know. As Stanley Dance wrote recently, Ellington was a bandleader and he played music to please the people. And if he went out of his way to write extended pieces, it was not only for his own personal satisfaction, but it was a contribution he felt he was making. And I still consider them important pieces even though they may not be considered jazz.

PL: Schuller points out that one of the most outstanding extended pieces that many people forget to mention is "Reminiscing in Tempo," that it was totally rejected when it was first performed—as a tribute to his mother who had just passed away—and that the piece is virtually perfect in structure. He feels that many people, even when discussing Duke's extended works, tend to forget about that one.

JV: Yes, along with "Creole Rhapsody." Those are both indeed extended works. But whether they're considered jazz or not, it doesn't matter. We're talking about Duke Ellington. And when you talk about Duke Ellington, you're talking about *music.* No boundaries.

PL: How do you view the importance of preserving his recorded legacy? Describe how the Library of Congress acquisition came about.

JV: I had been discussing the storage and disposal of my collection with John Hasse and Smithsonian for a number of years, but they were busy going after other things. They finally decided on what they were willing to pay for the collection, even though they apologized and said, "We know it's worth more, but this is all we can afford." At that point, my friend Rob Bamberger who works in the legal department of the Library of Congress contacted Sam Brylawski. He's the head of the Recorded Sound division. They paid me a visit and examined the collection, and made a very generous offer. So I said, "By all means, the collection goes to the Library of Congress."

I had good feelings about the Library anyway. I had gone there right after World War II with the woman who would become my bride. We went to look over the Library of Congress recordings of Jelly Roll Morton, and I realized that they were on the scene as far as music was concerned, long before Smithsonian even developed some of their own ideas. The only thing I feel badly about is that if my collection had gone to the Smithsonian, it would've been there along with

Duke's manuscripts and Ruth Ellington's contributions such as Duke's piano. But I feel that in the Library it has a better chance of being heard by people. Smithsonian has things that are still locked up in boxes that have never been uncrated. At the Library, people who make arrangements in advance with Sam Brylawski can come in and listen to anything they want to hear in the collection.

PL: So the collection is accessible to anybody.

JV: You have to make arrangements ahead of time, and you yourself do not handle the material. They have technical people who put you in a listening room, a very good one. They set it up and you press a button and hear whatever you ask to hear, and repeat it if you want to hear it again and so forth. That's the way they work.

PL: When someone goes to hear something at the Library, how do they know what their choices are?

JV: Most who go are serious students of Ellington, or musicologists. They need to be reputable, honest, and someone that the Library doesn't mind coming onto their territory. They need a legitimate reason, not just the kicks of coming in and listening to something. It has to be in conjuction with something that they themselves are working on. They want to hear a specific performance and they know it's in my collection, and most of it has finally been put on computer, so that even people on the Internet have access to what is in the collection. So they know beforehand and they call Sam or send him a letter requesting a chance to hear specific things. You can call Sam at 202-707-8465. He's a very bright young man. If he isn't there, you can leave a taped message. This is all done free of charge. It depends upon the availability of manpower. That's a big consideration since the Library is so understaffed.

PL: When your collection went to the Library, you kept your CDs?

JV: The CDs in my collection up to 1991—when the acquisition took place—were handstamped by the Library. They belong to the Library, but I'm allowed to keep them until I go to the Great Beyond. They have everything else: my films, my videotapes, all my record formats. The only things I kept were my research papers and books.

But a lot of people started feeling sorry for me [laughs], and I have a collection of about a thousand Ellington LPs right now in my music room upstairs. And most of them are mint copies, believe it or not. I have a lot of close friends who wanted to make sure that I wouldn't be culturally deprived [laughs]. Of course, it didn't please Barbara to see all these LPs coming into the house.

PL: After yours had all gone out!

JV: Exactly [laughs]!

PL: What will you do with the CDs that you acquired after 1991?

JV: I haven't made up my mind [laughs]. If my kids inherit them, they may auction them. But if everybody is comfortable with what we have, I would also donate them to the Library.

PL: What is your favorite format? CD, shellac, vinyl, tape?

JV: Shellacs to me are the greatest because they're the closest to the original thing, and if you have good equipment . . . my God, you'll hear things that sound as vibrant and as great as anything that's even being made today.

PL: What about after shellac was no longer used?

JV: After shellac, there are some very outstanding analog LPs, and of course there are some very outstanding CDs. As far as video quality, this will all go to a new format like DVD shortly, and people will be able to enjoy a digital format of watching TV.

PL: How about cassette or other audio tape?

JV: Unfortunately, cassettes are on the way out. They do have a place. There are some important things that have been stored on cassette, especially things done privately by various people, but unfortunately the collectors today are overwhelmingly going to compact disc.

PL: How about DAT?

JV: Jack Towers and I are both very high on DAT because the quality is there, as well as the shelf life, although you can't predict the same thing for cassettes. Certainly the overall quality is superior. It is so good that most studios still use DAT for their original transfers before they make their CD masters.

PL: Vinyl has seemed to be resilient.

JV: Vinyl has been resilient, but if you go to some serious record shows you can buy a lot of records in beautiful condition for about two to three dollars apiece now. A lot of people who are not serious collectors feel that if something comes out on CD, they don't need the LP anymore. Of course, this could be the farthest thing from the truth if a lousy job was done in preparing the CD.

PL: Like in *The Blanton–Webster Band.*

JV: Of course.

PL: Regarding videotapes, I don't see too many commercially available videotapes on Ellington.

JV: Certain things have been licensed, and certain things are in public domain. Karl Emil Knudsen in Denmark has produced some gorgeous videotapes that are available on import, and I would imagine that Allegro handles them. He's got magnificent original prints. But a lot of the later things are held privately in the hands of collectors. I turned over almost a complete collection of Ellington on film and video to the Library, but I started collecting rather late. I went to Harry Carney's funeral, and I was so touched watching his wife bend over in front of everybody and kiss him goodbye, that I decided I wanted a complete set of visuals of the band so I could go back and see my old friends over the years. And I found a lot of extraordinary original film. Many things were thrown out when news photographers would tape certain things at the Rainbow Grill or Carnegie Hall. After they used what they wanted on the air, they'd just scrap it! We were lucky to find a few things that were not scrapped.

PBS made a documentary called "Reminiscing in Tempo" that has since repeated on A&E. It's interesting, and it runs for two hours. It was in A&E's Biography series. They did two separate hours of Duke, combining the original PBS show with some comments by Dr. Logan's widow and a couple of others. I have some credit on it, along with Steven Lasker. It was well produced, although there are some goofs in it that shouldn't have been. They have the wrong year for "Jump for Joy," 1940 instead of 1941. But they've got some very rare footage, home movies that were made by Harry Carney and others. You see the guys playing baseball. It's nice. You may be able to purchase a copy from them.

PL: What are the best books that have been written on Duke? And some of the worst?

JV: Mark Tucker's two books are outstanding—the early years, and the critical anthology. A book written by an English newspaperman, Derek Jewell, who loved Ellington and was a personal friend of his, is an honest appraisal of Duke and the people around him. Many people don't like it for that reason. I think it's one of the most accurate. Eddie Lambert wrote a couple of small books, and his critique finally came out in time for the centennial, *A Listener's Guide.* It's a crime that it took so long for it to come out, it's a beautiful critique of Duke and the people who played with him, right alongside Derek Jewell's book.

The most accurate book is Klaus Stratemann's *Duke Ellington Day by Day and Film by Film,* published by Jazz Media in Denmark. It's a complete itinerary of Duke's professional activities, and it's a massive volume, not meant for the average reader. But on a factual basis, it is the most authoritative record of Ellington's career. Beyond that, I think the discographies are important. Jazz Media has one which runs from 1942 until the end. The Timner discography is more thorough, but does not list actual issues on any of the titles. Duke's own book, *Music Is My Mistress,* could have been a lot better except for the fact that he procrastinated so long and didn't write a single thing. Then he got Stanley out on the road with him while he was traveling and they threw it together in a couple of months.

PL: Many people feel that his own book doesn't give enough personal insight.

JV: It doesn't. It honors some of the people who were around Duke a lot, but it does not really cover everything that people want to know about Duke Ellington.

PL: What aspects of Duke's music and career are going to have the most lasting impact into the next century?

JV: Definitely his most popular compositions that he wrote over the span of his life, because they are in the same vein as Gershwin. Certainly some of his extended works will survive for the next century. They'll be performed by symphony orchestras all over the world.

PL: Is there significant progress being made with live repertory performances of his work?

JV: It's slow but steady. I'm sure there are at least ten to fifteen concerts worldwide every year by groups who manage to obtain the original orchestrations, or have musicologists reorchestrate them to be performed. It depends on how talented the musicians are. The most important thing is that they have a strong feeling about the music, because anybody who knows music and plays an instrument can play the notes, but it has to sound Ellingtonian. It cannot sound like something just picked up.

PL: This is something Gunther Schuller feels very strongly about. Since Duke was what I consider to be the first democratic composer, or post-Western composer, who wrote pieces for specific individual players, it is challenging for new players to recreate those sounds. Gunther pointed out that it can be done with respect and authenticity, and with the full knowledge that it's not possible for anyone to step into the shoes of a Johnny Hodges or a Cootie Williams.

JV: Someone who has come close is Bob Wilber. He does his "Bechet legacy," and his "Hodges legacy," and he plays very close to the vest on these things. He has a feeling for it. I also respect Wynton Marsalis because he is a very strong influence in keeping Ellington's music alive. He's a busy guy involved in so many different things, but he's taken the time to study the Ellingtonian aspects of all this.

PL: George Gershwin and Ellington are both justly celebrated as brilliant twentieth-century American composers with their own respective strengths. But unlike Gershwin, or any other modern composer, Ellington's career included live performances around the globe for half a century as conductor and leader of his own orchestra. Combining this relentless travel schedule with his staggering compositional output, I feel that this truly makes him unique.

JV: It makes him much more than unique, and it's something that kept him going. He would have withered up and died years before he did if he didn't have such drive and compulsion, such energy to carry on. He used to joke and say, "I pay these guys to play my music, because I want to hear it the way they play it." That's the way he said it. I don't think there's a parallel between Gershwin and Ellington, although a lot of people consider "Black Beauty" to be more of a Gershwin-type composition than an Ellington, but I don't believe that. The only thing I know for a fact that Ellington took credit for and did not write is the portion of "The Controversial Suite" called "Later." This was written and arranged by George Handy. But when you listen to it, it's very interesting. It is so un-Ellingtonian that you can tell he didn't have his hand in it at all. But the way they scored it is just beautiful.

PL: What do new musicians and composers have to learn from Duke?

JV: Young people can learn the importance of a composer like Ellington, and the legacy that he left behind when he died. When we had the Ellington conference in England in 1985, a high school band came over, and they did very well on some of his charts. In Chicago, at the 1998 conference, there was another high school band that were impressive. Not only is it important for these young people to see the scores, but I personally hope that there will always be some format of recording around so that they can listen—just listen—to the music, to see if they can glean something out of it. And hopefully that's going to happen. That has always been one of the basic motivations for my efforts.

PL: And what do you think they can glean from it that they can apply to their own musical journey?

JV: I think that the musical values—the beauty and the sadness—of the entire Ellington chain of material from beginning to end will always have a profound effect on people. But the people have to be encouraged, and they have to find the time to sit down and listen—the same way that even an old cat like myself listens to Bach and Beethoven. And I've heard these things all my life. I think that future generations also have to listen to Ellington.

PL: So they have to be exposed to the music, hopefully in schools.

JV: School is the best place for it.

The Legacy

ALTHOUGH THE MUSIC AND LEGACY of Duke Ellington will be preserved through education, publication of scores, live performance, international conferences of the Ellington societies, discographical and scholarly research, and preservation of the recorded legacy, the most important impact that Duke Ellington can have in the future is how new artists learn from his example—not to imitate Ellington, which would only be nostalgia, but to do as he did: find their own inner voice, seize the moment, take risks, break rules, and become masters in their own right. If musicians can learn from Ellington's constant search for new ideas and modes of expression, then we will be blessed with artists who have something powerful to say in their own language. Wherever this happens, Duke Ellington's spirit is alive and well.

Ellington would never approve of a world of Ellington imitators, but rather of a world of musicians who are following their own path just as he did. Although Jelly Roll Morton was an earlier example of a composer in the jazz tradition, Ellington was certainly not imitating Morton when he broke away from convention and composed his extended piece "Reminiscing in Tempo." Stevie Wonder was not imitating Ellington when he wrote his tribute to the Maestro, "Sir Duke." The most fundamental way that Ellington lives in our culture is in the way that he has influenced modern musicians, especially the ones we have examined: Stevie Wonder, Steely Dan's Walter Becker and Donald Fagen, Miles Davis, Sun Ra, James Brown, Sly Stone, George Clinton, Prince, Frank Zappa, and Charles Mingus.

Of course, this book has not even scratched the surface on any of these artists and their contributons. What has been given here is only a guide. Readers who are unfamiliar can begin by hearing for themselves the Ellington-inspired pieces that have been cited for each artist, such as Stevie Wonder's "Sir Duke," Steely Dan's version of "East St. Louis Toodle-oo," or Zappa's "Little Umbrellas." Further research will reveal greater treasures, and there is much more to learn from each of these artists who have inspired their own movements. It is up to each reader to hear for themselves how Duke Ellington has influenced these musicians, and how they have each taken Ellington's methods and applied them in new ways. But although they have each followed their own path as pioneers in their own right, none of them would have done exactly as they did without Duke Ellington. It never ceases to amaze me how Ellington has had such a pervasive impact on types of music that most people would never directly associate with the name Duke Ellington. This speaks to Ellington's greatness.

But there has been an unfortunate generation gap in our modern culture, with most sixties and post-sixties music appealing to a different audience than the ones who began listening to Ellington in the earlier days. Such a generation gap never existed in our culture before this century. Many younger people are not familiar with Ellington's work, and many older Ellington listeners are not interested in the rock, soul, funk, or avant-garde jazz produced by the artists examined here who share this common thread of Ellington influence. Duke Ellington himself would have continued to do whatever was necessary to bridge this gap between younger and older audiences, between not only "jazz" and "classical," but between "jazz" and "rock" as well.

Stevie Wonder himself said in a 1999 *Rolling Stone* interview: "I wish the old would listen to the young, and young to the old. Look at the gap between rap and blues. They are very similar, but people can't see across the gap. In their raw form, they're both crying out to be heard. They're about the pain of life. One might use a vulgar word, whereas the other might say 'my baby,' or 'my man,' but they are both about crying out. It is as if people do not want to hear, to confront the reality of what another generation's pain is about, old or young." Stevie himself has certainly done his best to close this generation gap, especially with genre-bending songs like "Sir Duke."

If one can listen to music without prejudice or expectation, then one can understand what Ellington meant when he said that there are only two kinds of music: good music, and the other kind. Regardless of labels or genres, if it sounds good, it *is* good! How many Prince fans listen to Duke Ellington, although Prince himself is certainly a student of Ellington? How many Ellington fans listen to Prince, although Prince was called "a modern day Duke Ellington" by Miles Davis? When Ellington fans can open themselves to the new directions taken by rock composer/bandleader Frank Zappa, they will discover where Ellington's innovations have taken root in Zappa's universe. When Zappa fans can open themselves to the groundbreaking work of Ellington, they will discover some of the roots of Zappa's experimentation within popular music. In the midst of today's musical diversity, there is a bigger picture where everything comes together, and at the center of this intersection is Duke Ellington. But despite the brilliance of these artists, none have equalled the timeless and beautiful music of Ellington. He is still the greatest of them all.

Luther Henderson

THE FIRST TIME I HEARD composer/arranger/educator Luther Henderson speak was at the 1998 Ellington conference in Chicago. He spoke about Ellington's spirituality, his unique ability to communicate to his musicians, how his methods of communication go back to the beginning of time, and how modern society can learn from Ellington's example as a great leader and communicator. Luther's knowledge is based on his experiences when he was asked to rearrange many of Ellington's extended works for symphony orchestras: "Harlem," "Night Creature," "New World A-Comin'," and "Three Black Kings," among others. Because these pieces were among Ellington's most personal expressions, Luther, a graduate of the Juilliard School of Music in New York, was able to interact creatively with Duke in a way that few others have, with the obvious exception of Billy Strayhorn.

Luther's background made him the perfect person for the job. His parents were musicians and educators, and Luther was exposed to the music of Ellington and Gershwin at an early age. He saw jazz as a merging of African "folk" music with European concepts. But he soon discovered that the Ellington, Basie, or Lunceford approach to orchestration was unconventional, and was not taught in schools. In fact, Juilliard prohibited its students from playing jazz at all. But he did receive the best in formal classical training there, and would simply go home and copy jazz arrangements from records or by memory from live shows he had attended. By this time, Luther was playing piano in Mercer Ellington's band. The two had become childhood friends when Luther's family first relocated from Oklahoma to Harlem. So Luther had the best of both worlds: the structured environment of Juilliard and its emphasis on the European musical tradition, and his liberal education playing and listening to jazz on the streets of New York City in the late thirties.

Luther explains how he made many of his choices when he worked on those arrangements. But he was not the only one to collaborate with Ellington in this way. Luther discusses the intimate creative relationship between Ellington and Billy Strayhorn, and how nowhere else in music history have two composers worked together so closely that it is virtually impossible to distinguish one's contribution from the other. Although Luther feels that Ellington gave Strayhorn the proper amount of credit for his work, he also believes that the general public is still largely ignorant of Strayhorn's work. Thanks to David Hajdu's Strayhorn biography *Lush Life*, this is starting to change. But Luther points out that Strayhorn was never comfortable in the spotlight to begin with, and was quite content to let the charismatic Ellington "take all the bows." Nevertheless, Luther maintains that Ellington offered Strayhorn financial stability, creative stimulation, and a chance for his music to reach more people than it may have if Strayhorn remained on his own.

Unfortunately, the father and son relationship between Duke and Mercer was not always as reciprocal. Having grown up with Mercer, Luther believes that Duke's overwhelming success was impossible for Mercer to compete with. Although a talented musician and composer in his own right—as well as the band's manager after 1964—Mercer's contributions were inevitably overshadowed by the groundbreaking achievements and global adoration of his father. This is regrettable, because Mercer composed some of the band's best pieces: "Things Ain't What They Used to Be," "Moon Mist," and "Blue Serge." He also served as a kind of talent scout, helping develop Billy Strayhorn's initial role in the Ellington organization, among many other important musicians who started with Mercer—including Luther Henderson and Butch Ballard.

Luther reiterates that above all it was Ellington's natural leadership and communication skills that enabled him to assemble such a multitude of talented individuals and inspire them to express themselves through *his* work. It is important to remember that Ellington took all the bows because he took all the *risks*. Ellington was a true pioneer, and it is easy for followers to do what pioneers have already done, but pioneers have nobody to fall back on but themselves. It was Ellington who took a chance when he extended "Reminiscing in Tempo" over four 78rpm sides, or when he unveiled "Black Brown & Beige" at Carnegie Hall, or when he brought his sacred music to Westminster Abbey. If Ellington must take the blows, then Ellington must take the bows. But in doing so, Ellington always acknowledged his musicians and allowed them to receive their fair share of the applause, and worked hard to give each of his players the material that would showcase their individual talents. This communication between group and

12. Duke on the bandstand with orchestra: "He felt that he should be respected in the same way as European classical composers"—Luther Henderson.

leader is the essence and foundation of Ellingtonia, and is where Henderson feels that Ellington embodies the American principle. But the implications of this are worldwide.

⊙∞∞∞⊙

PL: What was your musical background before you arrived at Juilliard School of Music?

LH: I was born in Kansas City, but we lived in Oklahoma. My parents were educators, and my father taught in Normal as well as other places like North Carolina. We moved to New York when I was about four years old, because my older sister was registered for school there. My family was musical, but not in a professional way. My mother played piano, and my father led a choral group called the Henderson Quartet with some of his brothers and sisters. They would travel to state fairs in the summertime and raise money for the schools. There was always music in my family, and I heard a little bit of everything.

I was not a child prodigy; I was simply interested in music. I worked with a private teacher, until I got bitten by the Ellington–Gershwin bug when I was in high school. Piano was my instrument, but I was always more interested in writing simply from listening to the music of the time. I would sit down and try to copy Jimmie Lunceford arrangements, and certainly Ellington. But what really struck me was when my parents took me to see the original production of "Porgy and Bess." Gershwin's approach to theater truly amazed me.

I was growing up like most kids in New York at the time, affected mainly by the folk music that we now call "jazz." Ellington's influence grew even stronger, because I had become close friends with his son Mercer. We lived in the same neighborhood. But one could not possibly live in Harlem and not know Ellington's music. He was a real force back in the thirties. "Black and Tan Fantasie" was the first Ellington piece that had an impact on me.

PL: What were the characteristics of that piece that impressed you?

LH: In retrospect, it's very hard to identify. I simply had a visceral reaction to it. There was something special about the spirituality of this folk music. Jazz is a folk music combining European and African elements. It speaks directly to the soul. That's where the term "soul music" comes from. That is what attracted me. Ethnic folk music is very infectious. It's the base material of any musical culture, the iron ore before you get the steel.

PL: How did you get to know Mercer Ellington?

LH: We lived in Sugar Hill, where most upwardly mobile New York black families moved in the early thirties. Mercer lived on Edgecombe Avenue. We were more or less on the same block, and we got to be pretty good buddies. We attended high school together, and we were both on the track team. Of course, I had heard his father's music for some time.

PL: What was your first impression when you finally met Duke?

LH: Like almost everybody else, I was in awe of this icon. And I think that's where some of the strain between Mercer and his father came from. Duke Ellington was a certifiable genius, and genius is notoriously self-centered. There are probably very few true geniuses of history that were able to maintain a functional family life. Without going too far into this, I feel that Mercer's relationship with his father could have been better. There are some problems with Mercer's book on Duke. There is some bias. But he was certainly not a parent-basher along the lines of *Mommie Dearest*. He wanted more than anything to be a part of Duke's musical world. Mercer was a bright and talented musician who happened to be the son of a man who was lionized around the world. In later years, he helped his father manage the band. But as an individual, he was trapped in difficult circumstances. Duke was the king, and Mercer was the son who could not inherit the empire. And that can be very difficult on a child. In all fairness to both men, that's what I think.

PL: How did you finally arrive at Juilliard?

LH: Coming up in a family of educators, it was assumed that my sister and I would have a college education. In high school, I scored very high in geometry, and I decided to be a mathematics major. But when I went to City College, I realized that I had to do a tremendous amount of studying for the higher level calculus and mathematical analysis. By this time, I was playing some gigs in the Village with Mercer. So I finally persuaded my parents to send me to Juilliard since I had to have a degree, although I was prepared not to have one. I wasn't an A student like some of my genius friends. I auditioned for Music Education in the fall, and I started there in 1938.

My experiences there were rewarding, but not exactly what I needed. I would have preferred taking some non-degree courses in composition. There was also no jazz allowed in Juilliard at that time. If you wanted to practice jazz or blues in the rehearsal room, you had to have one of your friends keep an eye out for a faculty member coming down the hall, because if you were caught practicing jazz you could get expelled. That has changed now. Fifty years after I graduated, in 1992, they wanted me to teach a course called Topics in Jazz. Things have changed. Juilliard became aware that their students were not always being prepared for the professional world. Other conservatories were teaching people how to do studio work and jazz. Juilliard was one of the last to do that. The fact that they're going that way is a good sign. Jazz is a serious art, and a product of the United States. It's a shame that you have to go to London or Paris to find out more about jazz than you can learn here.

When I studied Music Education, my major was piano. I had to pass the regulation Bach, Chopin, Mozart, the classical repertoire. If you passed a certain level in that music, you could continue. I took orchestration there, but as far as jazz was concerned, you learned it on the street. The Juilliard training was good for me because I could assimilate the European method as opposed to the African or jazz method. There's a big difference between the disciplines and conventions of folk music and more "evolved" music that has theory and different techniques of writing. For years people felt that jazz music could not be written down. John Hammond was one of the main spokesmen in that camp. If it was scored, it was not jazz.

The only way you could learn to orchestrate jazz back then was to try to copy down what you heard. When I saw "Porgy and Bess," I came home and tried to write it down on scrapbooks from memory. I would take Basie records, or Fats Waller records, and try to copy them down. You also learned a lot from hanging around the bands and watching what they were doing. It was time consuming, but when you've got the bug, time doesn't mean anything. However, I was never obsessed with details. If people asked me to do Basie or Ellington, it usually sounded more like me. Copying jazz is problematic, because you're copying a performance. Performances are generally not repeatable.

PL: But in the case of Ellington, many of his pieces have no improvisation. They're written out.

LH: Yes, but how did they get to be that way? Yes, he would write a theme, but his band was his instrument. His pieces were written to feature specific players with specific talents. This was new to the European tradition, but not the African tradition. The process is by rote, intricate harmonies executed by ear. So you learned by hanging around and using your ears. The technique of jazz orchestration had to do with who was there. I don't think you can find anything by Ellington that doesn't have some passages that were originated by concepts of the featured players.

PL: What about pieces like "Reminiscing in Tempo" or "Ko Ko?"

LH: I would be willing to bet that what Duke had originally written down was primarily thematic in nature. Duke would come in with charts of a certain theme, and the band would expand upon those themes with their own methods of phrasing. Of course, Duke was not the only one to do that. Basie and Lunceford did the same thing. The only people in jazz who really wrote everything out were Fletcher Henderson and Don Redman. They were the movers that took jazz from pure improvisation to the practice of arranging. Ellington wrote what he heard, and would direct Cootie or Hodges to do things a certain way, and they would know.

When I first began translating Ellington's music for symphony orchestras, my Juilliard training taught me that I should write everything out. That's what I did, and the musicians played it very nicely, and Duke complimented me on it. But he said, "You don't have to write all those notes for Sonny Greer. I will *tell* him what to do." He would communicate with them! This is pure folk tradition, not just African. This is what happens when people get together to express themselves in a group. The musicians get together and respond to each other. But there can be a leader, and this is what makes Ellington the embodiment of this tradition.

PL: Had you met Strayhorn by this time?

LH: Oh yes, I met him at Mercer's house when he came to join Duke. Mercer and I had been playing together. Billy Strayhorn was there, and so was Lionel Hampton—who would play piano with only his two index fingers, as if he was playing vibes with mallets! That was extraordinary, I've never seen anything else quite like that.

Strayhorn and I became quite close. He studied privately in Pittsburgh, and was originally hired as a lyricist. But when he arranged "Flamingo" for Herb Jeffries, that was a revelation for everyone. He did a lot of theater of Pittsburgh, but mostly studied privately. Of course, he studied classical music, and we would compare notes about arrangements. I was still in Juilliard, but eventually I became a vocal coach. Then I went into the Navy.

After the Navy, Duke and Strayhorn recommended me to Lena Horne, and I became her accompanist and arranger between 1947 and 1950. During the three years that I worked with Lena, I also did the symphonic translations for Ellington on "New World A-Comin'," "Harlem," and "Night Creature." Along with those, I did some piano copies like "Love You Madly." I was credited with the arrangement, and some people mistakenly believed that I composed it.

PL: How did Ellington approach you to work with him?

LH: He knew that he was writing music that could be orchestrated for symphonic performance. And because he knew that I had graduated from Juilliard, he used to call me his "classical arm," although I didn't have a lot of experience at the time. I think he knew that what he was doing should be appreciated by the entire artistic community. He felt that he should be respected in the same way as European classical composers. That's what he was working on when he approached me. But I certainly wasn't the only person who helped him in this way, and after the short time that I did work with him, I began to get more into theater and other things. So our collaboration lasted briefly, but it was very fruitful for both of us.

Toward the end of his life, I helped him again with "Three Black Kings." He wanted to do it for the Dance Theater of Harlem, which was starting with a new company. He would write a lead sheet and then say, "Why don't you take it from here and do this transition?" He would do this much more with Strayhorn than he ever did with me. He did it with his sidemen. He would write down a theme and tell one of his players to do something with it. Most of what I did for him were pieces that had already been performed by his band. After all, they were his instrument. I had a tape recorder, he would give me lead sheets, we would talk about what he wanted to do, and that was it. It may sound vague, but that's the way it worked.

PL: Ellington had some misgivings about formal musical training and how it affected a person's natural creativity, but he did say that Juilliard was an exception. Is that another reason why he placed his trust in you?

LH: I think so. Juilliard imposed on creativity to an extent, but they did draw the line. I would like to see all schools teaching classical players how to improvise with jazz, and jazz players how to submit themselves to classical. Ellington really embodied that principle.

PL: What did you do with "Night Creature"?

LH: I did the symphonic adaptation. There was a sketch, and I listened to it and reorchestrated it. This was for the Carnegie Hall performance with the Symphony of the Air. I had already reorchestrated "New World A-Comin' " and "Harlem" for his band and the NBC Symphony Orchestra with Toscanini conducting. I would write down what his band played, and then what the orchestra would play, tacit or double. One of the problems—particularly with "Harlem"—was that by the time I took it all down, the band would be out on the road and the concept would be changed considerably. I would have to readjust as the changes came about. With "New World," I would do the opening line with strings instead of trombone and saxophone, things like that. This was the process. You would take the theme, realizing that it was originally for his band, and decide what would work for a symphony orchestra. Many things you wouldn't double. A given line in "Night Creature" you may want to do with flute or piccolo instead of piano, or bassoon instead of upright bass. That's how it worked. Duke gave me the freedom to choose which instruments in the symphony orchestra would assume certain parts. I would make my choices for instrumentation based on my own best judgment, hoping that it was good enough. Apparently it was, because Ellington was pleased with my work.

PL: How did Tom Whaley fit into this process?

LH: Tom was what you would technically call a copyist. But it was much more complicated than that. He would interpret Ellington's scores, which were very strangely written. Duke would write things in various clefs and octaves that were not necessarily what they were supposed to mean. Tom knew exactly how to decipher them. He knew where to leave blank bars, without filling them in. He was not just a copyist. He was the link between Ellington's original mental conception on the lead sheets, and the sheet music that ended up on the bandstand.

PL: Describe Billy Strayhorn's role.

LH: Do you have a few weeks to spare? I worked with them on a musical called "Beggar's Holiday." Ellington was commissioned for the composition, and John LaTouche wrote the lyrics. Many of the themes were written by Ellington, some by Strayhorn. There was one place where a ballet was required, but Ellington was on the road at the time. Strayhorn was there supervising the orchestra, and we shared adjoining rooms at the time. I remember Duke and Billy talking on the phone for a little over an hour about the ballet. Strayhorn hung up, stayed up for a few hours, and wrote it. That's just one example of how the two of them had this special kind of continuity, where you couldn't always tell who did what.

Many times Duke would write eight bars and then Strayhorn would write the next eight bars, things like that. I don't think there is any collaboration between two composers in musical history similar to theirs. It was so unique. And what's interesting is that no matter what they worked on, it bore the Ellington stamp. He was that kind of genius—you were anxious to express yourself through him. That's what he did. I think with Strayhorn it worked both ways. Duke used to play a lot of Strayhorn's pieces, so there was a great artistic empathy there, and a great opportunity for Strayhorn to express himself in a way that he could probably not have done anywhere else. I didn't realize this until recently. It may have seemed at the time that Stray-horn was being taken advantage of, but I don't feel that way today, although advantage was taken on a certain level. For years the general public didn't know that "A-Train" was written by Billy Strayhorn. Even today, many lay people know "A-Train" as a Duke Ellington piece. Many people still don't even know who Billy Strayhorn is. That's not good at all, and I think it's starting to change.

Concerning the debates as to whether Strayhorn received enough credit for his work or not, I agree and disagree at the same time. Duke and Billy had what I call a symbiotic relationship. They each had needs to be fulfilled, and I think they both fulfilled the other's needs. Strayhorn would say, "Ellington is very good at taking bows, so I'll let him do all of that." We must remember that Strayhorn's life in Pittsburgh was not happy, he needed to get out! We realize this now after reading the exceptional *Lush Life*, which is required reading for anyone seeking an understanding of Billy Strayhorn. We understand now why he wrote the song "Lush Life" when he was still a teenager. Once he joined with Duke, he didn't have to worry about anything. And Ellington would take all the bows. Why? If you ask any public relations person, the press will mostly never try to promote more than one name. They're not going to promote Ellington/Strayhorn, they're going to promote Duke Ellington. This is not unusual. Benny Goodman was not a composer, but "Sing Sing Sing" is known as a Benny Goodman recording. This is by no means the way things should necessarily be, but it's simply the way things are.

There is some merit in these debates in an abstract sense. Elling-ton took advantage of Strayhorn, just like he took advantage of Johnny Hodges or Harry Carney, or anyone else in his group. He utilized their talents. This is what he did. This was part of his genius, not just in what he could write, but in convincing these exceptional musicians to do things his way. Again, this is the essence of folk music. An arranger doesn't write Aretha Franklin's vocal solos. It comes from her. A composer has to know and feel some empathy toward what the performer does. You appeal to them by virtue of what you write and what you say. It's also a business of rote.

Of course, Strayhorn's compositions were not all jazz. Many of the things he wrote for Lena, and things he wrote before he left Pitts-burgh, are really miniature compositions in more of a Gershwin vein. He provided Ellington with what he needed, and Ellington provided Billy with what he needed in his personal life. So I think it was a fair exchange. By the way, I think it's a shame that Ellington had to hire me or anyone else to do his symphonic adaptations, because I'm sure that he would have done them in a very inventive way himself. But he simply didn't have time to do that. His spirituality, his metaphysical drive, didn't have the time or inclination to deal with that kind of work. His head was too full—he was trying to write plays, film scores, and so on.

PL: Your work with Ellington was strictly on the side of adapting his band pieces for a symphony orchestra? Did you ever go the other way? Did you have any involvement with adapting Tchaikovsky's Nutcracker Suite for the Ellington band, or the Grieg piece?

LH: No, that was strictly Strayhorn and Ellington.

PL: You've said that jazz is essentially a folk tradition. I feel that jazz has always been a dynamic and unifying force that is not only beautiful music to listen to, but that also expands our awareness of what it means to be human. Duke Ellington strikes me as being the first composer to recognize the fact that his players were real human beings. He composed music that took into account their individual stengths and weaknesses. For this reason, I regard Ellington as the first truly democratic composer, or perhaps the first post-Western composer. I believe that we can take his concept of what makes an orchestra and expand it to a social level.

LH: I couldn't agree with you more. I happen to feel that of all the arts, music is the most accessible in any language or region. Spirituality and metaphysical energy are synonymous, and music is an extension of this metaphysical communication. Without stating any specific religious beliefs, the basic energy that powers the universe is the flow between plus and minus, between all living beings. For that to survive, there has to be motion. This motion is not just physical, it's metaphysical. All living beings—plants, animals, human beings—have spiritual communication, and the arts are the vehicle or the tools with which we dispense this knowledge.

The most essential communication happens one-to-one, mind-to-mind, spirit-to-spirit. Musical communication is spiritual communication. And it's one-to-one, handed down from generation to generation. With the advent of technology, printing press and other things, it all changed. But the generations that have grown with basic folk traditions are generally the physically oppressed. The oppressors generally have the physical prowess. The ones who are oppressed generally have the metaphysical advantage. The Romans conquered the Greeks because they wanted their culture, their knowledge. The same with the Japanese and Chinese. Europe and Africa. People find ways to survive. Oppressed people must utilize and manifest metaphysical power to survive.

Ellington was one of the embodiments of this kind of communication I am talking about. I don't know of anyone else who had it to that degree. Once in a while you find a conductor who may have it. Ellington knew about this communication of spirit. Whenever he met someone new, he could tell from their first encounter exactly who that person was and how they fit into his scheme of things. He could communicate to them, even if they didn't understand it. They might walk away from a conversation with Duke thinking, "What was he talking about?" His communication was spiritual. It's no coincidence that his music is so inspirational for the entire world. If the entire human race could learn this kind of give and take, this kind of spiritual communication between minds, which is the essence of jazz or any folk music, then we wouldn't be going around killing each other.

The 1998 Ellington conference in Chicago had musicologists describing Ellingtonia. I prefer to call it *Ellingtonia* because his compositions are part and parcel of his people. If I write something down for a trumpet player, and I'm looking for a wah-wah sound, I'll write "a-la Cootie Williams" on the score. I write those words if I want someone to get that particular sound. After all, the sound of those players is one of the fundamental aspects of Ellingtonia. This is the basic kind of communication for mankind. The musicologists at the conference drew parallels between political events and Ellington's music as it reflected the changing times, the same way one would have analyzed the music of an entire nation. You see, Ellington really embodied the musical spirit that is the United States of America. It's the merging of the European and African traditions. He's the essence of that musical culture. The basic folk portion of that is no different if it's Chinese or Ukranian or American. The connection is the same.

Several years ago I travelled to China with my wife who is a theater director. This was before the Beijing massacre. We heard a Chinese Dixieland band in Shanghai, and they were the worst sounding Dixieland players you ever heard in your life. But their spirit playing the music together was so great, by the time they finished their set with "Saints Go Marching In," everybody got up and started doing a Congo line around the room! The geographical distance didn't mean anything when it came to the spirit of the communication. If people could be involved in this kind of communication with each other—politically and culturally—there will always be differences, but at least we would have a better chance to embrace and deal with these differences in a less destructive way.

PL: How do you feel about Duke's Sacred Concerts and the spiritual impulses behind them?

LH: Of course, Strayhorn had died just before the Second Concert was completed, and Dr. Arthur Logan died when Duke was working on the Third. I think they are his ultimate expressions of himself, and they should be *received* in the spirit in which they were *conceived*. It was his truest expression, in virtue of the relationships he experienced with his musicians—with Cootie, Carney, Hodges, Strayhorn, perhaps even me. They are very important pieces. I think someone will make the mistake of trying to recreate rather than trying to reinterpret these Concerts. Is it okay to try to do Coleman Hawkins's "Body and Soul?" That's an individual performance. The Sacred Concerts have to be taken in the same way.

PL: There is a strong undercurrent of darkness in those Concerts.

LH: Ellington didn't want to die! He believed in God, but he didn't want to die. That sadness comes from how his life progressed, especially in the later years. His last years, from Strayhorn's passing to the end, were difficult years for him. He started losing all of the people he loved. He wrote all the lyrics to these Concerts, and he may not be a poet laureate, but this was his truest expression of himself as he evolved through the years with his band and everybody else that was around him. I may be doing some work on these Concerts for a project that has not yet been solidified. I'll have to think about how I should proceed, but I may not proceed at all. I very well may decide not to do anything. Maybe nothing should be done with these Concerts, maybe they should just stay on the records and that will be the end of it. I don't know.

There is some sadness in spirituality, but that doesn't mean that it's bad. You can't have all glad and no sad. You have to have some polarity to have motion. "Don't get down on your knees to pray until you have forgiven everyone!" I saw the Concert at the cathedral with Bunny Briggs. "David Danced Before the Lord" brings you back to the primal rhythm, the drums, the jungle sounds. That's where it all came from. Look at what's happening with hip hop music today.

PL: Many people feel that Ellington's music was too complex for the masses. How do you see his more extended pieces like "Night Creature" as having a direct link to African music? Some people would say that this music is the farthest thing from "jazz."

LH: You just said it. The fact that anyone, John Hammond or anyone else, has to say that it's not jazz means that they will never understand it! The message of "Night Creature" or similar symphonic pieces— the messages about the creatures, the birds—is really just an evolution of the basic jungle sounds, the human sounds of the voice, the rhythmic sounds of percussion. These basic sounds from the dawn of mankind, from which everything springs, have not changed. Ellington and all folk musicians are still in their "primal" stages, extending their techniques into the more "evolved" conventions and structures that we have today. And for the most part they are succeeding. Why should someone have to make a comparison?

Mozart was also prolific, as well as Bach. They're not the same as Duke Ellington, but they appealed to people in much the same way. They evoked visceral and emotional responses. There was a sharing of spirituality. What defines any great artist is this sharing of spirituality with anyone who experiences the work. This is what makes it great. Not everybody can do that. I compare Ellington to any composer, because he has permeated the globe! Haydn wrote "Twinkle Twinkle Little Star?" I don't think so. I think that was a folk song, you know what I mean? The Clock Symphony didn't just come out of his head, it came out of his experience.

PL: Gunther Schuller talks about the criticism he has received for wanting to perform Ellington's music with a repertory orchestra. Critics tell him it's a Eurocentric rather than an Afrocentric approach.

LH: OK, and what's wrong with that? Why can't it be Eurocentric? Why can't it be Sinocentric, like the Chinese Dixieland band? Why is that bad? It only makes it bad when we're programmed to feel that anything different from our own culture is bad. As long as we feel that way, we're never going to get together and communicate! We have to be able to walk in each other's shoes for a little while. Wynton's band at Lincoln Center could never play like the Ellington band, no matter who they get. That doesn't mean that they don't play great! There are some great players out there, and why should they stand still? Custodialising is good in its way, but it's not the same thing as creative continuity. It's more of an intellectual approach, which is fine, but it's not living experience.

I think jazz should always be required in music schools. I think that classical players have to learn how to play jazz. When I was teaching graduate students at Juilliard, I asked how many of them had taken any courses in improvisation or keyboard harmony. Maybe three or four out of twenty would be able to extemporize on anything, and that's ridiculous because improvisation is where it starts before it gets written down. Anyone who ever observed Ellington practicing at the piano can tell you that. Improvisation first, scoring second.

You can't tell me that Bach, with all of those preludes and fugues that he played every Sunday, didn't make those things up. He couldn't do it every week like that. Bach was a jazz musician, that's what he did! When you do it enough times, it's like "A-Train." All of those solos become part of the composition, like "Cotton Tail," or any of those pieces.

PL: What do musicians of the next century have to learn from Ellington's music? What is there for future generations?

LH: We need to teach the essence of Ellingtonia, which is the essence of artistic communication. We must apply it to ourselves. We need to learn how to improvise and play with one another like a great jazz band. That applies to a great symphony orchestra. Are you familiar with conductor Simon Rattle? I saw him do a Haydn symphony at Lincoln Center with his Birmingham Orchestra, and people stood up and gave a standing ovation! I've never seen people do that for a Haydn symphony. It was because it was infused with this communication. Some conductors have that ability. After the concert, I spoke with Rattle and said, "What you've got there is a jazz version of Josef Haydn!" Why? Because the people in the orchestra were all younger people, they were all enthused. They were brought from Birmingham after training with Simon, they were proud to present this music, and they made a whole new thing. And that's what is to be learned from Ellington—to make a whole new thing. His reach far exceeded his grasp, but he always kept reaching, and we've got to keep on reaching towards the future. We have to keep trying to learn to communicate. That's the message of Duke Ellington.

Afterword

Ellington took the music of the African-American experience, and transformed it into a music that expressed the experience of all Americans. He reached out to everyone regardless of race. He said, "*The* people are *my* people." Ellington was regal in bearing, but retained the common touch. He was disturbed by racial prejudice, but reacted by setting a positive example of excellence and leadership: always well dressed and well spoken. His actions and bearing spoke louder than words. He had a tremendous ability to rise above adversity. He kept pushing forward because he had to: the creative life was the only life he knew. He was a diligent, disciplined, hard-working artist, who stopped at nothing to excel and perfect his craft—a model for musicians, and people in general.

After all, Ellington was a revolutionary because he was a great communicator who believed in the human spirit. He knew that his musicians were real people, with real strengths and weaknesses, and real feelings. He was the first composer to structure a piece around a specific player's sound. Suddenly composition became more of a collaborative process. Unlike Mozart or Beethoven, Ellington's music was not composed for just any orchestra to play, where the musicians have no personal connection with the composer. It wasn't about one man; it was about a group of people working together. He was the first democratic composer.

Jazz was the first indigenous American art form, a music of free expression and self determination. Although this is what the United States has always struggled to achieve, it is far from an everyday reality. People are still judged by their physical appearance in America. We still have a long way to go before our communities begin to emulate the harmonious give and take of the Ellington orchestra. It may seem naive or utopian on the surface, but if we can apply Duke Ellington's model of an orchestra to our social structure, then our workers and homeless people will be seen as more than cogs in a machine, but rather as real people with real needs.

"Freedom is a word that is spoken and sung, loudly and softly all around the world, and in many languages. The word freedom is used for many purposes. It is sometimes even used in the interest of *freedom.*" These are Ellington's words from the Second Sacred Concert, where he reminds us that the word "freedom" is not always used for the sake of freedom itself. Things are not as they appear on the surface. Ellington had to endure a great deal of criticism, particularly in his own country, because his music had grown from the African tradition, which is still not considered as aesthetically refined as European classical music.

And yet, Ellington's music touches the very essence of what Thomas Jefferson envisioned for the United States: each person contributing freely while considering the needs of the group, striving for the goal of spiritual and social harmony within diversity. This is why Ellington's music must be taught in schools, and why jazz desperately needs increased funding through government grants and art programs, at least on an equal level with European classical music—which in reality has much less to do with our multicultural society than Ellington's music does. Music coming from an African tradition can never be judged by European standards. But if it's music that communicates the human condition, as does Ellington, then it can be called classical music.

At the present time, there is a return to a more conservative approach in jazz and popular music, where commercial appeal and record sales are the bottom line. Ellington was a pragmatist, and realized that he had to write his share of hit songs in order to survive and keep his orchestra together, so that his more personal works could see the light of day. But Ellington came before the onslaught of the video era, where physical image plays an important role in marketability. Because music has become a multi-million dollar industry, money is invested in whatever sells the most, leaving little if any room for experimental music. Although the media has traditionally preferred to promote one person as opposed to a group, things changed with the arrival of the Beatles. Suddenly it was possible for a group of musicians, writing their own songs and playing their own instruments, to receive equal media exposure.

There was a great deal of room for experimentation with this concept, which coincided with the technological advancements of LP records and FM radio. Suddenly it became more acceptable for artists to expand on the innovations introduced by Ellington with his extended works. Where Ellington was criticized for "Black Brown & Beige" in 1943, rock composer Peter Townshend of The Who was praised for his rock opera *Tommy* in 1969. This artist-friendly environment lasted from the mid-sixties to the early eighties, when video music networks replaced radio as the number-one selling point for records.

The number of successful *bands* as opposed to singers with backing musicians has gradually declined, at least in terms of media exposure. Whereas people knew that the drummer for the Beatles was Ringo Starr, the public today has no idea who plays drums for most of today's video stars. This goes against everything that Duke Ellington stood for in terms of individual musicians getting the recognition they deserve. Ellington also believed that while it was important to have commercial appeal, it was also necessary to take risks and go against the stream in pursuit of one's own artistic vision, otherwise music would cease to evolve as an art form.

This is another reason why George Clinton and the P-Funk orchestra remains the closest creative link to Ellington in today's context: every musician has something special to offer that cannot be duplicated, and the focus is on the organic quality of the music and the interaction with the audience. A live P-Funk concert may not be everyone's cup of tea, but if one can look through the costumes and loud guitars, it is highly recommended for those who wish to know where the spirit of Duke Ellington lives in today's music, particularly in a concert setting.

The Internet is beginning to turn the tide. With the technology allowing music to be distributed freely through cyberspace by anyone with access to a computer, without the need for record companies, independent artists are beginning to sell their own music online. Unlike television, the Internet does not discriminate artists based on physical appearance. An artist's sales are generated solely by musical merit. While this can never be a substitute for live performance, it certainly gives musicians more freedom of expression. If Ellington were alive today, he would be taking full advantage of this new technology and its uncanny ability to bring people together regardless of race, gender, age group, or religion. But Ellington *is* alive in the music of today's artists who are continuing to break down whatever barriers stand in their way. Perhaps the Internet revolution will eventually bring a new tide of experimentation and freedom in music, taking the emphasis away from the physical image of the star, bringing it back to the writers and musicians.

One thing is certain: wherever people get together to communicate with each other and express their spiritual beliefs through music, Duke Ellington will be there. The twentieth century was the century of the people. Global communication and world wars brought people together under the best and worst of circumstances. The arts of the twentieth century encompassed people from every walk of life. Music became a medium of expression for the common man. Songs written by working class people became classics that are still sung today. Secular music was combined with sacred. Styles and genres converged, and new forms were born. Music opened up for everybody who had something to say, even if they were just singing the blues. Duke Ellington best captures the spirit of the twentieth century because he was an artist of the people, from rich to poor, black to white and every color in between. He was inspired by people, composed for people, performed for people, and loved people "madly." No matter who you were, Duke had something special for you, something to communicate to you. And as Luther Henderson says, communication is the message of Duke Ellington. As long as people can find ways to talk to each other, musically or otherwise, Duke Ellington's message is getting through loud and clear.

Although this is the kind of statement that inevitably raises suspicion, I believe that Duke Ellington is the most complete musician of all time, for the simple reason that he did it all. He was a composer, orchestrator, arranger, bandleader, conductor, accompanist, and soloist, and he did all of these things exceptionally well. Even more so than Ives, Copland, Bernstein, and Gershwin, Ellington has embodied what is best about being an American musician, capturing the essence of freedom in music, freedom with discipline. He took a musical form in its relative infant stages, developed it, perfected it, and elevated it to the stature of classical music. Then he set the precedent for that musical form to be combined with other forms of music. Quite apart from his musical accomplishmens, his achievements as a self-taught innovator opened the door for limitless experimentation in modern music. He not only spoke to African-Americans, but to all people. In Duke's eyes, everybody was somebody. But in the end, he was the King of All. He was Sir Duke.

Bibliography

The books and magazines that were consulted during the writing of this book include the following:

Duke Ellington, *Music Is My Mistress,* Doubleday, 1973
Mark Tucker, *The Duke Ellington Reader,* Oxford 1993
————, *Ellington: The Early Years,* University of Illinois, 1995
Janna Tull Steed, *Duke Ellington: A Spiritual Biography,* Crossroad, 1999
Rolling Stone (issue RS 830–31)
Brian Sweet, *Steely Dan: Reelin' in the Years,* Omnibus, 1994
Miles Davis, Quincy Troupe, *Miles: The Autobiography,* Touchstone, 1990
John F. Szwed, *Space Is the Place: The Lives and Times of Sun Ra,* Pantheon, 1997
Rickey Vincent, *Funk: The Music, the People, and the Rhythm of the One,* St. Martin's, 1996
Liz Jones, *Purple Reign: The Artist Formerly Known as Prince,* Carol, 1999
Ben Watson, *Frank Zappa: The Negative Dialectics of Poodle Play,* St, Martin's, 1995
Ravi Shankar, *Raga Mala: The Autobiography of Ravi Shankar,* Genesis, 1997